A Lexicon of JEWISH COOKING

A c
food

PAT

Co

Library of Congress Cataloging in Publication Data

Shosteck, Patti.
A lexicon of Jewish cooking.

Bibliography: p.
Includes index.
1. Cookery, Jewish. 2. Fasts and feasts—
Judaism. I. Title
TX724.S53 1979 641.5'67'6 79-50995
ISBN 0-8092-7698-4
ISBN 0-8092-5995-8 pbk.

Published by Contemporary Books, Inc.
180 North Michigan Avenue, Chicago, Illinois 60601
Manufactured in the United States of America
Library of Congress Catalog Card Number: 79-50995
International Standard Book Number: 0-8092-7698-4 (cloth)
0-8092-5995-8 (paper)

Published simultaneously in Canada by
Beaverbooks
953 Dillingham Road
Pickering, Ontario L1W 1Z7
Canada

On the Day of Judgment, we will be asked to give account of every good thing which we might have enjoyed and did not.

—The Talmud

Contents

L

M

O

P

R

S

Acknowledgments

My special thanks go to research librarians at the Library of Congress, Washington, D.C.—Ellen Murphy, Feige Zylberminc, and Myron Weinstein of the Judaic Section, Everett Larsen of the Hispanic Division, and Leonard Beck of the Rare Book Division; to the staff at YIVO in New York City, especially to Dina Abramowicz; to Yiddishist and translator (even of Old German) Aaron Seidman, Rabbi at George Washington University Hillel Foundation; Yiddishist, scholar, and columnist for the *Jewish Daily Forward (Der Forverts),* the late Murray Frank; translator, friend, and fellow student of the Hebrew language, Walter Golman; Italian scholar and translator, Claire Iacobelli; Yiddish translator, Dora Yocelson; and to the publisher of the *Jewish Week of Greater Washington,* Joseph Hochstein.

How blessed I am that my world is peopled with those whose total lives are devoted to the study and interpretation of Jewish belief, history, and culture. I am indebted to them, very especially to Emanuel Mandel for sharing information about the life and culture of Hungary, pre-World War II; to Rabbi Max Ticktin, Professor of Modern Hebrew Literature at George Washington University, for his pointed insights; to Rabbi Oscar Groner, International Director of B'nai B'rith Hillel for his thoughtfulness, concern, and interest; and to Barbara Kirschenblatt-Gimblett, Professor of Folklore, University of Pennsylvania; Dr. Moses Aberbach, Professor, Baltimore Hebrew College; Dr. Graenum Berger, American Association for Ethiopian Jews for sharing helpful information.

Closer to home, I wish to thank Sherry Talbot who typed the manuscript and Fran Anderson who sometimes shared the task, Connie Maas for her editorial assistance, Rebecca Malcolm for her interest in historical pictorial material and her drawings of historical challah shapes, and Florence Einhorn who collated the pertinent bibliographical materials.

For help in the testing and modern adaptation of recipes, I want to thank Roz Chidakel, Cookie Friedman, Selma Heizler, Shari S. Neufeld, Barbara Ridberg, Cele Ridberg, Betty Rosenberg, Barbara Shefter, Baruch, Motaram, Gail, and Yashir Shirazi, Ginette Spier, and Grace Stern.

Closer still, I am forever indebted to the sources of my inspiration: Herschel Shosteck, mentor and morale builder; my wonderful children, Eron and Deborah; and especially my mother, Marion Miller, who passed on to me her love of cooking, and my late father, Leon Miller, who imbued me with his love of learning and all things Jewish.

Introduction

Thousands of books have been written on the subject of food. Thousands more will, no doubt, be added to shelves already flabby from supporting so much verbal gluttony. Why, then, yet another?

Most books which focus on food are recipe collections, "how-to" manuals devoted to teaching readers to prepare food or preserve it, freeze it or ignore it. This book is also a "how-to." But more importantly, it is a "how-come," devoted to providing answers to the innumerable questions which are constantly asked about this fascinating cuisine, questions that to date have been rarely answered.

If only these questions were as easily answered as that infamous answer offered by the fictional rabbi of Chelm to an equally infamous question: When asked one day by a congregant why the oceans were so salty, he opined: "Because of all the herring that live there!"

The biggest question of all is, of course, why are Jewish foods Jewish? Jews prepare spaghetti and pizza, quiche, pita, and sauerbraten. That doesn't make these foods Jewish. What does make certain foods "Jewish" is the intricate melange of historical circumstance, religious law, regional custom, and taste, which over the centuries has contributed to transforming recipes to symbols, instantly recognizable and, above all, shared by both the people who prepare the food and the ones who eat it. Not just edible mixtures of ingredients, the recipes have become part nourishment, part cultural road sign, and part fulfillment of a ritual, ultimately bestowed with a significance which is much greater than their capacity to fill one's stomach.

This not being Chelm where answers come so easily, I continue to answer the basic question in the several hundred pages which follow. Indeed, the question and its answer are the subject of this book.

In the process, since it is only right that a Jew answer one question by asking another, I have raised and commented on other questions:

—Why do Jews make such a fuss about food?

—Why is food so important to Jews?

—What influence has the Jewish dietary law (*kashrut*) had on making this cuisine unique?

—What were the foods of the Bible and do Jews still eat them today?

There are answers to each one of these questions, interesting answers which to date have required of those who try to answer them something of a scholar's zeal and commitment.

But not all of what there is to say about Jewish food can be answered in response to the questions I have just listed. Some of what has to be said concerns the questions that few of us think to ask: Why did Jews "invent" gefilte fish or pay such great tribute to as lowly a vegetable as the carrot? The purpose of this book is to offer answers to these questions, too.

Then there are the recipes, the really authentic recipes that are the outcome of this fascinating blend of religious precept, custom, and gastronomy. They are part of this book, too, for as entertaining and as informative as the answers to all these questions may be, it is equally rewarding to understand the cuisine by preparing the foods that are a part of it.

Since this book is a lexicon, it is organized alphabetically. Yet unlike conventional lexicons, in which the words of one language are listed and defined, this one, reflecting as closely as it does an almost unceasing historical pattern over thousands of years of displacement, flight, and dispersion, contains words from several languages.

Many of these words are taken from Yiddish, the language of Eastern European Jews and their descendants, or are "Yiddishized" versions of foreign terms. Since millions of Eastern European Jews immigrated to North America and Canada in the late nineteenth century and early twentieth century, it is the cookery of these Jews that Americans, Jewish and non-Jewish alike, think of as being Jewish. This book, written by an American Jew of Eastern European background, reflects this bias.

Yet, this book is much more than a detailed exploration of Eastern European cookery. Reflecting the breadth of Jewish culture throughout the world, it contains words other than those from Yiddish or what Leo Rosten calls "Yinglish" (bagels, blintzes, and lox qualify as Yinglish). Words of Spanish, Russian, English, Hebrew, and Arabic origin appear here as well.

Certain words appear again and again. If they are food terms, the repetition is a signal that the foods are extremely important. Challah, for example, appears over and over again. So do *tscholent* and matzah. Nonfood terms also appear repeatedly. Rather than define them each time they appear in the text, here is a brief definition of these commonly used terms:

Ashkanazic and *Sephardic:* Once the term Ashkanazic referred to Germany, the Jews of Germany, and their descendants living in other countries. Over the centuries it has come to mean much more. It now refers to the culture, folklore, social institutions, and people of Northern and Eastern Europe, and their descendants. It is also used to distinguish the Jewish people and culture of the areas mentioned above from Sephardic traditions, people, and culture. Sephardic refers to the descendants of the Jews who lived in Spain and Portugal, before their expulsion in 1492, and their heritage.

b.c.e. and *c.e.:* "Before the common era," and "of the common era," corresponding to b.c. and a.d.

Midrash: This is a word meaning to go beyond the literal meaning of the Bible in order to find new or inner meaning. Generally, the plural term, *midrashim,* refers to the literary and scholarly rabbinic writings set down during the period which began following the completion of the Talmud, and ended with the closing of the great Jewish schools in Babylonia in 1040 c.e.

Mishna: The word means repetition or doctrine, and refers to the body of Jewish law that had been orally transmitted over five and a half centuries, from the time of the scribes to the redaction of Judah ha-Nasi in the third century c.e. The Mishna was compiled in Palestine by approximately 150 teacher-scribes called collectively the *Tannaim.*

Shtetl: This is a Yiddish term meaning small town. The *shtetl* began to take shape in Eastern Europe in the Middle Ages when Polish nobles allowed Jews to settle in their private towns. Soon, Jews constituted the majority in many of these towns. There Jewish culture and tradition were left to develop and prosper nearly unhindered for many centuries. Life in the *shtetl* was intimate and revolved around the home, the market-place, and the synagogue. Because of economic and social problems as well as persecution, *shtetl* life began to decline in the nineteenth and early twentieth centuries. During World War II, most Eastern European Jews were killed and with them the *shtetl*, too, ceased to exist. However, the influence of the *shtetl* remains pervasive and can be seen today in the attitudes, customs, and folk beliefs of many Jews, and in modern Jewish art, literature, and, of course, food.

Talmud: This is the Hebrew word for "study" or "learning." Between 200 c.e. and 500 c.e. various scholars, called collectively the *Amoraim,* wrote discussions and commentary on the Mishna; these were called Gemara. Generally, the term Talmud refers to both the Mishna and Gemara. During the early period just mentioned, two distinct Talmuds emerged, one called the Jerusalem Talmud and the other the Babylonian Talmud. They differ somewhat in interpretation of the Oral Law as well as in language. The Babylonian Talmud is more highly regarded than the Jerusalem Talmud because the latter is incomplete.

Torah: Torah literally means "teaching" or "law." Moses is said to have received the Torah, or Written Law, on Mount Sinai during the forty-year period the Jews wandered in the desert following their exodus from Egypt. Tradition also has it that Moses was given a detailed explanation and analysis of the Written Law which was passed down from generation to generation and later became known as the Mishna or Oral Law. Thus, in the modern usage, Torah usually refers to both the Written and Oral Law, i.e., the Hebrew Bible as well as the entire body of Talmudic writings and interpretations.

Of course, this book is not the last word on Jewish food, just the latest. There are many gaps left to be filled by future research and discovery. The largest gap of all will never be filled: a gaping wound left by the Holocaust in Europe during World War II—the murder of six million Jews—which resulted in the near destruction of an entire culture. We can learn from survivors and surviving sources about what once was. But where food is concerned, even the best recollection is no substitute for the real experience of eating the food made by its creator. What might have been everyday contemporary experience has, regrettably, become history.

Metric Conversion Tables

U.S. LIQUID AND VOLUME MEASURES AND METRIC EQUIVALENTS

1 teaspoon =	5 milliliters
1 tablespoon =	15 milliliters
1 ounce =	29.5 milliliters
1 cup (8 ounces) =	237 milliliters
1 pint (16 ounces) =	473 milliliters
1/5 gallon or "fifth" =	¾ liter
1 quart =	.946 liter
½ gallon =	1.9 liters
1 gallon =	3.78 liters

U.S. DRY WEIGHT MEASURES AND METRIC EQUIVALENTS

1 ounce (avoirdupois) =	28.35 grams
¼ pound =	113.4 grams
½ pound =	226.8 grams
1 pound =	454 grams
2 1/5 pounds =	1 kilogram
5 pounds =	2.27 kilograms

Adafina

For nearly five centuries, the cooks of Madrid have enjoyed preparing a hearty soup they call *cocido madrileno.* No less than sixteen ingredients go into making it, at least half of them various kinds of meat and poultry. At the top of this feast fit for the likes of Gargantua goes the *pelota,* a giant meatball that is fried before being added to the *cocido* and cooked for a little less than an hour to be served to diners who must be on the verge of starvation to eat such hefty fare.

Cooking a *cocido,* a word which in Spanish means boiled soup (taken from the word for boil, *cocer*), is a multi-stepped process. First the chickpeas are soaked overnight, drained, and tied in a cheesecloth sack. Then they, the meat, chicken, and marrow bones are added to a huge kettle of boiling water, along with carrots, leaks, and a mint sprig. Later the sausage, cabbage, rice, and a clove of fried garlic are added, all topped by the *pelota.*

Now, turn the clock back at least 500 years, to a time when Jewish culture thrived in Spain. Take out three of a *cocido's* usual ingredients—the ham, bacon, and pork sausage—substituting for these non-kosher ingredients several eggs, raw and still in their shells. Add more flour or meal to the *pelota,* making of the ball a dumpling rather than a meatball. Layer the ingredients in a capacious pot before the cooking process begins, set the pot into a bed of hot coals or Sabbath oven, cover the pot with more coals, and let the ingredients bubble and simmer for hour upon hour.

Now the dish is not *cocido* but the uniquely Jewish dish *adafina* (say *ah—dah—feena*) or *dafina,* its name coming from the Arabic *dafana,* a word which means to cover or bury and, possibly, the ancient Hebrew word, *tzafun,* meaning "to conceal." Sacred writings dating from Biblical and post-Biblical times stated quite emphatically that fires could be kindled only before the Sabbath began. Writings from Talmudic times stated just as emphatically that eating hot food on the Sabbath was a good deed (mitzvah). The Jews of ancient times created a rather resourceful solution to what could have been a dilemma. Food for the Sabbath was partially cooked over a hot fire. Then the cooking pot was wrapped in thickly woven pieces of cloth or animal hide and placed in (not on) the fire or inside a special portable Sabbath oven. Placed so, the cooking pot became hidden from view by the surrounding bed of coals or by the oven itself.

Uncovered, the aroma and taste of *adafina* enticed Jew and non-Jew alike. Compared to the sardines, toasted cheese, and foul-smelling mutton, foods which a fourteenth-century Spanish poet, Juan Ruiz, claimed were the ordinary fare of his countrymen, eating *adafina,* "The Jew's Stew," he called it, was as good as feasting royally. On Saturday the Christians would cry to get invited to sit at a Jewish table to feast on it. "Pork their knives would refuse to cut," he exclaimed, knowingly. It was the *adafina* they hungered for.

Unfortunately, by 1492, a little more than a hundred years after Ruiz's lines had described so lustily the hungry longings of *adafina*'s non-Jewish devotees, the Spanish Inquisition forced the conversion of thousands upon thousands of its Jewish creators. In fact, once Torquemada was appointed Grand Inquisitor by Queen Isabella, cooking food overnight in an oven, a sign of Jewish practice, was an act which if discovered led to certain arrest. Pork, forbidden and much despised, now had to be added to the stew by *converso* cooks as a sign that, yes, their conversion to Catholicism had indeed taken place. Eggless and boiled, *adafina* became *cocido,* akin to other Spanish stews like *puchero* and *olla podrido.*

If the *conversos* in Spain altered the contents of the *adafina* in order to protect themselves, the Jews who fled the country by 1492 to relocate in Italy and North Africa did not. The original dish is prepared to this day in Morocco and is called by the same name. In fact, a dish similar to it is prepared by observant Jews everywhere in the world at exactly the same time of the week and using virtually the same recipe.

Elsewhere, however, its name is *tscholent.* But that is yet another story.

ADAFINA

Since outdoor wood or coal burning Sabbath ovens are a rarity these days, the following recipe can be prepared simply and authentically using an ordinary modern gas or electric oven.

4 tablespoons olive oil
2 cloves garlic
⅓ cup raw rice
2 leeks, white portions only, diced
2 pounds lean, boneless lamb, cubed
½ roasting chicken, cut into serving-sized pieces
1 or 2 marrow bones
6 eggs, raw and unshelled
3 carrots, peeled and quartered
1 mint sprig
1 small head cabbage, trimmed and quartered
½ pound kosher garlic sausage or salami, cut into thick chunks
½ pound chickpeas, presoaked overnight
Salt and pepper to taste

1. In a large pot, sauté the garlic, leeks, and rice in the oil. Remove from heat.
2. Layer remaining ingredients, leaving the chickpeas for last. Add 2 cups of water. Put the chickpeas in foil or a cheesecloth sack and place at the top.
3. Prepare the *pelota* and place it at the very top of the *adafina* ingredients. Cover.
4. Place in a 300-degree oven and cook for 3 hours. Reduce oven temperature to 150 degrees and keep warm until ready to serve.
   Note: The Sabbath law specifies that a food prepared for eating on the Sabbath must be at least ⅓ cooked before being placed in a warming oven or on top of a lighted burner where it can become completely cooked. Three hours is sufficient time to cook the adafina *completely so judge partial cooking time accordingly.*
5. When ready to serve, remove the *pelota* carefully and place it in the center of a large soup tureen. Surround the dumpling with remaining ingredients and serve into soup bowls.

Makes 6 to 8 servings.

PELOTA

¼ pound lean beef or veal, ground twice or macerated in a food processor
1 egg
Bread crumbs
2 tablespoons olive or vegetable oil
Nutmeg
Ground cloves
Salt and pepper

1. Mix meat, egg, and enough bread crumbs to form a compact ball. Add seasonings to taste.
2. Form into a large dumpling, adding more bread crumbs if needed to maintain the shape of the dumpling, and roll in bread crumbs.
3. Brown in oil.
4. Add to *adafina* ingredients and cover the pot.

Albondigas

If ever there was a place called Camelot for the Jewish people, it existed in a city in North Central Italy called Ferrara during the time of the Italian Renaissance. Jews came to Ferrara as refugees from the Spanish Inquisition, as immigrants from Bavaria and Central Europe, and as exiles from other Italian towns. Many came as outcasts, searching for a gentler, less fearsome life.

In Ferrara they found it and were able to settle into the life of the city as free, prosperous citizens. For almost ten decades, the entire sixteenth century, they were accorded the rank and respect they had sought for so long. Their success enabled many of them to achieve financial independence which, in turn, led to a general prosperity. They developed a taste for beautiful homes, retreats to country villas, and leisure time pursuits, among them the study of astronomy, geography, and poetry. Many of them became intellectual lights. And in the midst of all this economic success, there came a religious freedom rarely accorded to Jews living in the Diaspora. Sixteenth-century Ferrara boasted ten synagogues, one of them housed in a villa given to the Jews to be used for just that purpose.

While it is true the enlightened time of the Renaissance encouraged pursuit of the highest ideals of mankind, a more practical mutual backscratching could not be ignored either. The Italians needed the Jews for economic reasons; the Jews needed the Italians for social reasons. The whole setup was a perfect example of the delicate balance which can be struck between people and which can work to the mutual benefit of all concerned.

One Italian family in particular, the House of Este, worked diligently to promote and protect Jewish interests. The Este family accepted the Jews as neighbors and equals. Perhaps they dined together at banquets held at the Este family's beautiful table, exchanging pleasantries and philosophies as fruity Italian wines sloshed in tall goblets and huge platters piled high with food elaborately arranged were served before them.

So intertwined were the social lives of the inhabitants of Ferrara that on one of those platters was served a Jewish dish, "*A Fare Vivanda alla Hebraica, di carne,*" a recipe most probably brought to Italy by Spanish and Portuguese Jews fleeing the Inquisition. In Spain they would have called the dish *albondigas.* The recipe appears in a fine little book called, simply, *Libro Novo,* first printed in 1549 in Venice, a book written for a member of the illustrious Este family, Ippolito d'Este, the Cardinal Duke of Ferrara.

History, of course, sadly notes that the happy ever-aftering of Ferrara did not come true. By the end of the sixteenth century, persecution, distrust, and suspicion replaced friendship and economic cooperation. Camelot had vanished. Yet the recipe for a giant meatball with a glorious and succulent past remains, printed on a page which today is as brittle as a piece of uncooked pasta.

ALBONDIGAS

A Fare Vivanda alla Hebraica, di carne—Meat Dish, Hebrew Style

Take three pounds of boneless veal (without skins and nerves), and chop into small pieces. Add a mixture of crushed oily herbs, raisins, and a bit of spice of each kind. Mix everything together and cut in half. Add between these two halves the yolks of four hard-boiled eggs, and shape into one ball. Cook this in a soup with crushed oily herbs, some nutmeg, and enough saffron to give it color. Serve one or two slices according to size, on slices of bread, if you wish.

—*Libra Novo,* Venice, 1559

3 pounds boneless veal, finely chopped or ground
2 teaspoons dried tarragon (or ½ cup fresh tarragon leaves), crumbled
1 teaspoon fennel seeds
¾ cup white raisins
¼ teaspoon ground cloves
½ teaspoon cinnamon
1 teaspoon salt
Pinch mace
4 hard-boiled egg yolks

Gravy:
2 cups water
½ teaspoon nutmeg
¾ teaspoon fennel seeds
1 teaspoon tarragon
⅛ teaspoon saffron
½ teaspoon salt (or to taste)

1. Mix veal with 2 teaspoons tarragon, 1 teaspoon fennel seeds, raisins, cloves, cinnamon, mace, and salt.
2. Shape mixture into one large ball. Cut the ball in half. Remove the whites of 4 hard-boiled eggs and press 2 yolks into each half of the ball. Reshape into one large ball.
3. Measure remaining ingredients into a skillet and mix. Place ball in liquid, cover, and cook over very low heat for 1½ hours.
4. Place toasted bread into the bottom of a soup bowl topped by a slice of the meat and a small amount of the gravy.

Makes 6 servings.

Almond

Be not like the almond tree for it blooms before all trees and produces its fruit after them.

—*The Book of Ahikar,*
Fifth century b.c.e.

In southern Egypt during the fifth century b.c.e., there was a legendary man named Ahikar who was famous among the Jews for his wisdom. The profound philosophy of his early life was recorded in a book named after him. As he grew older (and wiser still), he grew sad because it became apparent that he would have no child of his own. Eager to have an heir to his legacy, Ahikar adopted the son of his sister.

Ahikar's counsels to his son became a part of *The Book of Ahikar* and more than ever it was poured over as a rich source of wisdom. In it Ahikar observed the virtually unique nature of the almond tree. The tree actually bears its fruit during the first two months of the year, well before any leaves appear. But the fruit itself does not ripen until late summer. From this phenomenon Ahikar drew his advice to his son. Sadly, this and the other lessons of Ahikar must have fallen on deaf ears, for he eventually was forced to disown his own son. The third part of *The Book of Ahikar* chronicles the curses of an old man. Ahikar had grown sadder, but wiser still.

While Ahikar was indeed correct in observing that the true fruit of the almond tree does not ripen until late summer after the outer shell has dropped off, there is a short time while the fruit is still green but when the shell itself is edible. It is this interim period of ripening that the Talmud takes note of in describing Jeremiah's vision: "Just as 21 days elapsed from the time the almond sends forth its blossom until the fruit ripens, so 21 days passed from the time the city was breached until the Temple was destroyed."

The almond is one of the two nuts mentioned in the Bible. The other is the pistachio. The almond was considered to be one of the "choice fruits of the land" sent by Jacob to the ruler of Egypt (Genesis 43:11). So important to the Jews was the little nut that it was included in the motif which decorated the golden candlesticks of the Tabernacle.

Probably originating along the South Mediterranean coast between Mesopotamia and Algeria, the almond has been considered to possess a wide assortment of qualities. Thousands of years ago cooks discovered that almonds could be ground into a flour or paste which could be used as a substitute for flour to make unleavened sweet cakes at Passover, the week when not even a single bread crumb can be used in food. It is used this way to this day by the North African Jews. The ancient Greeks believed that eating almonds would prevent intoxication (if only it were true!). Maimonides, the great twelfth-century Jewish physician who was influenced by the ancient Greeks, attributed to the almond " . . . the property of guarding the exteriors of the brain."

Of all the numerous recipes which use almonds, marzipan is perhaps the one which gets the most attention in Sephardic-Jewish homes, *mandelbrodt* in Ashkanazic-Jewish ones.

MANDELBRODT

5½ cups flour
4 teaspoons baking powder
½ teaspoon salt
1 cup sugar
1 teaspoon almond extract
½ cup vegetable oil
3 eggs
½ cup orange juice
1 teaspoon finely grated orange rind
1 cup sugar
¼ cup ground cinnamon
2 cups chopped walnuts or almonds
Apricot or strawberry preserves
Dried apricots, cut into small pieces (optional)

1. Sift together dry ingredients.
2. Make a well and add almond extract, oil, beaten eggs, and orange juice. Blend together. If dough is too sticky to handle, add more flour. The dough should be stiff enough to roll out easily.
3. Divide into four parts. Roll out one part at a time on a floured board or table. Brush with oil.
4. Mix cinnamon and sugar together and sprinkle over the dough. Spread preserves, sprinkle with chopped nuts and chopped apricots.
5. Roll like a jelly roll. Seal ends. Brush top with oil and sprinkle with cinnamon-sugar.
6. Bake at 350 degrees for 45 minutes on oiled cookie sheets. Remove from sheet at once and place on rack to cool.

Makes 48 one-inch-wide pieces. This recipe freezes exceptionally well.

MARMALADE OF EGGS THE JEWS WAY

Take the yolks of twenty-four eggs, beat them for an

hour; clarify one pound of the best moist sugar, four spoonfuls of orange-flower water, one ounce of blanched and pounded almonds; stir all together over a very slow charcoal fire, keeping stirring it all the while one way, till it comes to a consistence; then put it into coffeecups, and throw a little beaten cinnamon on the top of the cups.

This marmalade, mixed with pounded almonds, with orange-peel, and citron, are made in cakes of all shapes, such as birds, fish, and fruit.

—Hannah Glasse, *The Art of Cookery Made Plain and Easy,* 1751

Aphrodisiacs

Until the turn of this century, venereal cookery had always had its place in Judaism and included a truly astonishing number of substances, most of them common foods like artichokes and almonds, beets, pomegranates, and fried onions, but others so awful that it is difficult to imagine that ingesting them could have resulted in anything but celibacy.

Through the ages, into concoctions drawn primarily from Greek, Arabic, Roman, and German sources went such purported sexual stimulants as sparrows' brains and galanga roots, garlic buds, rooster testes, and sea holly. They were a-brewed and a-stewed apparently by women but almost always imbibed by men who, enjoined by Jewish law to perpetuate the human race, took the traditional view that ingesting a particular food or recipe ensured not just their performance or virility but their fertility.

The distinction is an important one. Non-Jewish sources have always emphasized the aphrodisiac's power to promote desire. The official Jewish attitude, espoused throughout the centuries by the rabbis and gleaned primarily from the Talmud and later writings, took account of desire for desire's sake. But in keeping with both the goal of procreation and a very straitlaced view of sexuality, the rabbis actively rejected the notion of using an aphrodisiac to promote any more desire than what was absolutely necessary to ensure the act of sexual intercourse taking place. Lust for its own sake was (and still is) totally contrary to Jewish teaching. Fruitfulness, on the other hand, is a blessing.

So, too, did mainstream Judaism steer clear of the medieval Moslem view of aphrodisiacs as drugs. In treatise after treatise, several written by no less a Jewish personage than philosopher-physician Moses Maimonides (who wrote down his medical discoveries more for his Arab patrons and patients than for his fellow Jews), are hundreds of recipes for potency using such ingredients as pigeons' eggs, marrow bones, almond milk, asparagus seeds, rose petals, and even chicken soup. Judging from the breadth and depth with which the subject of potency was treated, the lack of it must have been one of the great problems facing the medieval Arab man, that seemingly hapless practicer of polygamy!

Of the love essences, extracts, witches' brews, and potions that must have run like gurgling rivers in the imagination and kitchens of medieval Europe, there was also an official Jewish disdain. But, again, the Jews of Europe living in the Middle Ages weren't always as unconcerned about their love lives as the rabbis would have wanted them to be. In fact, the pages of Jewish medical treatises of the time are filled with descriptions of various mixtures which would aid and abet desire. One fifteenth-century codex written in Yiddish contains an astonishing number of recipes for aphrodisiacs: 408 potions to ensure cohabitation; 528 to promote love; 547 to keep the love of one's wife; 547 to prevent one's wife from desiring another man; and a startling 1,204 to be used to induce one's destined mate to come to his bed!

One love recipe recommended washing with (not drinking) kosher milk.

> For love, take the milk of a kosher, first-born cow, and wash your face with her milk. On the same day an angel will come to you, and all your words will be heard, and all your wishes fulfilled.

Another made unusual use of cabbage picked before sunrise plus a few nondigestibles strewn or slept on rather than eaten.

> If you want to cause the woman who is destined for you to come to your bed, take a cabbage—it must be picked

> before sunrise—and take a shingle from the roof, or straw, and some earth from under the doorstep. When you go to sleep, place the cabbage under your head and the shingle on your body, and scatter the earth around your bed, and say the following: "Shingle that covers me, cabbage that wakes me, I charge you in the name of the Lord, God of Israel, to bring my love to me so that we may drink mead and wine. An angel should bring her and show me her form as she walks the earth." And when you wish to send her back, say "I charge you to go from me in the name of Michael, Raphael, and Gabriel." She will leave you.

These and thousands of others were the product of a curious blend of Germanic folk sources, Biblical and Talmudic references, and Hebrew phrases taken from the vast array of mystical literature, all put down in medieval Yiddish.

Nowadays, brewer's yeast eaten straight is about as raunchy a potency potion as we'll allow ourselves. Currently, the entire lore of aphrodisiacs, Jewish and non-, is treated as quaint historical nonsense. Masters and Johnson have taken over where slept-on cabbage left off. But beyond technique, in this collection of old-fashioned elixirs written on a page of parchment in ruinous condition may be a recipe which really works. It may reek of galanga roots and require the munching of raw asparagus seeds. But, if rediscovered, the recipe may one day be as sought after as sparrows' brains and sea holly, especially if it's kosher.

AN APHRODISIAC

> Avicenna and other physicians besides him mention certain kinds of beneficial sweets and behold, we have put together out of them a sweet which is mild in effect and tastes pleasant, and which has in practice proven itself successful and this is its preparation: Pine, pistachio, and almond kernels, of each two ounces. Sesame fried together with its peel; eruca seed and seed kernel of melons, of each one ounce, sugar and skimmed bee honey four liters. Fry all kernels with sesame oil then the sweetness congeals to halvah as is usual. However do not make the fire too strong. And let the master know that all these foods prepared for the purpose of sexual intercourse must be taken at the end of the bath, in fact, if it is possible to

drink thereafter three ounces in measure of good smelling wine, this is all the more effective for the purpose intended, and also to put fat on the body.

—Moses Maimonides, *Treatise on Sexual Intercourse,* twelfth century

Apple

I said: "I will climb up into the palm-tree,
I will take hold of the branches thereof;
And let thy breasts be as clusters of the vine,
And the smell of thy countenance like apples;
And the roof of thy mouth like the best wine,
That glideth down smoothly for my beloved,
Moving gently the lips of those that are asleep."

—Song of Songs, 7:9–10

"And . . . she took of the fruit . . . and did eat . . . and she gave also unto her husband, and he did eat" (Genesis 3:6). So the trouble began. A rather simple story about the Garden of Eden, Adam and Eve, the serpent, and a piece of fruit has had more impact on us than any other. It is understandable, then, why every single word of this Biblical passage has been read and reread, studied and scrutinized, explained and elucidated.

Although the heart of the controversy involves God and two all-too-human creatures, scholars have focused almost as much on the fruit. Indeed, for centuries Jewish scholars have written bushels indicting not just the apple, but also the peach, citron, apricot, quince, lemon, fig, grape, wheat, nut and, of all things, the mandrake as being the *real* forbidden fruit, all because the Bible was never clear on what fruit was actually eaten. But after all has been said and done and written, in most people's minds, the apple is the culprit.

Ah, the sweet taste of the apple and the look of it: In Jewish mystical and legal writings, the apple's image is polished to a high gloss, its essence overpoweringly sensuous.

Just a few chapters after the story of Adam and Eve appears, the verse, "the smell of my son is as the smell of a field which the Lord has blessed" (Genesis 27:27), is interpreted as referring to the fragrance of an apple orchard. In the Talmud the Jews of ancient Israel are compared to an apple tree. In the mystical writings of the Kabbalah, "the orchard of holy apples" signifies the most sublime holiness. The *tappuach* is an attribute of God, synonymous with beauty because, says the body of medieval mystical writings called the *Zohar*, beauty "diffuses itself in the world as an apple." In the Middle Ages so special was it that incantations would be etched into the tough skin of each piece before it was eaten.

The importance given the apple, sweet and juicy, luscious and tempting as it ever was, is most apparent at the time of the new year. In the traditional Jewish New Year preparations, the apple dipped in honey takes on a special meaning: "O Lord, that the year just begun be as good and sweet a year." According to some, the two are a symbolic combination equaling "the Field of Apples" (in Hebrew the *sadeh shel tappuhim* or *chakal tappuhin*), the metaphor used in Jewish mystical writings to describe the biblical Garden of Eden.

FRESH APPLE CAKE

1½ cups fresh diced raw apples
½ cup shortening
½ cup brown sugar
½ cup granulated sugar
1 egg
1½ cups sifted flour
½ teaspoon baking powder
½ teaspoon baking soda
½ teaspoon salt
½ teaspoon cinnamon
¼ teaspoon nutmeg
⅛ teaspoon cloves
½ cup buttermilk

Topping:
½ cup brown sugar
½ teaspoon cinnamon
½ cup chopped walnuts

1. Cream shortening and sugars. Add egg and beat well.
2. Resift flour with baking powder, baking soda, salt, and spices. Add to creamed mixture alternately with buttermilk.
3. Fold in apples. Turn into a greased 9-inch-square baking pan. Mix together topping and sprinkle over batter.
4. Bake at 350 degrees for 40 minutes or until cake springs back when touched.

Makes 12 servings.

APPLE STRUDEL

Dough:

3¼ cups all-purpose flour
¾ cup hi-gluten flour*
4 sticks margarine or butter (1 pound)
1 cup ginger ale
Pinch of salt
1 teaspoon grated lemon rind
1 teaspoon orange juice
Dash ground cloves
1 cup melted margarine or butter

Filling:

6 large tart apples, cored and seeded
½ cup seedless raisins
½ cup walnuts, pecans, or almonds
1 cup brown sugar
2 teaspoons cinnamon
1 teaspoon grated lemon rind

1. Sift the flour. Add margarine, ginger ale, and remaining dough ingredients (except melted butter or margarine) and stir to form a soft ball. Place on a floured board and knead for 10 minutes. Cover with a warm cloth and let stand for 30 minutes. While the dough is resting, make the filling.
2. To make the filling, chop the apples, raisins, and walnuts coarsely. Add remaining ingredients and mix well.
3. Cover a table or large counter with a clean, smooth tablecloth. Sprinkle flour over the top of the cloth. Roll out the dough as thin as possible without tearing it, making sure that it is not sticking to the cloth. If you want a very thin dough, pull from the edges all around the dough by placing your hands underneath the dough, palms down, and gently stretching the dough over the backs of your hands.
4. Brush melted margarine over the stretched dough, place the filling in an even roll the full length of the dough and within two inches inside the edge. Fold the two-inch piece over the filling, and then lift the cloth over the filling so that the dough will roll over the filling. Gently flatten dough edges against filled roll. Close off the edges by pinching them gently.
5. Cut pastry to fit pans or cookie sheets. The pans should be greased well. Brush tops of the strudel with margarine

*Available at health-food stores in 2- and 5-pound sacks.

and bake at 375 degrees for 35–45 minutes, or until golden brown. If top looks dried out while baking, brush on more margarine. Cool partially and mark into 1 to 1½ inch pieces. Cut when cold.

Makes 36 large pieces.

Vanilla Sauce

2 cups milk
4 egg yolks
1 tablespoon cornstarch
¾ cup sugar
⅛ teaspoon salt
2 teaspoons vanilla
1 teaspoon rum or to taste

1. Heat the milk in the top of a double boiler until just below the boiling point.
2. Combine egg yolks, sugar, cornstarch, and salt, beating well. Beat the hot mixture gradually into the yolks.
3. Return to double boiler for 5 minutes and cook over low heat, stirring constantly until thick. Cool. Add vanilla and rum. Reheat to lukewarm just before serving. Pour around (not over) individual servings of strudel.

Makes 2 cups.

Artichoke

One day, while contemplating the appearance of the artichoke, a vegetable decidedly strange-looking and shriveled, the ancient Roman Pliny screeched: These are the most "monstrous productions of the earth." Obviously, he had never tasted them.

Eventually, Romans of all ages came to love the taste of the artichoke, although it took fifteen hundred long years for them to do so. In particular, they came to favor artichoke "cooked the Jews' way," *carciofi alla giudia,* a simple dish dating from the Renaissance, prepared by frying the youngest, most tender artichokes of all in a bath of hot olive oil. Between the Via Avenula and the Piazza di Monte and the Ponte Quattro

Capi, within the area of the old Jewish ghetto of Rome, a visitor to any one of several restaurants can still find *carciofi alla giudia* prepared following a 450-year-old Jewish recipe.

It was the French artichoke that the Renaissance Jews relished, by the way, a vegetable reintroduced into Italy by Catherine di Medici.

CARCIOFI ALLA GIUDIA—DEEP-FRIED ARTICHOKES

Young artichokes, those having a very small choke or no choke at all, are the most desirable ones to use to prepare this recipe.

4 young artichokes
3 large cloves garlic, minced
4 cups olive oil, for frying
Salt and pepper

1. Remove stiff outer leaves. To remove tough, pointed leaves at the top of the artichoke, cut crossways about ½ inch from the top of the point. Remove stem. Discard leaves and stem. Wash artichokes and drain dry.
2. Over a medium flame, heat olive oil in a deep saucepan or fryer. Add minced garlic. Carefully place artichokes, two at a time, into oil. Fry until crisp, about 20 minutes. Remove from oil and drain on absorbent paper. Repeat using 2 remaining artichokes.
3. Dust lightly with freshly ground pepper and salt. Gently flatten leaves to look like an open flower.

Serve as an appetizer.

B

Bagel

To the market we must run
Bagelach *to buy*
To smear them with butter
Father and Mother
Should lead you to the marriage canopy.

—19th century Jewish folksong (Russian)

Said Israel Baal Shem Tov* one day to a simpleton who didn't understand the value of bagels: "There are many non-Jews in the wheat field where you work. Take the bagel which you carry with you and throw it toward them. You will see how they will come to you."

And so it happened that only an hour after the simpleton had left the famed Hasidic master, he fell into a swiftly flowing river. The non-Jews were far away at the top of the mountain. How was he to let them know that he was drowning? Then he remembered that in his pocket was a roll with the power to save him, its round shape a symbol of life itself. With his last bit of strength he threw it to the people on the mountain. And, with the help of the Almighty, just as the Bescht had told him, the people came to save him from drowning in the river.

Which all goes to show you as one pundit proclaimed several decades ago, a bagel (even a soggy one) is much more than a doughnut with rigor mortis.

The hard, chewy roll, the name for which comes from a German word meaning bracelet or ring, for hundreds of years—from medieval times until the second decade of this century—doubled as an amulet of great and amazing power.

*The founder of the European Jewish mystical religious movement called Hasidism. He was also called the B-e-s-c-h-t, the acronym for Baal Shem Tov, meaning master of the Good Name. He lived in the eighteenth century in Eastern Europe.

Long before it was transformed from mere roll with a hole to miraculous lifesaver, the dense, chewy circlet of baked dough (an undainty morsel if there ever was one) was given to women about to give birth as well as to the midwives who attended her. A chaser of evil spirits, of demons, of the Evil Eye, in Germany's eastern provinces and in Poland during the seventeenth century, a bagel was life insurance for the superstitious.

Traditionally, bagels have been boiled and baked just as they are today, in large commercial ovens, to be eaten by everyone in town, not just Jews. In Europe, especially in Eastern Europe, they were sold in the crowded marketplace of each city and *shtetl* by bagel sellers who carried dozens of them stacked one on top of the other on long sticks.

The bagel's special reputation, altered somewhat to include the power of granting prosperity to its eaters and pocketers, made its way across the Atlantic to North America steerage class in the late nineteenth and early twentieth centuries. New immigrants were known to boast to their relatives still in the Old Country that not only were the streets of New York paved with gold, they were also lined with pushcarts piled high with hot bagels. What better sign of good fortune was there, after all?

Before World War II, a bagel had rarely been known to run in the same circles with lox (smoked salmon) or cream cheese. You ate a bagel with butter. Period. But in the years following the War, again a time when outward signs of prosperity were greatly sought after, the bagel was paired off with a fish with a very high price tag per pound. Just in case the rest of the world didn't understand that having a bagel on one's plate meant prosperity, it would understand that, if a person could afford to eat lox, he or she was well-to-do.

So lox became the bagel's stand-in, a more obvious sign of good fortune. It helped, of course, that the combination tasted wonderful, especially when the two halves of a bagel, slathered with cream cheese and layered with lox, bracketed sliced sweet onion, cucumber, and fresh tomato as well.

BAGELS

3½ to 4 cups all-purpose or unbleached flour

2 teaspoons salt

2 packages (2 tablespoons) dry yeast
1 cup lukewarm water
2 eggs, separated
3 tablespoons sugar
3 tablespoons vegetable oil
3 quarts boiling water
1 teaspoon cold water
Poppy seeds or sesame seeds

1. Sift flour and salt together. Add yeast to ½ cup lukewarm water. Stir into flour. Reserve 1 tablespoon of egg yolk in a cup and beat remaining eggs lightly. Add sugar, eggs, and oil to remaining water and blend with flour mixture.
2. Mix to form a dough, adding more flour if necessary to make it firm. Flour hands and turn dough out onto lightly floured board. Knead until smooth and elastic (5–10 minutes).
3. Place in an oiled bowl, cover, and let rise at room temperature until doubled in bulk (about 1½ hours). Preheat oven to 425 degrees.
4. Punch down the dough and knead again until all air is pressed out and dough is smooth.
5. Pull off pieces of dough and roll into ropes about 7 inches long by ¾ inch thick. Form into rings, moistening ends and overlapping them; press ends to seal. Let stand for 10 minutes.
6. Slide a few at a time into the hot water. Turn after one minute and remove with a slotted spoon after one more minute.
7. Mix egg yolk with the cold water and brush tops of bagels with the mixture.
8. Place bagels on oiled cookie sheets and, if desired, sprinkle with poppy or sesame seeds. Bake for 20 minutes or until golden brown.

Makes 15 bagels.

To make a lox and bagel sandwich: Cut each bagel in half crosswise. Slather cream cheese on each inner half. Layer one half of bagel with lox (belly or Nova), a slice of sweet onion, a tomato slice, and several cucumber slices. Top with other bagel half and serve.

Baladur

In the medieval yeshivas of Mainz and Prague, Cracow and Rome, Hamburg and Paris, year after year, for century upon century, sat the Rabbinical Student—young, old, eager, indifferent, brilliant, slow, and often forgetful. Facing him in some small unheated room, poorly lit by a candle or two, would be the Rav—the great teacher, the Talmudic Scholar—relentlessly drilling a passage of Gemara, or a specific legal commentary into a brain already crowded with other passages, other commentaries.

The Scholar would address the Student, calling him Velvel or Moshe, Abraham or Yankel. "Tell me, what is the opinion of Rabbi Hayyim?" Or, "Does not Rabbi Zvi-Hirsch say otherwise?" Sometimes the Student would struggle for the answer, obviously floundering; and the Scholar, sensing all in but a moment's time, would be displeased.

"You must do better. Review, review your studies; then you will have no need even of *baladur,*" he would implore.

"*Baladur.* Ach!" The student would then chide himself for forgetting even the *baladur* today, forgetting to mix the ingredients for it. No wonder his mind was in such a state!

Passed down through the centuries from scholar to scholar, the various recipes for *baladur,* or small *baladur* as it was usually called, reached far into the German Jewish scholarly communities of the Middle Ages. Thought by the Moslems to be a highly effective memory strengthener, the original recipes were based on the use of nuts from the family of trees and shrubs called anacardia. (The cashew is in this family.) In the yeshivas of Germany, where having a good memory was of incredible importance since much of what one learned may never have been committed to paper but was transmitted orally from community to community, the benefit of *baladur* became legendary.

The proverb, "Review, review your studies, and you'll have no need of *baladur,*" became erroneously attributed to the Talmud, and the original recipe containing the specific nut of the anacardia plant was supplanted by ingredients much closer at hand. Ultimately, those who used it came to think of the various concoctions called *baladur* as being distinctively Jewish.

The first formula was simple to prepare as long as the Student knew how to multiply:

> Eat hazelnuts for 9 days beginning with six and adding six more each day.

The second depended on arithmetical knowledge, a strong stomach, and a passing acquaintance with two short passages from the Bible:

> Eat pepper seeds for 9 days, beginning with one seed and doubling the dose until it reaches 256 seeds on the 9th day; and each time before you consume them, recite Deuteronomy 33:8–11 and Psalms 119:9–16.

The third, suited only for a stomach lined by cast iron, is a real recipe, much like the ones found in Jewish medical texts of the Middle Ages:

> Grind cloves, long peppers, dates, ginger, galanga-root, and muscat nuts in equal quantities, beat them with olive oil into a paste, and eat a little every morning before breakfast.

Could one, did one, ingest these unsavory sounding formulas every day of one's scholarly life, or just when the memory seemed to be lapsing acutely? Did the Student know when to stop or did eating *baladur* and, as a result, remembering, give one a life-long dependence on its properties? Historians are silent on this subject, ignorant perhaps, or, without their own dose of *baladur*, forgetful of what they might once have known.

Barnacle Goose

The barnacle goose is a real goose all right. But the word barnacle is a misnomer, a corruption of the word Hibernia, meaning Ireland. The Hibernia goose is a migratory bird which lives in the Arctic region during the winter. Every year it flies south in large flocks to spend the summer on the western shores of the British Isles. During the Middle Ages, possibly as early as the eleventh century but certainly by the twelfth, a strange legend evolved concerning the Hibernia or barnacle goose. Perhaps because it rested with dozens of others of its flock in the high branches of trees, the story was circulated that the barnacle goose actually grew directly from the tree trunk itself, attached to it by its beak. Less popular was the notion that the barnacle goose grew from a seashell.

Said Gerald of Wales, the original conqueror of Ireland and twelfth-century expert on the habits and importance of barnacle geese:

> There are here many birds that are called "Barnacles" (*bernacoe*) which in a wonderful way Nature unnaturally produced; they are like wild geese but smaller. For they are born at first like pieces of gum on logs of timber washed by the waves. Then enclosed in shells of a free form they hang by their beaks as if from the moss clinging to the wood and so at length in process of time obtaining a sure covering of feathers, they either dive off into the waters or fly away into free air. . . . I have myself seen many times with my own eyes more than a thousand minute corpuscles of this kind of bird hanging to one log on the shore of the sea, enclosed in shells and already formed . . .

As improbable as these notions were, even more improbable was the use to which they were put, for the myth of the barnacle goose served to further undermine the extremely strained social and political relationship between Christians and Jews in twelfth- and thirteenth-century England. Nothing was too absurd to be used to heap abuse on the much-hated and reviled Jews. So it was that the barnacle goose was hauled out, invented perhaps, to offer proof to the Jews of the Immaculate Conception. "Born of pieces of gum, on logs of timber," they were, and eaten by the bishops because they were "not flesh nor . . . born of the flesh," said Gerald. "Be wise," Gerald continued, "Be wise wretched Jew."

> Be wise even though late. The first generation of man from dust without male or female (Adam) and the second from the male without the female (Eve) thou darest not deny in veneration of thy law. The third alone from male and female, because it is usual, thou approvest and affirmist with thy hard beard. But the fourth, in which alone is

salvation, from female without male, that with obstinate malice thou detestest to thy own destruction.

Blush, wretch, blush, and at least turn to nature. She is an argument for the faith and for our conviction procreates and produces every day animals without either male or female.

No Jew would have taken seriously the link Gerald made between the barnacle goose and the Immaculate Conception. But many did take seriously the question of the fowl's suitability as food and went so far as to write nearly a dozen legal opinions concerning its ritual fitness for their table. Caught up in the muddle created by the bird's being considered by the Christian community as neither meat, fish, nor fowl, the rabbis of the time investigated the problem with the Jewish scholar's usual thoroughness and seriousness, yet never agreed on the final classification of this strange creature.

Their debate sounds today like a borscht-belt comedy routine, but there can be absolutely no doubt that the opinions were rendered in absolute seriousness. If, as Gerald of Wales and practically everyone else opined, the barnacle goose did in fact grow on trees, and if it could be eaten even on meatless fast days by the Christians of England and Ireland, then perhaps, thought several less-than-distinguished medieval rabbis, Jews could eat it in the same way they ate fruit—as a *parve* (neutral) food. Yes, this group wrote after looking into the matter and deciding to move with the tide, the barnacle goose did not have to be ritually slaughtered. It wasn't meat. Nor did it have to be eaten separately from milk or cheese.

Other rabbis of the time who surely must have smelled a rat (or was it a barnacle goose?) discussed the matter, feeling compelled to form some opinion about it, pro or con (typical of scholarly rabbis, after all), and dispatched the barnacle goose to the place where they felt it rightfully belonged according to Jewish law: to the ritual slaughterer if Jews were to eat it at all and to a table where no milk foods would be served.

Yet another group of learned medieval Jewish scholars regarded it as shellfish and forbade its being eaten at all. Even the *Shulchan Arukh,* the masterful sixteenth-century compilation of Jewish laws, a code which governs Jewish practices to this day, contains a passage which alludes to the phenomenon of the barnacle goose, ruling that birds which grow on trees are not permissible as food since they are regarded as creeping things, a category of forbidden foods set down in the Bible.

Beets

Ubiquitous in Jewish cuisine, vying for first place with cabbage, beets have been savored from ancient times to the present, from Babylonia to Baghdad, Bessarabia to Brooklyn, Brest-Litovsk to Baku, by the likes of the kingly and wise Solomon, the learned Talmudist Hanina, and especially by the ordinary folks who have eaten beets in incredibly creative forms.

Grown most often in climates where summers are extremely short (notably in Northern and Eastern Europe), beets have always taken well to being preserved so that a family could make excellent use of them for wintertime food. In German and Eastern European Jewish homes, throughout the centuries, beets were used in delectable soups, jams, and marinades. Naturally sweet, they were also used to make candy and, as such, provided a welcome relief from a rather sour-tasting peasant diet.

Today, beets are associated with four dishes often eaten in Jewish homes where the antecedents are Ashkanazic: borscht, *rosl, roslfleysch,* and beet *eingimakhts* (preserves). Borscht really is a Russian dish, *rosl* is a dish with a fascinating, if confusing, Polish-Jewish-Russian background, and a good *roslfleysch,* according to some, doesn't have a beet in it. Beet *eingimakhts* are preserves eaten traditionally at the New Year for two reasons: because the preserve is sweet and because the Hebrew word for beaten back—*salek*—is associated with another Hebrew word *selek* (beet) in the following phrase: "We eat the *selek* on Rosh Hashonah so that our enemies will be beaten."

BEET EINGIMAKHTS

8 cups beets, peeled and quartered
6 cups sugar
2 cups honey

5 teaspoons ground ginger
2 lemons, sliced thin
2 cups coarsely chopped walnuts or almonds

1. Cook beets in boiling salted water until almost tender. Cut into small cubes, or julienne if preferred.
2. In a large saucepan, combine sugar, honey, ginger, and water. Stir gently over low heat until sugar has dissolved.
3. Bring to a boil, add beets and lemons. Lower heat and cook gently until beets begin to have a transparent look and mixture is extremely thick, about 1 hour.
4. Add the nuts and cook for another 5 minutes.
5. Pour beet mixture into sterilized jelly glasses. Store in a dark place to preserve beautiful beet color.

Makes 18–20 8-ounce glasses.

Blintzes

Contemplating the eating of a plate of blintzes is not quite like receiving a love letter but there are certain agreeable similarities. First, it's nice just to look at the envelope and anticipate the delights within. Blueberries, maybe? Pot cheese mixed with butter and cinnamon? Brandied strawberries, perhaps? Soon the envelope becomes too difficult to resist since it's what's inside that counts. Finally, if the news is as good as you hoped it would be, comes the sweet aftertaste. Not completely satisfied, you anticipate another and then another. All of this should give you some idea of why no one ever uses the singular form of this word, *blintzeh* (rhymes with *mints—eh*).

The postmark is Ukrainian on all the envelopes, by the way, and rare now, since the date is an old one, ancient probably. In Russia *blinis* (pancakes) have been traditional Lenten food, the basis for this custom apparently dating from ancient times when the coming of spring's equinox was greeted with joy and celebration. The round shape of blintzes and *blinis* reflected the round shape of the sun.

The season for blintzes filled with cheese, according to the Jewish calendar, is the time of Shavuot when recipes using dairy products are traditional. Also the rolled blintzes, if placed side by side in pairs on the plate, suggest the tablets of the Law given to Moses, the event which is commemorated on Shavuot.

Jewish food chauvinists consider crepes to be French blintzes. However, there is an abundance of historical evidence (much of it in medieval books of Jewish law) to support the theory that the two foods, so very alike, really developed independently of one another with a probable common source. A pancake, after all, has been around for a long, long time.

THE BASIC PANCAKE RECIPE

3 eggs
½ teaspoon salt
1 cup water or milk
1 cup sifted all-purpose flour
Butter, shortening, or vegetable oil

1. In a large mixing bowl, beat the eggs thoroughly. Add salt, water or milk, and flour. Beat until smooth.
2. Melt ½ teaspoon butter, shortening, or oil in a 5-inch or 6-inch skillet over medium heat. Pour into the skillet just enough batter to make one thin pancake. This will be about 2 tablespoons.
3. Now work quickly. Tilt the pan to coat the bottom and fry the pancake until firm. It should not be brown. Cook on one side only. Carefully turn the pancake out of the pan and place bottom side up on a clean thin towel.
4. Continue with remaining batter, greasing the skillet as needed. This recipe will make 18–20 pancakes.
5. Place 1½ tablespoons of any filling on one end of the pancake and roll it up as you would a jelly roll, folding the edges inside to form an enclosed pocket for the filling.
6. At this point, you may freeze or refrigerate the blintzes for future use. When ready to serve, fry in shortening until golden brown or bake them in a greased baking dish at 425 degrees until brown.

BASIC BLINTZES

Prepare basic pancake recipe. Fill with the following mixture: 2 cups dry cottage cheese (or substitute drained creamed cottage cheese), 1 egg, 1 teaspoon softened butter, 1 teaspoon grated lemon rind, ½ teaspoon vanilla, and 2 teaspoons sugar. Fry or bake and serve with sour cream.

APPLE BLINTZES

Prepare basic pancake recipe. Fill with the following mixture: 2 cups finely chopped, peeled apples, 1 tablespoon ground almonds, ¼ teaspoon salt, 1 tablespoon brown sugar, ¼ teaspoon ground cinnamon, 1 tablespoon lemon juice, 1 unbeaten egg white, 1 tablespoon apple wine (optional). Fry or bake and serve with a topping of cinnamon sugar.

BLUEBERRY BLINTZES

Prepare basic pancake recipe. Fill with a mixture of 1½ cups well-drained cooked or canned blueberries, 1½ tablespoons all-purpose flour, 1 tablespoon sugar, and ¼ teaspoon ground cinnamon. Fry or bake and serve with whipped cream.

RHUBARB BLINTZES

Prepare basic pancake recipe. Fill with strawberry preserves. Fry or bake blintzes. Prepare fresh rhubarb as follows: remove leaves, wash, and cut into 1-inch pieces. Place cut rhubarb over water in the top pan of a double boiler. Cover and steam for 20 or 25 minutes. Do not stir. Add ½ to ¾ cups sugar. Remove from heat and add cinnamon or ginger to taste. Spoon over warm blintzes.

Bokser

Every day a Heavenly Voice comes forth and says: The whole world is supplied with food on account of my son Hanina, while he is satisfied with one kab *of carobs (⅓ of a peck) from one Sabbath to the other.*

—The Talmud

When Jews say *bokser* they are not referring to a 200-pound man of muscle wearing oversized mittens and satin shorts. He's a *baak—ser. Bokser* (say *bawk—ser*) is the Yiddish word for carob, the word most commonly used by Jews to describe the seed pod which they eat in its absolutely natural state.

Nutritious? Absolutely. Appealing? To taste a carob pod's cloying sweetness is to make the thought of eating salt herring pleasurable. To chew it is to invite a trip to the dentist. To swallow it presupposes a digestive system perfectly ordered and on the alert.

Yet beyond the pod lies a cornucopia of international recipes, opening up luscious gastronomic possibilities which the Jews have rarely explored.

For centuries the Arabs have extracted the sweet syrup from the tough leathery carob pod and used it, rather than sugar or honey, for making a syrup for baklava or *kadaif*. Delicious. A thousand years ago, the French and English were pulverizing carob pods (brought back from the Crusades) and mixing the powder with heavy or "clouted" cream to make nutritious substitutes for animal flesh. Scrumptious. Today, powdered to a talcumlike fineness, health food devotees use it as a chocolate substitute in everything from "Tiger's Milk" to candy bars. Not bad.

But to this day the Jews, always aware of the foods being eaten by non-Jews living closeby, have eaten the dense pod just as it comes from the tree and always on two special holidays of the year, Lag Ba'Omer and Tu Bishvat; on Lag Ba'Omer because on that day it is traditional to remember a very ancient story, and on Tu Bishvat, the holiday of trees.

From a people so concerned with the taste and form of what they have chosen to eat comes this seeming lack of interest in the carob's versatility. Accidental? Of course not. Jews resist the culinary possibilities for one reason alone: to taste, to bite into a food that practically bites back, and to remember that in the second century c.e., two men, Rabbi Simeon bar Yochai, a student of Rabbi Akiba, and his son Eleazar, having been chased into hiding in a cave in the hills of ancient Israel by the Romans, survived, according to legend, for twelve long years on nothing more than the pods of the carob tree. If Simeon and Eleazar could manage twelve years of the stuff, the tradition goes, two days of *bokser* make for a very small sacrifice indeed.

Miraculous occurrences in Judaism are not abundant. What happened to Rabbi Simeon and his son has always been considered one of those rare miracles, particularly by the Kabbalists, the Jewish mystics who consider Rabbi Simeon to be their earliest and most important contributor: credited with authoring the *Zohar*, the collection of mystical writings and teachings, pupil of the famous Rabbi Akiba, and outspoken in his hatred for his Roman oppressors. Tough, hardy, and thick-skinned yet sweetened by a love of learning and abiding faith, to describe Simeon is to describe the food on which he sustained himself.

By the way, Jews don't call *bokser* carob. *Bokser* is *bokser* where Yiddish or "Yinglish" is spoken. Otherwise, Jews usually call the food *dibbs* in North Africa, *charuv* in Israel, or even St. John's bread in Europe and the U.S., the latter name bestowed on carob by anonymous medieval authors in the belief that the "locusts" St. John the Baptist ate were actually carob pods.

Borscht

A few centuries ago in the hinterlands of Russia, a solitary Jewish traveler, tired and hungry, came upon a modest cottage. Knocking on the door, the traveler intended to ask—beg, if necessary—for a meal. An old Jewish woman cracked the door open and replied that there was practically no food in the house, either for her or for the unexpected traveler. Desperate yet quick witted, the Jewish traveler spotted a stone near the hearth.

"If you will allow me, I can make a meal for the two of us to share using only the stone."

Driven by hunger and curiosity, the woman agreed, thinking that perhaps the man might possess some magical powers. The traveler chopped some wood. He entered the house, lit the fire, and put a huge pot of water on to boil. To the woman's astonishment, the young man next threw the stone into the pot. The two hungry strangers stood in front of the fire watching the stone simmer. "*Bobbe,*" suggested the traveler, "a dash of salt will most certainly help." The woman obliged. "*Bobbe,*" the traveler continued, "perhaps a potato . . . a carrot . . . a beet . . . some cabbage . . . a parsnip . . . whatever you have." The woman obliged again. When they finally sat down to share the meal, the woman was delighted and exclaimed, "What a fine meal made using only a stone!"

"Stone soup," as first named in this old tale, describes a soup made from just about any odds and ends which are left in the kitchen. Borscht is considered a "stone" soup. Its name is derived from the old Slavic word for beet. Yet, many recipes for borscht are prepared without beets. Some rely solely on a combination of vegetables, some add meat, some brag of green peppers and tomatoes.

Borscht can either warm one's innards or cool one's kitchen. Hot borscht usually has meat with a thickened consistency, much like a stew. Cold borscht usually is a conglomeration of vegetables with a thin, watery stock. While there seems to be no historical basis linking beet borscht to predominantly Jewish foods, its popularity is link enough.

HOT BEET BORSCHT

3 pounds lean brisket
1 large onion, sliced
1 clove garlic, mashed or minced
2 carrots, pared and sliced
1 parsnip, pared and sliced
2 teaspoons salt
1 teaspoon pepper
Water to cover
8 beets, washed, peeled, and sliced
4 potatoes, pared and cubed
1½ cups chopped fresh tomatoes
1 tablespoon lemon juice
1 tablespoon sugar
3 whole allspice seeds
Salt
Pepper

1. Place beef, onion, garlic, carrots, parsnip, and seasonings in a large soup pot. Cover with cold water and bring to a boil.

2. Reduce heat, cover and simmer for 1 hour. Skim off fat.
3. Add remaining vegetables, seasonings, and more water if necessary. Cover and simmer for 45 minutes more. Check seasoning. Serve hot.

Makes 8 servings.

COLD BORSCHT

8 to 10 fresh beets with beet greens
4 scallions
⅓ cup lemon juice
4 tablespoons sugar
1 tablespoon salt
Water to cover (about 2½ quarts)
1 pint sour cream
1 small cucumber, peeled and chopped
1 scallion, chopped fine
1 tablespoon fresh chopped dill or 1 teaspoon dried dill weed
1 teaspoon salt

1. Wash, peel, and slice the beets. Chop the greens coarsely. Chop the scallions. Place ingredients in a large soup pot.
2. Add lemon juice, sugar, salt, and enough water to cover the vegetables completely.
3. Cook over medium heat for 1 hour. Correct the seasoning and chill until ready to serve.
4. In a separate bowl or blender, combine remaining ingredients. Mix or blend well and chill.
5. Serve when borscht and sour cream mixture are thoroughly chilled. Use the sour cream mixture as a topping for the borscht.

Makes 6 to 8 servings.

Bulke

Bontshe Schweig (Bontshe, the Silent), the fictional character created by Yiddish writer, Isaac Leib Peretz, was the most humble of humble men. Never one to blow his own horn while he lived, when he got to Heaven he could do no better. Implored to speak up on his own behalf, Bontshe in Heaven was as quiet as he had been on earth. Most of all, Bontshe was silent, the most silent of all the souls in Heaven.

On earth, Bontshe's deeds were the kind that gained him no notoriety. Even if he had been exceptionally talented or wise, he would not have spoken of it. When others tormented and offended him, never once did he shout or scream at them in anger. He didn't speak at all. When he was trampled by a horse, he remained silent. When he was ridiculed and taunted by his wife, not once did he speak up. And when he went to Heaven and faced the angels, he was as tongue-tied as he always had been.

Bontshe, the angels said, now that you are here you may have whatever you want. Tell us what you want. Anything at all.

Silence.

They insisted. They beseeched.

Finally, as if from a place as far away as the farthest star and as close as a homely, bleak room cluttered with the effects of the personal pain of one man's life, came the answer.

In a supplicating manner he responded, merely to say that he, Bontshe Schweig, Bontshe the Silent, who could now have the pick of all that might be his in Heaven as there was not for him in life, now, please, if you please, that all that he wanted was . . . a *"bulke mit putter,"* a hot roll with butter. So then, after all was said and done, wasn't it best now to ask only for the possible which, simple though it was, would be more sweet and satisfying eaten here in a peaceful Heaven. It would be, thought Bontshe, reward enough for a man so humble.

Bulke (say *bull—ke*) is a Yiddish word of Slavic derivation and means roll. *Zemmel,* a Yiddish word which also means roll, comes from German. Both words apply to the same kinds of small breads, usually made from an extra batch of challah dough on Fridays to feed to hungry children awaiting a Sabbath feast, or of whole wheat dough during the week. The rolls are made in various shapes: in twists to imitate braided challot, birds with raisins for eyes, and round for Rosh Hashonah and Yom Kippur to symbolize an everlasting life without beginning or end.

BULKES

To make bulkes: Follow directions for preparing challah dough, through Step 4 (see Challah). Shape according to the following directions. Then, follow challah dough directions Steps 6 and 7, reducing baking time to 15 minutes or bake until tops of *bulkes* are golden brown. Makes about 3 dozen rolls.

To shape bulkes: Little challah loaves. Roll three small (tennis-ball size) portions of dough into ropes and then braid as you would braid larger loaves.

Birds. Shape a small portion of dough into a long rope. Tie the ropes as if you were making the first knot in the process of tying your shoes. Shape one end into the head of a bird. Flatten the other end for the tail feathers, making shallow cuts in the "tail" to represent feathers. Place raisins in the eyes.

Crescents. Roll out dough and cut into triangles. Starting with wide edge, roll toward a point. Gently shape dough ends toward one another.

Cabbage, Stuffed

See Holoptsches.

Carnatzlach

Carnatzlach (say *car—nots—lock*) are meatballs that are liberally laced with black pepper and hot paprika and contain enough garlic to assure their eaters complete isolation until the taste's worn off. The combination of ingredients marks the dish as being of Roumanian origin and but for the overwhelming presence of garlic, *carnatzlach* are dead ringers for Russian and Middle Eastern ground meat kebabs.

CARNATZLACH

1½ pounds chuck steak, ground
4 or 5 cloves garlic, minced
1 teaspoon paprika
½ to ¾ teaspoon pepper
¼ cup matzah meal
¾ teaspoon salt
1 egg

1. Mix all of the ingredients together and form into balls or oblong rolls.
2. Grill or broil until slightly charred but not dry.

Makes 10 2-inch-long pieces.

Carrots

How amazing is a Jew's delight in elevating the most ordinary foods, those eaten with dulling regularity in the homes of the poorest of families, to the most precious of delicacies, to be relished on the High Holidays and regarded as special, symbolic, and enobling. Magical, actually.

Forbidden time and time again throughout their long history from falling back upon magic and sorcery to explain the events which shaped their lives, many Jews, particularly those who lived during the Middle Ages, believing in God and Torah, were nevertheless all too ready to use whatever else was at hand to help along their meager and often frightening existence.

The Torah was revered, looked upon with awe. The discussions of the Talmudists were placed on a plane above the ordinary. There was respect for these and a respect for learning. But there was a distance, too. It was sometimes impossible to see one's own experience of living in a small village in Eastern Poland or the Ukraine as being at all similar to the life of King David or the heroic efforts of Deborah. Also, the Jews of Eastern Europe lived in constant physical fear. Life was difficult, so difficult at times that it became imperative to know everything about life, not only Torah and Talmud, but the shapes of the trees and the way the winds blew, the disposition of each inhabitant of one's village or neighborhood and even the numerical equivalents of certain words. All could affect one's life. Even the seemingly mundane had strange and unpredictable power over one's fate.

How one behaved at a wedding or funeral was said to determine one's future. The degree of a mother's concern for protecting her newborn son before his *Brit* (ritual circumcision) and the kinds of amulets she placed under her pillow to ward off the Evil Eye were thought to make the difference between ensuring his life or death. The chairs around a dining table had to be placed in special ways and covering the table with a cloth on the Sabbath became a way of protecting one's family from the evil spirits.

So, too, what one ate could determine one's fortune, not only in the physical sense, but in the spiritual and economic sense, too. Food, the way it was stored, prepared, served, and eaten, particularly on holidays, had as much significance in medieval Jewish life as did the particular prayers said on those holidays.

One such food, carrots, a lowly food one must admit, dug up from the ground just like a common potato and regarded today as just another vegetable from the plot out back, became in the eyes of the superstitious a carrier of the message of Rosh Hashonah, the message of hope, abundance, and the multiplicity of God's blessings.

Lowly, yet. But also sweet and golden, tough as the coin of the realm and in Yiddish called *mehren,* a word which is also used to mean multiply.

Centuries ago the European Jews made the most of the coming together of two word meanings and the look and taste of a simple garden vegetable. From the food they made *tzimmes,* compote, carrot soups, cake and candy, even jam. To consume these delicacies was to taste the carrot's sweetness and make its reputed powers one's own, not just for now but for a golden, prosperous future.

OLD-FASHIONED CARROT SOUP

This recipe is often made for one of the meals eaten on Rosh Hashonah, the Jewish New Year, especially among Jews of Polish and Russian background.

6-pound stewing chicken or ½ of a stewing chicken and 3 pounds beef flanken or beef soup meat
2 large onions, sliced
2 pounds carrots, grated
6 stalks celery, sliced
1 pound large dry lima beans, washed but not soaked
½ pound pearl barley
2 tablespoons salt, or to taste
1 teaspoon white pepper, or to taste
Water to cover

1. Combine ingredients in large soup pot. Bring to boil, reduce heat and simmer, covered, for 2 hours, stirring occasionally.
2. Taste for seasoning, adding more salt, pepper, and water as needed to cover ingredients.
3. Cover and cook for at least 3 additional hours, stirring occasionally and checking for correct seasonings.

Makes about 7 quarts.

Challah

Challah brings nourishment to the whole world.

—The *Zohar*

And the Lord spoke unto Moses saying: "Speak unto the children of Israel, and say unto them:

'When ye come into the land whither I bring you, then it shall be, that, when ye eat of the bread of the land, ye shall set apart a portion for a gift unto the Lord. Of the first of your dough ye shall set apart a cake for a gift; as that which is set apart of the threshing-floor, so shall ye set it apart. Of the first of your dough ye shall give unto the Lord a portion for a gift throughout your generations.' "

—Numbers 15:17–21

Activity, bustle, and anticipation are all part of a traditional Jewish Friday morning. In front of the great gray, soot-darkened synagogue on Douhanyi Street in Budapest, the wide pavement is swept with the quick, nervous movements of an elderly man guiding a pushbroom. As early as 5 a.m. shoppers dot Jaffa Street in Jerusalem, the long main thoroughfare that ends at the walls built in the time of the Hasmoneans. Sometimes abrupt and always rushing like mad, the marketers scurry into the tiny cupboard-size shops to buy candles and wine for the Sabbath before going to work.

In Fez, eggs are delivered to noisy crowded households by young boys who sell the pearl-colored ovules one by one as if they were as precious as the great jewels of a medieval calipf. And in Montreal, the servants of well-appointed Jewish households exchange greetings in suburban supermarkets as they buy 10-pound sacks of white flour in wrappings marked with English and French labels.

Everywhere, in perhaps as many as thirty languages—could it be more?—in French, English, Hebrew, Spanish, Yiddish, Greek, Ladino, Persian, Hungarian, Arabic, German, Swedish, Italian, and so many others, there is talk on a Friday morning. Much of it is about the usual things, like the weather, for example. It's cold, it's warm, snowing, raining, damp, or dry. On Kibbutz Bet Hashittah, talk may be about the *hamsin,* the still air that settles over the Eastern Galilee at summer's height. In Iowa, in midwestern singsong cadence, the conversation may focus on the snowstorm coming out of the Northwest.

There is also talk of money and work, of schedules and school, of parties and change for the bus, of politics and geometry. Snatches of conversation in the early Friday morning rush.

And there is movement: out to the car, the bus, the donkey (Jews get to wherever they are going by many means). There is dressing, breakfasting, and cleaning.

But, central to it all is the cooking, beginning always with challah, at the bakery or at home, not only because making bread takes time but also, perhaps most of all, because the spirit and creative energy of the cook are strongest first thing in the morning. The challah gets the best of it.

How can it be that the recipe for the Sabbath egg bread is virtually the same in Buenos Aires as it is in Sydney, in London, Bucharest, or Los Angeles? But it is. First there is the yeast, large chunks or dustings of it that must be dissolved in warm water the way sugar is in a cup of hot tea. The combination yields spongy, aromatic thick foam, bubbly and pockmarked like the uneven surface of a flat moon.

Like yellow puffed suns in a succession of summer skies, the egg yolks wait in their whites for the time when they will be beaten with oil, mixed with water, and beaten to a standstill in a mound of flour. First they are added to the yeast. Then the flour, poured from big sacks or small, is added to the yeast and eggs.

Challah can by ancient law be made from wheat, barley, maize, spelts, or oats. But white flour is the flour of the rich, and on the Sabbath, by tradition, a person should settle for no less than it.

A little more water, some salt, saffron for the Sephardim, liqueur by the American gourmets, more sugar or honey by the Lubavitcher Hasidim who like their bread sweet; all the ingredients are added until the mixture objects to the process and demands a rest.

It gets pummeled instead. Kneaded and squeezed, stretched and pounded, the challah dough in the skillful hands of its creator is infused with air and vitality. Only then is it set aside while the cook waits for it to grow fat and bulbous with a life all its own.

Meanwhile, the hands that have handled the dough are caught up in other tasks: scraping carrots and parsnips for a soup, chopping fish or liver, piling meat and beans into a pot for the next day's *tscholent.* And then it is time for the challah again, the best time, for the cook becomes sculptor, plucking hunks of risen dough to shape or roll, pile or mold.

So old is the art of shaping bread that it goes back to a time when shepherds grazed their flocks on the hills of Judea where the large, modern city of Jerusalem now stands. This was the time when the maker of the dough, before she baked the challah, would separate a tiny portion of each loaf to offer to the priests (*kohanim*) rather than burn it as has been the practice since the destruction of the Temple.

An Israelite woman living in the days of Moses, or her counterparts living one century, five centuries, or ten centuries later, in the days of Joshua, Deborah, Samuel, Jeremiah, Daniel, and throughout much of the Biblical age, shaped round after round, each no bigger than a tea cookie, convex and hollow, similar to modern *pita.* The process was a careful one, its outcome little loaves as unadorned and spare looking as the flour from which they had been prepared. Many hundreds of years would pass before challah would become the dense, intricately shaped breads we know today.

The practice of shaping loaves in the non-Jewish world goes back to the time of the Pharaohs and perhaps earlier. Rounds, cubes, braids, pyramids—Egyptian bread loaves were a study in solid geometry. These shapes and others—lyres, rings, even farm tools—were added to the repertoires of the Greeks and Romans. In the Middle Ages in Europe the craft was at its height, done for amusement or to symbolize an historic or religious event. The Jews, clearly not the creators of the idea of telling a story with bread dough, borrowed the idea and developed it into a language all their own.

By the late Middle Ages, their *challot* became elaborate creations, shaped with more than just sustenance in mind. They were the much-prized ceremonial breads of the Sabbath, made to look as special as they tasted. Often, each curve of their surface had a deep religious and unique symbolic meaning, going far beyond mere decoration. Because Jews lived in so many different countries of the world, wide variations in shape emerged over the centuries. But the source for most of the variations was the religion shared by all Jews. No matter where they lived, Jews prayed to the same God and read the same holy books in the same sacred language. Like the fairy-tale characters who found their way home by following a little trail of crumbs, the Jewish people, unsettled on the land, used the many shapes of Sabbath or holiday challah to direct them toward the one constant force in their lives, their God.

For the Sabbath, the German Jews made their *challot* round as a freshly minted coin, sprinkling the top of each loaf with *kimmel* (caraway) or poppy seeds. Or they made them into elongated breads shaped to resemble an egg and placed a little dough chain on the top. Polish Jews made elongated loaves from thick ropes of sweet dough and brushed egg over them with a goose feather. In Russia many Jews followed the custom of forming the dough into braids so that exactly twelve bumps were prominent, to signify the number of showbreads which, according to Hasidic legend, were placed in the portable Tabernacle during Biblical times. Many Jews follow this custom today, particularly Hasidim of Russian background. As a variation of this same custom, others made two loaves of six bumps each and covered the breads with seeds to represent the gift of manna given by God. The two loaves signified the double portion of the manna gathered on Friday for that day and the following Sabbath day.

In Central Europe—Hungary, Rumania, Turkey, Greece and the Greek Isles, the countries ruled by the Ottoman Turks—the challot were braided and sometimes shaped into crescents and called *kipfel*. In North Africa, women would sculpt *challot* into uniquely Sephardic shapes—flowers, logs ringed with dough—adding a touch of their own creativity to make their loaves as distinctive as a signature.

Holiday breads were even more elaborately crafted and varied from one geographical region to another. Some incorporated the design motifs of the surrounding Christian and Moslem cultures, as in the crown or turban shaped bread baked on Purim. Yet most were uniquely Jewish, the central theme of each a line from the Hebrew Bible, a Jewish folk belief or a practice associated with the particular holiday when the challot were prepared.

On Purim in Central Europe, a braided loaf took on a new meaning and symbolized the ropes of the gallows which figure so prominently in the Biblical Book of Esther. On Shavuot, in Eastern Europe, it was common well into this century to press a seven-rung dough ladder across the top of an elongated challah loaf to symbolize the seven heavens torn open by God when the Laws were transmitted.

Particularly at the beginning of each new year, the dough sculptor's task became a true labor of love, a transmission of hope and faith in the future from heart to hand to food to God. Never just the rote behavior of a woman in her kitchen, making the challah and separating the little piece of dough (also called the challah) from it before baking was a special obligation, one of the three *mitzvot* (commandments of God) she was obligated to perform. In particular, the fashioning of a loaf of holiday bread was an expression of her own longings for peace, prosperity, and good fortune.

In Eastern Europe the most popular New Year's season challah shape was the circle. It was used to signify the hope for a good and complete New Year. Sometimes a ring of dough was placed on top of the round loaf, or even a coin. Also popular were spirals and ladders to symbolize the reaching up to heaven. The wings of angels, birds' heads or birds' wings were other Rosh Hashonah and Yom Kippur motifs.

Of them all, perhaps the most interesting was the loaf often prepared for Hashona Rabbah, the seventh day of Sukkot, the Feast of Tabernacles. An extended hand coming as though from the inside of the loaf seemed to reach out toward heaven, molded in this way to receive the written judgment given by God on this particular day, twelve days after Yom Kippur.

In our own day, the *challot* are often less elaborate, but the ritual and preparation surrounding them are carried out with the same kind of fervor and concern as they were 500, 1,000, or 2,000 years ago. Late on a Friday afternoon, the youngest hands in the household move one, sometimes two, or as many as four freshly baked *challot* from kitchen to dining table. They set them on a board to be covered with a small cloth as white as the cloth which covers the table, to symbolize the whiteness of the manna which fell into the white desert of Sinai. Then they place the wine nearby, along with the candles to be lighted and blessed at sundown, the beginning moment of the Sabbath or any special festival. A blessing will be said over the wine before the meal begins; a blessing will be said over the challah at the beginning of the meal.

The kitchen is alive again with activity as all the other foods are readied for the meal. But soon, in keeping with the striving for ease and peace on these special days, the activity will be replaced with leisure, the bustle with tranquility, and the anticipation with a mood of relief that, finally, the work of this day and all the others which have led up to it can be enjoyed to the limit.

CHALLAH

2 tablespoons (2 packages) dry yeast
1 cup warm water
½ cup granulated sugar
½ cup vegetable oil or margarine
2 tablespoons kirschwasser or brandy (optional)
3 eggs, beaten, plus 2 egg yolks
1½ teaspoons salt
5 to 6 cups all-purpose flour
Poppy, sesame, or fennel seeds

1. Dissolve the yeast in warm water. Add sugar, oil, and liqueur, and mix well.
2. Add 3 beaten eggs, reserving the 2 extra egg yolks for glazing the tops of the challah.
3. Add salt and gradually add flour.
4. Knead for 10 minutes, to form a smooth, pliable dough. Place in a greased bowl, cover and let stand in a warm place until doubled in bulk, about 2 hours.
5. Put dough on floured board or cloth, shape into two medium-sized loaves, and place on two greased baking sheets.
6. Cover and let rise up to 2 hours. Coat with egg yolk and sprinkle with seeds.
7. Bake in preheated 375-degree oven for 30–40 minutes, or until top is golden brown and breads sound hollow when touched.

LOW CHOLESTEROL CHALLAH

This is a dairy recipe since the commercial egg yolk substitute used in it contains non-fat dry milk.

1 tablespoon active yeast (or 1 package dry yeast)
1 cup warm water
2 to 3 tablespoons sugar
2 teaspoons salt
⅛ teaspoon saffron
½ cup melted margarine, cooled (or ½ cup unsaturated vegetable oil)
¾ cup egg yolk substitute
4½ cups flour, unsifted
Poppy or sesame seeds

1. Melt margarine and cool.
2. Meanwhile, dissolve yeast in warm water. Add sugar, salt, and saffron.
3. Add margarine (or vegetable oil), egg yolk substitute, and 3 cups of the flour. Stir until well blended.
4. Gradually add remaining flour. Knead on a floured surface until the dough is smooth and elastic, about 10 minutes.
5. Place in a greased bowl, cover and let rise in a warm spot until double in size, about 2 hours.
6. Punch down and knead for a few minutes.
7. To make one large braid, divide into three equal pieces. Roll each piece into a long rope.
8. Braid the three ropes together and pinch ends to seal. Place on a greased baking sheet and let rise until double in size, about 1 hour.
9. Brush with liquid egg yolk substitute and sprinkle with poppy or sesame seeds. Bake in a preheated 375-degree oven for 25 minutes.

Makes one very large or two medium-sized loaves.

Chanukah

Eat foods dainty and fine,
And bread baked well and white,
With pigeons and red wine,
On this Sabbath Chanukah night.

—Medieval Sabbath Zmira (tablesong)

During the shortest days of December, when the nights are long and dreary, the Jews celebrate Chanukah (say *ha* to rhyme with pa—*new*—*ka* to rhyme with ma), the Festival of Lights. The holiday is celebrated each year to remind Jews of the turbulent days of the Macabees and their fight for religious survival in the year 165 b.c.e.

The word Chanukah means dedication in Hebrew and refers specifically to the rededication of the ancient Temple after it had been desecrated by the Syrians.

Chanukah is also the holiday of lights, hence the name Festival or Feast of Lights. These two elements of the holiday—the rededication of the Temple and the emphasis on light during the dark days of winter (the days closest to the winter solstice)—are fused in a well-known story about a little cruse of oil. When the Temple was desecrated and the eternal light which burned in it snuffed out, the story goes, the Macabees were able to salvage from the devastation one little cruse of oil which burned for eight days and nights until more oil could be prepared.

From this story comes the practice of lighting candles for eight days, one for each day of the holiday, and the custom of eating foods cooked in oil.

The most common food eaten on Chanukah among Jews of Eastern European background is the latke or potato pancake. Today in Israel and Morocco, *soofganiyot* (fried jelly doughnuts) are popular. In Western Europe, the typical foods are fritters; in Hungary, *kolatches;* in the Middle East, *kadaif* and flat fried sweet cakes.

Goose is another typical Chanukah food in Europe but not in the United States where latkes get all of the cook's attention. Historically, goose grease and *gribenes* (cracklings) were the much-anticipated Chanukah delicacies of the Eastern European *shtetl,* savored a dab or a piece at a time until the small supply had run out.

Noodles and potato kugels prepared with a huge dollop of goose fat were other Chanukah delights.

In the days when poor medieval Jews had to use eggshells instead of bronze menorahs used by the rich to hold the little tapers of Chanukah, another food custom became associated with Chanukah—that of eating foods made with cheese. The custom apparently arose in the fourteenth century. Jews of the Middle Ages explained the custom in the *Shulchan Arukh,* the Code of Jewish Laws, by connecting it with Judith. According to the Hebrew version of the Apocrypha, Judith, a daughter of the Hasmoneans, was able to eat at the banquet table of Holofernes, the leader of the Syrian forces. While she dined on mild dairy foods, she fed Holofernes salty cheese and wine to quench his thirst. When he became drunk, she beheaded him. Eating foods made with cheese is done to remind Jews of her heroism.

Cheesecake

Two lifelong friends, recently widowed, planned a trip to New York. Each had her heart set on doing something she'd dreamed of doing for years. The Jewish woman was determined to treat herself to Lindy's famous cheesecake; the Irish woman was intent on saying her prayers at Saint Patrick's Cathedral. Their friendship started to totter, since neither could agree on which place to go to first, yet neither wanted to part company even for a short time. Finally, the Jewish woman, being a bit more mellow, suggested a compromise. "I'll go with you first to Saint Patrick's," she ventured, "if you promise you'll light a candle and pray that there is still some cheesecake left for me at Lindy's!" The prayers were said and answered. Their friendship endured. In fact, it is said that the light for Lindy's cheesecake still burns near the altar of Saint Patrick.

Cheesecake is likely to show up on the table during Shavuot. It is during this combined commemoration of God's giving the Torah to the Israelites and of the Spring Harvest when dairy foods play an important role. According to one tradition, the ancient Israelites had to wait so long to receive the revelation of the Law at the foot of Mount Sinai that their milk curdled and only cheese was left for cooking.

ORANGE-FLAVORED CHERRY CHEESECAKE

Crust:

1½ cups graham crackers or cornflake crumbs
¼ cup sugar
½ cup softened butter or margarine

Filling:

1½ pounds cream cheese, at room temperature
1 scant cup granulated sugar
Finely grated rind of 1 medium orange
4 eggs, separated
2 tablespoons sifted flour
1 cup light cream
⅛ teaspoon salt
1 teaspoon vanilla
½ teaspoon almond extract

Topping:

1 21-ounce can cherry pie filling
1 teaspoon almond extract
Dash of orange flower water (optional)

1. Mix crust ingredients together in food processor or with a fork, making certain that butter or margarine and crumbs are well blended.
2. Press blended crust ingredients against the bottom and sides of a greased 9- or 10-inch springform pan.
3. Using an electric mixer at medium speed (not a food processor), beat cheese until smooth. Add sugar and rind. Beat in egg yolks and add remaining filling ingredients. Mixture should be perfectly smooth.
4. Beat egg whites in small, deep bowl, adding a pinch of salt while they are being beaten. Beat until moist peaks form and you can invert the bowl without the egg whites slipping out.
5. Fold egg whites into cheese mixture and pour filling into crumb crust.

6. Bake in a preheated 325-degree oven for 1½ hours or until the cake is dry to the touch and is very firm. When it is done, a knife inserted into the cake will come out clean.
7. Turn off heat and allow cake to remain in oven for 30 minutes more. It is normal for the cake to sink somewhat as it cools.
8. Remove from oven and cool to room temperature in pan. Remove sides of pan carefully. Slip a spatula between bottom of cake and cake pan bottom and slowly move the spatula underneath the entire cake. Using pancake turner, slip cake onto a serving plate.
9. Mix filling ingredients together and spread over top of cake.
10. Refrigerate a minimum of 3 hours but, for best results, overnight.

Chicken Soup

As far as possible the meat [eaten] should be that of hens or roosters and their broth should also be taken, because this sort of fowl has virtue in rectifying corrupted humors, whatever the corruption may be, and especially the black humors, so much so that the physicians have mentioned that chicken broth is beneficial in leprosy.

—Maimonides, *Treatise on Accidents,*
12th century

Just at the time when the winter snows had further barricaded the little *shtetls* of Eastern Europe, walling them off with mounds of heavy whiteness that grew larger and more impenetrable with each passing week, and just when the mood of the inhabitants had grown weary of cold and dark nights—Chanukah with its glowing candles had been celebrated long before—a welcome piece of news would be passed excitedly from household to household, a bit of pleasing information which promised a change from the drudging pace.

There was to be a wedding in the community, soon, the

week after next. Suddenly, the crunch of one's footfalls on the thickly packed snow made a little music, the everyday talk in the marketplace had a lilt of expectation to it, and the taste of a meager slice of black bread made one dream of the wedding feast to come.

The news would reach the neighboring villages, the beggars, the traders passing through town, and even those townfolk who hadn't spoken to the groom's parents for years. A wedding feast was for everyone; this one would last a week. There would be a *badchen* and four musicians, dancing and, most especially, platters heaped high with the specialties of the cook. These were, of course, the foods everyone expected to eat at a wedding. There could be nothing omitted if one wanted to avoid the jealous spite of next month's gossiping.

The lively hum of activity was everywhere, but especially in the home of the bride's family. Feasts came often enough, thankfully, at Rosh Hashonah and Chanukah, Purim and Pesach; but these were family gatherings and not for the dozens of people who were always invited to a wedding.

What could not be made at home would be brought to the communal bake house. First prepared were the festival white-flour loaves, the *challot.* Laced with beaten egg yolks, the strands of dough from which they would be made were woven into an intricately layered design that would soon turn golden brown from the heat of the oven. Then the fish would be chopped, spiced, and molded into perfectly round balls, symbolic of the shape of the universe and the ongoing nature of life. Cauldrons steamed and the aroma enticed.

Chickens were captured. Two of them might be carried in the wedding procession as a sign of fertility, to observe a custom almost two thousand years old. Others would be slaughtered, picked clean of their feathers, and gutted. In some communities, the bride and groom would break their prenuptial fast with a roasted piece of one, along with an egg. Still others would be placed in a huge cooking pot, to be made into a soup that would soon gleam in the bowls, the golden globules of fat forming a thick veil that would protect the essence underneath, the *gildene yoich,* the golden chicken soup. So valued was this golden liquid that the wedding feast itself would always be called by that name, as if the cakes and brandy, fish and challah, chicken and liver were no more than third cousins, twice removed, obviously the less important guests.

The soup is still treasured by Jews throughout the world, drunk in great gulps to fend off colds (thereby earning the name "Jewish penicillin") and prepared almost universally as part of many Sabbath meals. Some Jews have never called it *gildene yoich,* some in their lifetimes never knew the soup was ever called by that name. Yet just as lovingly will Jews call it chicken soup and know that the soup is, ineffably, more than hot broth in a bowl.

CHICKEN SOUP

A 3- to 4-pound broiling chicken, cut up or whole
3 quarts water
1 large onion, peeled
1 large carrot, peeled and sliced
2 stalks celery, coarsely chopped
A few sprigs dill
A few sprigs parsley
1 tablespoon salt
¼ teaspoon white pepper
¼ teaspoon garlic powder

1. Place all of the ingredients in a large soup kettle. Bring to a boil, lower the heat, and simmer, covered, for 1 hour or until chicken is tender. Add more salt, as necessary.
2. Remove parsley and dill, and chill in order to allow fat to cake at the surface. When ready to serve, remove the fat and reheat.

GILDENE YOICH

1 4-pound roasting chicken, with giblets, neck, and feet
Water to cover
3 onions, sliced
1 small parsnip, cut in rounds (optional)
3 large carrots, roughly chopped
6 stalks celery, cut in 1-inch lengths
1 bay leaf
6 peppercorns
1 tablespoon salt or to taste

1. Cut the chicken into about 9 pieces. Do not remove the fat.
2. Put the chicken pieces and remaining ingredients into a large pot and bring to the boil, lower the heat and simmer until the vegetables are very soft and the meat leaves the bone, about 3 hours.

Serve with soup mandlen, noodles, or farfel.

Chrain

Gefilte fish without chrain *is punishment enough.*

—Old Yiddish saying

If you, like Eliza Doolittle, pronounce the word *chrain* (say *kh—rain*) to rhyme with rain, Spain, and plain, you'll be saying it correctly but won't know a thing about it. Never has *chrain* been served on the plains of Spain. On the plains of Hungary, Poland, Roumania, Russia, and North America definitely, but never Spain. Never.

Chrain is grated horseradish root, moistened with a few drops of vinegar, sweetened with a sprinkling of sugar and, on Passover, colored with beet juice. It is invariably served with gefilte fish.

Chrain has a vast horde of devotees, but then there are those who find its powers too persuasive and its stinging effect on their sinuses too vexing to endure. Occasionally, more than one pundit has been heard to exclaim that it is for the sake of eating gefilte fish with *chrain* that four cups of wine are served during a Passover Seder.

Among Jews of European background, *chrain* is often included as the symbolic bitter herb on the Seder plate for Passover. Few would question its right to be there.

CHRAIN

½ cup grated horseradish root
½ cup hot beet juice
3 tablespoons white vinegar
2 teaspoons sugar or to taste
¼ teaspoon salt

1. Pour the hot beet juice over the grated horseradish and let soak until soft. Drain and cool.
2. Add the vinegar, sugar, and salt.
3. Check for taste by dabbing a small bit of the mixture onto a piece of bread, matzah, or cracker.
4. Refrigerate in an airtight container.

Makes ½ cup.

HORSERADISH STEW

Stew three pounds of meat in a pint of water; grate one large horseradish, add it to the gravy and some fine breadcrumbs, a little pepper, ginger and salt, with half a cupful of the best vinegar. It is very highly recommended by all who have tasted it.

—*The Jewish Cookery Book,*
Mrs. Esther Levy, 1871

Chremslach

It is a dish like this one which gives Jewish cuisine's detractors their heavy ammunition in the form of fritters oozing with oil, overburdened with matzah meal, and drenched in honey. Even a *chremsel* that had wings couldn't fly!

Neither could its culinary ancestor, *vermiculos,* a Roman dish of dough molded into short, fat chunks. Fried in oil and served with pepper and honey or with a ubiquitous Roman fish sauce called *garum, vermiculos* must have sunk into the very bottom of a Roman stomach, rendering the eater unfit for a visit to the bath, the Coliseum, or even the next room. Yet, unappetizing as it was, the recipe for *vermiculos* somehow survived in Jewish households for two thousand years sans the fish sauce but otherwise unchanged. It has taken its place gracelessly each year at the Passover feast.

The Jews of the Middle Ages Yiddishized the Latin name for the ancient Roman recipe. They also ate it regularly. We know they did because they wrote about *chremslach* (say *chrems* to rhyme with tens—*lockh*) in their books of Jewish law, calling it *gremlinish* in the Book of Pious (*Sefer Hasidim*), the medieval thirteenth-century German compilation of legal interpretations, or *vermesist* in French books of Jewish law written in the same period.

Interestingly, *vermiculos* is the ancient ancestor of yet another food very unlike *chremslach.* We know it today as *vermicelli,* the Italian word which means "little worms." In

Italian households the dough, which in ancient times had been more like formed farina, gradually became transformed by the fourteenth century, or perhaps even earlier, into thin strands of pasta, definitely a culinary improvement upon farina. Yet the Jews stuck tenaciously to the old Roman recipe for *vermiculos,* changing little more than its name.

That name, by the way, was to undergo several more etymological changes in Yiddish before it made it to the twentieth century as *chremslach* or, as some Jews still spell it, *grimsel.* But its basic ingredients have not changed from the days when the cooks of Rome made the dish with meal, mixed it with water, shaped it into "worms" of dough, fried it quickly, and doused it with sauce. This is one Jewish recipe with two thousand years of staying power!

GRIMSLECH

Chop up one half pound of stoned raisins and almonds, with one half dozen apples and one half pound currants, one half pound brown sugar, nutmeg, cinnamon, one half pound fat, the rind of a lemon, 2 soaked matzot or unleavened bread; mix all the ingredients together with 4 well beaten eggs; do not stiffen too much with the matzo meal; make into oval shapes; either fry in fat or bake in an oven a light brown.

—*The Jewish Cookery Book,*
Mrs. Esther Levy, 1871

CHREMSLACH

A slight modification here and there and Mrs. Levy's recipe becomes one of the best *chremslach* recipes ever. Baked *chremslach* are a wonderful treat, fried ones heavy and greasy.

½ pound white or brown raisins
½ pound almonds
1½ pounds apples, cored and seeded but not peeled
½ pound dried currants
2 cups brown sugar
Dash salt
¾ teaspoon nutmeg
2 teaspoons ground cinnamon
¼ pound (1 stick) margarine
Rind of 1 lemon, grated or chopped fine

2 soaked matzot plus ¾ cup matzah meal

4 eggs, well beaten
Matzah meal

1. Using the steel blade of a food processor, a grinder, or by hand, chop or grind raisins, almonds, apples, and currants.
2. Add sugar, salt, spices, margarine, and lemon rind.
3. Drain the matzah well, crumble and add along with matzah meal.
4. Add eggs.
5. Add more matzah meal as needed to form a pliable but firm mixture, free of any surplus liquid.
6. Form into balls, approximately 1½ inches in diameter, and roll each in matzah meal to lightly coat the surface.
7. Place on lightly greased cookie sheet and bake in a preheated 375-degree oven for 30 minutes.

Couscous

When the recipe comes from North Africa, has an Arabic name, and is cooked in a pot known as *la couscousiere*, you know that the dish is couscous—fiery in Tunisia, piquant in Morocco, ruby red and spicy in Algeria. Couscous is daily main course fare for most North Africans, Jew and non-Jew alike. The dish is a ten-course meal in one pot topped by another pot filled to the top with pebbly semolina grains that have absorbed the flavor of each ingredient below.

Into the bigger pot, the one which is placed directly over the fire, go cooked chickpeas or favas, and sometimes green peas. Braised meat (lamb, beef, and chicken) are added in combination with one another or individually, depending on availability and taste. Then the fun begins, for the vegetable variations are endless. Perhaps the cook chooses to use only onions, garlic, and leeks. But better yet is a couscous made from onions, garlic, and leeks, plus a whole bunch of celery, an entire zucchini, a small eggplant, and a turnip or two.

Startling and shocking to some are the seasonings: cumin in heavy sprinklings, an ample amount of freshly shredded ginger, and at the very least, a teaspoon of chili pepper.

Moroccans often sweeten the somewhat sour taste of couscous with a sprinkling of raisins, dark or light, and the Algerians augment the sauce with crushed tomatoes and sowings of cayenne.

At the end, swiping all the flavor, is the semolina, the couscous, steamed by the vapor from the melange cooking in the pot below.

COUSCOUS

If you can, use a special *couscousiere* to prepare this dish. Or improvise with a large saucepan for the meat and vegetables and a steamer or strainer which will hold the semolina so that it does not come into direct contact with the liquid in the bottom pot.

1 cup cooked chickpeas
1 pound couscous* (semolina)
1 pound lean lamb, cut into 1-inch cubes
1 pound beef flanken, cubed
2 carrots, cut into large pieces
1 onion, quartered
3 bay leaves
1 tomato, sliced
3 teaspoons salt
1½ teaspoons ground chili pepper
1 teaspoon ground ginger
2 teaspoons ground cumin
4 tablespoons olive oil
8 celery stalks, cut into large pieces
2 turnips, peeled and cut into large pieces
2 zucchini, cut into large pieces
2 leeks, white parts only, cut into large pieces
2 eggplants, cut into large pieces
⅓ cup raisins
2 tablespoons margarine

1. Pour the couscous onto a cookie sheet. Sprinkle with warm salted water. Work lightly between the fingers so that each grain is separate, moistened, and beginning to swell. Let the couscous rest for 15 minutes. Repeat this process 3 times.
2. Place the chickpeas in the bottom of the *couscousiere* with the lamb, beef, carrots, and onion. Pour in enough water to cover and bring to a boil. Reduce the heat, cover the pan, and simmer for 30 minutes.

*Available at Middle Eastern groceries and some supermarkets.

3. Add the bay leaves, tomato, salt, ground chili pepper, ginger, cumin, oil, celery, turnips, and zucchini.
4. Put the couscous in the upper pan and place it on top of the lower pan. Make sure that the liquid in the lower pan cannot enter the upper pan or the couscous will become lumpy.
5. Cover the *couscousiere* and place it over the heat. Simmer for 15 to 20 minutes, or until the vegetables are half cooked.
6. Add the leeks, eggplants, and raisins to the stew and add the margarine to the couscous. Continue cooking for a further 15 to 20 minutes, or until the meat and vegetables are tender. Do not overcook or the vegetables will disintegrate.
7. To serve, pile the couscous onto a large, heated platter, make a well in the center, and spoon the vegetables and meat and some of the sauce into it.

Serves 6.

D

Dill Pickles

Most Jewish children of Central and Eastern European background become dill pickle mavens before they have graduated to table food. At five months of age, they have been known to use a "¾ done" as a teething ring. At three years, they think that pickles actually grow in giant barrels. At four, they think that peppers and tomatoes do, too.

When they are five, they figure out that pickles are really cucumbers. When they get to six, they contemplate how great it would be to dive into a brine-filled, pickle-filled barrel. By the time they're nine, they've already fantasized the great Hester Street pickle heist a hundred times over, imagining what it would be like to eat a barrelful of Guss's best dills.

The onset of puberty in girls is marked at twelve by a newly acquired disgust for dill pickles (in boys this happens at fourteen) since, as everybody knows, pickles cause garlic breath. Yech! In late adolescence, a budding ecumenicism and liberal respect for others is marked by a return to pickles, but of the bread and butter variety.

It's only when a first job takes a Jew to a place where the only barrel in sight has been converted to a bar stool in someone's rec room that the reawakening takes place. But the longing for the food that is now so unobtainable becomes fulfilled only with a trip to the Pickle Barrel close to home. And so the cycle begins again, in order to satisfy a taste for garlicky, sour-pickled foods that has gone on in the European Jewish community for centuries.

KOSHER DILL PICKLES

This recipe makes 10 quarts of pickles. It can be prepared in a large crock or in 10 individual quart jars.

20 pounds small or medium cucumber pickles (about 3 to 6 inches long)
¾ cup mixed pickling spices
10 cloves fresh garlic
½ cup whole red hot peppers, cut into small pieces
20 sprigs fresh dill
1¾ cups kosher salt
2½ gallons cold water, or enough to cover cucumbers
A 5-gallon-capacity stone crock or wooden barrel, or 10 quart-size glass jars with lids

Preparation for using a crock:

1. Wash the cucumbers thoroughly, discarding any imperfect ones.
2. Place half the spices, garlic, peppers, and dill in the bottom of the crock. Fill the crock to within 3 inches of the top with washed cucumbers. Cover with remaining spice and a layer of dill.
3. Mix the salt and water together and pour over the cucumbers.
4. Place a plate, tray, or board over the crock to weigh down the vegetables. When the cucumbers turn olive green, are free of white spots, and are translucent inside, they are ready to eat or pack into small jars. The brining should take about 2 to 2½ weeks.

Preparation for using quart jars:

1. Wash the cucumbers thoroughly, discarding any imperfect ones.
2. Sterilize the jars and the lids.
3. Fill each jar with the following quantities of spice:

1 tablespoon salt
1 clove garlic, cut into thirds
2 small pieces red pepper
1 teaspoon pickling spice
2 sprigs dill

4. Add washed cucumbers to jars. Pour cold water over the cucumbers to cover.
5. Seal jars tightly. Pickles will be ready in about 2 weeks.

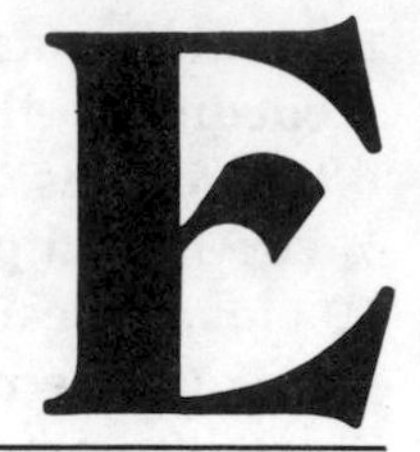

Egg

An ancient Jewish story tells of a woman who took her son to a cook and said to him, "Teach my son the trade." The cook replied, "Let him stay with me five years and I will teach him a hundred dishes made from eggs."

—Midrash Rabbah

In Jewish tradition the symbolic value of an egg has always been as important as the way it is prepared. The egg is a food of great contradiction. While its very existence suggests the initial stage of life, its shape has always suggested life's continuous cycle. The egg also appears at the *se'udat habra'ah,* the consolation meal following a funeral. At this meal, it is said to represent the bereaved "since they have no mouth" to express what is in their hearts.

The roasted egg occupies an equally important place on the Seder plate at Passover. This can be traced to the time of the First and Second Temples when by law a lamb or goat had to be slaughtered, roasted, and eaten by midnight. After the Temple was destroyed, the sacrifice became a more individual offering, with a roasted egg (*beitzah*) taking the place of the Passover festival offering. Good fortune, it is said, comes to those who eat this egg. But even on such a festive occasion, the egg stands as a reminder that joy is mixed with sorrow.

Other customs reveal just how important the egg was to the Jews historically. In Russia centuries ago, a Jewish bride who carried an egg in her hand was hoping for a large family; she ate it as an aphrodisiac. In seventeenth-century Germany, an egg was often given to the little Jewish child entering school for the first time. After the lesson, the egg, with a Biblical quotation from Ezekiel or the Psalms inscribed on its shell, was presented to the new student. Before the child could indulge, however, the words were read aloud by the teacher.

In the late Middle Ages in some areas of Poland, it was the custom for children to receive colored eggs on Pesach. Since paint or dye were taboo on this holiday, the eggs were boiled with hay or onion skins to produce the colors.

HAMINDAS (Brown Hard Eggs)

The egg, being *parve*—neutral, not a dairy or meat food—fits easily into the Jewish cuisine as well as traditions. It has always been used by Jews as a major source of protein.

This particular dish is often made for Sabbath lunch wherever Jews of Sephardic background live. Sometimes it is prepared for Tisha B'av or for the *se'udat habra'ah,* the consolation meal following a funeral service.

12 eggs in their shells
Skins from 3 medium onions
¼ cup vegetable oil

1. Place the eggs in a large pot and cover with water. Add the onion skins and oil.
2. Cook at very low heat for 6 hours. The oil prevents the water from evaporating quickly, but you will have to add more water from time to time. The onion skins will give the whites of the cooked eggs a soft beige color.

Einbren

Einbren (say *ein* to rhyme with mine—*bren*) is to Ashkanazic Jewish cookery what sour cream is to Russian cookery and béchamel is to French cookery. It is an augmenter, used to thicken those sauces in meat dishes which cannot be thickened with dairy products. The word *einbren* is a Yiddish one and refers to the brown paste that is made by heating oil or schmaltz together with flour.

EINBREN

1 tablespoon vegetable oil

2 tablespoons all-purpose flour

1. Over moderate heat, combine ingredients and fry until golden.
2. Add to hot cabbage borscht and roast meat dishes like *roslfleysch* or *gedempte fleysch.*

Farfel

Whoever was burned on hot farfel will blow at cold farfel.

—Yiddish proverb

Nowadays most of the noodles we eat come boxed and wrapped, store-bought and fashioned by unseen machines using procedures devised by design engineers who know next to nothing about food. Think of it: Italian *pastini* and cannelloni, *freselli* and *rigati, spaghettini* and *mostaccioli,* noodles shaped like conch shells and rolled into tubes as large as an arm, bow-tied, spinach-flavored, grooved and curlicued, Chinese fried and cellophaned, even Japanese *somen* with just a hint of sugar. Producing every noodle shape, size, and texture, including the finest gossamerlike threads and the thinnest vermicelli "worms," technology has made simple what was once a painstaking and time-consuming multistepped process.

Less spectacular, the list too short somehow to really impress, the Jewish contribution is packaged lokshen, mostly long and thin, fat and short, bowties—and one other, the strangest pasta of all, farfel (say *far—fell*), made by cutting large sheets of noodle dough to bits and then toasting them. The farfel bits become reconstituted to a soft sponginess when they are cooked with a savory liquid, traditionally chicken soup.

Until recently, before farfel was made by machine, the process took hours. Interestingly, the geographical location of its maker determined the manner in which it would be made.

Historians assert that Jews first learned to grate dough for farfel in medieval Germany, to cut farfel pellets from thin pieces of dough in Poland, and to chop noodle dough into tiny pieces in Lithuania. Best of all, they learned to eat farfel with pieces of fried chicken or goose skins (*gribenes* or *grieven*) in

Russia. Undoubtedly the country where Jews first ate farfel was Germany, where farfel was prepared from leftover pieces of unbaked bread dough.

In the United States, in Canada, and in Israel, the Lubavitcher Hasidim, a group of Orthodox Jews, consider farfel pellets to have a special roundness. They therefore make a special point to eat them boiled or baked at the beginning of each New Year. Also, these people who speak Yiddish as a first language link the sound of the Yiddish word *farfallen,* meaning all done, with farfel, and give the eating of farfel yet another purpose: For them, a taste of farfel should remind one of the hope that all misdeeds of the past year will be done and over with.

Another word for farfel is *flekn.*

FARFEL KUGEL

Farfel kugel was prepared in the Ukraine and Bessarabia for hundreds of years. The schmaltz was rendered goose fat and the *gribenes,* small, fried pieces of goose skin mixed with chopped onion and pieces of fat. Jews of European background relish it today but use schmaltz made of chicken fat.

3 tablespoons vegetable oil or schmaltz
1 large onion, finely chopped
2 cups finely chopped mushrooms
1 teaspoon lemon juice
2 cups dry toasted farfel bits
1 cup chopped gribenes
3 cups chicken or beef stock
1¼ teaspoons salt
½ teaspoon pepper

1. Heat the oil or schmaltz in a large pot. Add onions and chopped mushrooms and sauté for five minutes. Add lemon juice, farfel bits, and *gribenes,* and simmer for another five minutes, stirring well to mix.
2. Mix seasonings into soup stock and pour slowly over the farfel mixture. Cook covered over low heat until most of the moisture has been absorbed, about seven minutes, or turn into small (2-quart) greased baking casserole and place in a preheated 325-degree oven for 25 minutes. Serve immediately.

Makes 8 servings.

Fluden

"Dear Husband," said a Jewish wife the day before Rosh Hashonah, "I'd rather not go to synagogue but remain home instead where I will grate cheese for a fluden *and make a big dough for macaroni."*

—*The Fox Parable Book,* 1687

Seated around large trestle tables covered with tablecloths woven from flax, in rooms sparsely furnished and dimly lit, the Jews of twelfth-century France and the Rhineland often feasted like kings and queens, on cakes made from flour that had been specially fermented with grape skins, rich *gateaux,* crisp bits of sweet crackers called *oublies,* spongy cakes fried in oil, *chremslach, pashteten,* fat pigeons roasted first and then doused in salt water, wine from their vineyards, and liqueurs made from sweet cherries. Even the famed rabbis of the age, the Tosafists, were said to have studied the Talmud "with their stomachs full of meat, vegetables, and wine."

And *fluden.* This versatile dish which usually encased grated cheese between two layers of dough but occasionally was prepared by combining fruit and cheese (as it is to this day) or just fruit, like strudel, was first mentioned in the rabbinic writings of the tenth century and then again and again in the writings of the succeeding three centuries. *Fluden* (say *flew—den*) or *fladen* (from the word *plata* meaning flat) as it was also called, may have been a dish indigenous to Northern France, yet its similarity to Italian delicacies, notably lasagna, can't be overlooked. Indeed, the idea for *fluden* may have been brought to Northern France, an important center of Jewish learning, by the many Jewish families who traveled there from Italy during the early Middle Ages.

It is clear from the rabbinic writings of several centuries that, while the rabbis and their students sat in the synagogue studying Talmud and interpreting the Torah, perhaps settling a difference among them on the baking of a *fluden* of cheese in the same oven with a *pashtet* of meat, down the street in their homes their wives and daughters were preparing the very food the rabbis discussed. On Sukkot the women would place *rozini* (raisins) between a sweet dough; on Tisha B'av, particularly in

Germany, they used apples for the filling. For Shavuot, cheese filled the capacious rectangular pocket and the *fluden* became known as Mount Sinai cake. On Rosh Hashonah, too, cheese filled the *fluden* and butter dripped from its pores.

FLUDEN

This recipe makes one strawberry *fluden* and one blueberry *fluden*.

½ pound butter
¾ cup sugar
1 cake yeast (or 1 package dry yeast) dissolved in ¼ cup lukewarm water
5 egg yolks
1 cup evaporated milk
5½ cups all-purpose or unbleached flour
1 quart strawberries
1 pint blueberries
¾ cup granulated sugar
4 tablespoons flour
Milk
Butter

1. Cream butter with sugar. Add yeast which has been dissolved in lukewarm water. Add egg yolks, milk, and flour. Mix well and then knead into a soft, smooth, pliable dough. Let stand for 30 minutes.
2. Wrap and freeze overnight. One hour before you want to bake the cakes, remove dough from freezer.
3. Prepare strawberries and blueberries. Wash fruit and remove damaged portions and stems. Drain and slice the strawberries; leave blueberries whole.
4. Mix together ½ cup sugar and the 4 tablespoons flour, reserving remaining ¼ cup sugar. Mix with the fruit, using half of the mixture for the strawberries and half for the blueberries.
5. Cut the dough in half and place one section in refrigerator. Cut the dough you are working with into two equal pieces. Knead for several minutes and then roll each piece into a rectangle about ¼-inch thick.
6. Grease the bottom of a 9″ × 13″ baking pan and place one piece of dough in the pan, covering the bottom.
7. Brush a little milk over the surface of the dough. Scatter

strawberries over the dough. Dot with butter and spread remaining section of dough over the fruit. Brush top with a little more milk and sprinkle with sugar.

8. Repeat Steps 6 and 7 using the blueberries. Bake at 375 degrees for 30 minutes.

Serves 24.

Garlic

The most pungent pot herb of them all, garlic has been insistently aromatic and persistently present in the cuisine from Biblical times to this very moment. So widely, obtrusively, and continually has it been consumed over the centuries that the term "garlic eater" was, until quite recently, synonymous with the word Jew. In Roman times, Marcus Aurellius criticized Jews for exuding its smell. During the time of the Spanish Inquisition, there were even those who claimed that the Conversos, those Jews who converted to Catholicism to escape death or imprisonment, could still be recognized as Jews from the smell of garlic on their breaths.

Garlic's reputation as a restorative in Biblical times led the Pharaohs' building foremen to the practice of feeding great quantities of the cultivated herb to the Jewish pyramid builders in an effort to keep those overworked and hapless souls from falling down on the job. But the overriding reason for garlic's high profile historically was the outcome of another, though related, attribute: its purported powers as an aphrodisiac. That it has been recognized early in recorded history as being an energy food for construction workers was absolutely beside the point.

Nowadays, garlic and love strike us as being an unlikely pair. But in Babylonia and Palestine, Athens and Rome, the two had a very steady and extremely satisfying relationship. In fact, they carried on for years, beginning in about the fourth century b.c.e., and ending with our own scientific age when it was no longer a mark of high intellect to profess a belief in aphrodisiacs (at least not in public).

If the matchmakers were clearly Greek and Roman, the coupling was uniquely Jewish. Particularly on Friday evening, on the Sabbath, was garlic to be savored, for it was thought to "heat" the body, at just the time the Jewish sages of both the Bible and Talmud believed was appropriate for enjoying conjugal pleasures. Eat garlic on Friday evening, Rabbi Ezra implored, since "it promotes love and arouses desire." Making every effort to comply, the Jews roasted the herb or ate it raw, boiled it, and mixed it with fish, meat, and even beets, so that the strong-tasting bulb more than insinuated its presence in the foods and hence on the breaths of its partakers. Once, Judah-ha-Nasi, the famous second-century Talmudist, even had to ask his garlic-eating students to leave his lecture room, so distracting had the wafting aroma of garlic become in the small space.

The Talmud provided the historical bridge which linked the ancient fondness for garlic as an elixir of love to the medievalists' equal regard for it. The great twelfth-century Spanish-Jewish scholar and physician, Moses Maimonides, never recommended the use of garlic in his *Treatise on Sexual Intercourse,* suggesting as a formula for success the eating of mutton, young doves, and sparrows' brains instead. But in thirteenth-century Germany, the traditional Sabbath fish was mixed with copious amounts of garlic. In Eastern Europe the Sabbath roast goose and chicken were stuffed with it. Only the wine seemed to escape a dose.

Not willing to look upon garlic as serving only one purpose, however, the Eastern Europeans reassessed it and gave to it an additional virtue, that of curative. Mixed with salt, oil, and pepper, it was regarded as a remedy for intestinal worms. But one would always need to handle the little bulb with care since, if peeled and left out overnight, the evil demons, whose fantasized presence the medieval Jew feared so profoundly, would contaminate the herb and poison those who ate it.

Today, garlic is a much-loved seasoning, present in many foods traditionally served on Friday evening, the reason for which should by now be clear. But to season the chicken soup or gefilte fish and expect to have happen what Rabbi Ezra suggested would? Never. To take the throb from a lower left incisor? Hardly. To cure intestinal worms? Not likely. As aphrodisiac and ingredient of popular medicine, garlic has lost its reputation to all but a few strict interpreters of the Talmud and practitioners of folk medicine. What a loss!

Gazoz

The one-word Hebrew equivalent of "two cents plain." In other words, seltzer, carbonated water, fizz. It is currently out of style, plain and totally unneeded in American soft drinks, since all are sold with the carbonated water premixed into them. But in Israel no one would think of taking a straight swig of the sweet, syrupy essences of orange, raspberry, lemon, grapefruit, grape, and strawberry which are sold in the tall glass bottles at every food store. One learns fast that a glass of those syrups won't be enjoyed without a spritz or two, or twelve for that matter, of *gazoz* (say *gaa—zoz*), or water if you're really desperate.

Israelis like to tell a story that tells exactly how they feel about *gazoz*.

Once, not too long ago, a Tel Aviv-ite wandered out into the dry, barren hills of the Judean Desert not far from Jerusalem, just to look things over. Expecting the hills to be dotted with cafés (and not the dry brush that really was dotting the sandy, rocky wilderness), he left himself unprepared for the inevitable need for water.

Soon his pace became halting as he staggered from one dry wadi to another, expecting a café to be just over the next rocky outcropping. His thirst became nearly unbearable with each desperate step.

"A drink, I must have something soon or I'll die," he shouted aloud.

And he trudged onward, wondering if the next step would be his last.

And then, with the very next step that took him over the hill, he spied what looked like a man. Weakly, he called out for help and fell to the ground.

There was another person out there in the desert, a Jerusalem-ite who had come prepared, his canteen strapped to his belt. But not prepared well enough as it turned out for, after he had given the wanderer a sip from his canteen, the hapless fellow lying on the ground was heard to say, "Pheww! Who can drink juice without a little *gazoz* in it?" And with that, he spit out the liquid and died.

Gedempte Fleysch

And Elisha came again to Gilgal; and there was a dearth in the land; and the sons of the prophets were sitting before him; and he said unto his servant: "Set on the great pot, and seethe pottage (the nezid*) for the sons of the prophets." And one went out into the field to gather herbs, and found a wild vine, and gathered thereof wild gourds his lap full, and came and shred them into the pot of pottage; for they knew them not. So they poured out for the men to eat. And it came to pass, as they were eating of the pottage, that they cried out, and said: "O man of God, there is death in the pot." And they could not eat thereof. But he said, "Then bring meal." And he cast it into the pot; and he said: "Pour out for the people, that they may eat." And there was no harm in the pot.*

—II Kings 4:38

Like a Jewish Marco Polo, Petachia of Regensburg savored many of the years of his life by staying in motion. Beginning his travels in about 1175, he made his way through Poland and Russia to the Crimea, from there to Armenia, Babylonia and Syria, and finally to his destination, the land of Israel. Although he kept a diary, the tales of his travels were written down by those who had been regaled, enthralled and entertained by Petachia's personal recital of his exotic experiences.

One of these tales must have shocked his Jewish listeners, for Petachia graphically described the custom he had observed among the travelers of Kedas in the Ukraine. Tucked under the saddles of their horses, he said, at just the right angle, went pieces of raw animal flesh. Urged to a gallop, the horses would sweat and the saddles would be pressed back and forth. Sweat and friction would "cook" the meat and the horsemen would dismount and have their dinner, such as it was.

Meat "cooked" and tenderized by saddles may be kosher (as long as it has been salted first), but it is the heat of a fire which must cook meat according to Jewish tradition—cook it until it is transformed into food which no longer resembles the flesh of a living animal.

The most prized Jewish meat dishes therefore are those that have been braised, pot-roasted, stewed, oven-roasted, boiled, or otherwise cooked *in extremis. Gedempte fleysch* (say *ge—*

demp—ta—flaysh), meaning in Yiddish potted meat, is one such dish popular especially among Jews of Eastern European background and with slight variations among those of Sephardic background. Its Biblical precursor may have been the *nezid* referred to in II Kings 4:38.

Tscholent and *adafina*, the prized slow-cooking dishes of Sabbath, are also dishes of braised meat. So are brisket of beef, *flanken*, *essig fleysch*, goulash, tzimmes, and the recipes which combine meat and a stuffing which fills its insides: veal breast, beef tripe (also called *magen* or *gipa*), beef spleen (in Yiddish, *miltz*), and beef lung.

In the United States and most of Europe, the preferred meat is beef or veal. In the countries which border the Mediterranean, lamb or goat meat is more popular.

GEDEMPTE FLEYSCH

3 cloves garlic, minced
2 large onions, chopped
1 tablespoon vegetable oil or schmaltz
4 to 5 pounds whole brisket, well trimmed (or 4 to 5 pounds flanken, chuck, or shoulder roast), cut into large chunks
1 tablespoon paprika
3 bay leaves
1 teaspoon salt
½ teaspoon pepper
1 tablespoon Worcestershire sauce
1 cup boiling water (or 1 cup red wine)
1 cup dried or fresh mushrooms, sliced
5 medium potatoes, quartered

1. In a large, heavy pot, sauté garlic and onions in oil until golden brown. Remove from pan and reserve. Place meat in pot and brown on both sides over moderately high heat.
2. Add garlic, onions, and remaining ingredients. Cover and simmer for 2 hours, stirring occasionally. Add potatoes and simmer for an additional hour.

Makes 8 servings.

VEAL BREAST

Marinade:

- 4 to 6 pounds veal breast, well-trimmed and slit crosswise to form a large pocket
- 3 cloves garlic, mashed
- 1 teaspoon salt
- 1 large onion, peeled and sliced
- 2 bay leaves, crumbled
- ½ teaspoon whole peppercorns
- 1 teaspoon paprika
- 1 cup dry white wine

Stuffing:

- 2 cups cooked white or brown rice (or 2 cups cooked bulghur wheat)
- 1 medium onion, coarsely chopped
- 1 tablespoon vegetable oil
- 1 teaspoon salt
- ½ teaspoon freshly ground pepper or to taste
- 6 pitted prunes
- 8 dried apricot halves
- ½ cup blanched almonds

1. Spread the veal breast and inside of pocket with garlic and salt. Place in large roasting pan and add remaining marinade ingredients. Cover and refrigerate for 8 hours, turning once after 4 hours. Strain liquid and discard remaining solid ingredients.
2. Preheat oven to 325 degrees.
3. Fry the onion in oil until golden but not brown. Place rice in large mixing bowl and add the fried onion, salt, and pepper.
4. Using a food processor or grinder, coarsely grind prunes, apricot halves, and nuts. Mix with rice, and taste for seasoning.
5. Stuff the mixture into the pocket. Since opening will be quite large and difficult to sew closed, cover opening with a piece of aluminum foil wrapped across the front of the breast and tucked underneath it. Add strained marinade to the pan.
6. Cover roasting pan, and roast for 2 hours. Remove cover, and roast for an additional hour, adding more wine if pan juices evaporate too quickly.

Makes 4 to 5 servings.

Gefilte Fish

There is an old saying in Judaism so simply and directly stated that it belies the complexity of the tradition behind it. "Without fish there is no Sabbath," goes the saying, taken from a table song (Zmira) of the thirteenth century. (The song itself is still sung today to celebrate the arrival of the Sabbath and the traditional evening meal which is such an important part of the day's observance.)

Yet as old as the saying is, the tradition behind it is even older. Tracing its history compels one to follow as convoluted a trail of lore and observance as Judaism has to offer until, at the end of the search, the bits and pieces that have been gathered along the way finally come together and the story becomes clear, its culinary significance unmistakable.

First, a discussion of the "fish" in gefilte fish, then the "gefilte."

You can go back to Genesis and the story of the Creation to find the first Biblical discussion of fish. "And God blessed them, saying: 'Be fruitful and multiply and fill the waters in the seas. . . .'" But it can be argued that the Bible mentioned hundreds of foods: fish but one of them. Yet, by the end of the Biblical era and the beginning of the Talmudic age, fish became more and more important to the Jews until, exceeding even its usual physical dimensions, it became inextricably linked with the Messiah who, according to ancient legend, would come to the righteous of Israel in the form of a giant fish from the sea, the Leviathan. Tasting its body would be reserved for the faithful, its head for those who had fulfilled the Law.

Preparing for its coming, the Jews of the period ate other fish and bread and wine at a particular meal known as the *cena pura,* or special supper, the soothing effect of its presence at the meal becoming more important as the times grew more unsettled and harsh. This was, after all, the Israel ruled by Rome; the Israel of the Zealots and the gladiators; the Israel of famines, plagues, syncretistic religions of every sort including, of course, the developing Christianity.

Pervasive, the practice of eating fish at the Sabbath meal became an accepted ritual, mystical in its implications, focusing on a hope of better days to come. So central to the observance of the Sabbath did it continue to be that an observant Jew of

Eastern European background to this day would not sit down to a Sabbath meal without it.

And that brings us to the "gefilte."

By accepting Jesus as the Messiah (often symbolized by a fish, the Greek word *icth(os)* means fish, or as a fisherman), the Christians fulfilled the longed-for hope of eating the Messianic supper. The Jews, of course, for whom the Messiah has not yet come, did not do and have not done anything of the sort. Instead, they have continued to hope for the coming and have continued to prepare Sabbath meals over the past twenty or twenty-one centuries since the serving and the eating of the *cena pura*—meals which almost always include fish. And, in the Jewish communities of Europe, South and North America, the fish invariably comes to the table minus its bones.

Why?

Enter the laws governing the observance of the Sabbath, as intricate and complex a body of legal tenets as any in Judaism. Most of these Sabbath laws have to do with defining for Jews what can and cannot be done on the day of rest. Work is not allowed and, according to Orthodox Jewish observance, eating a fish with the bones intact is work!

How can eating fish be considered work, you are moved to ask, puzzled by the obvious incongruity? Shuffling papers and weeding the garden are work. But eating fish? Never.

Again, the answer comes from the Talmudic period. Specified first in the Mishna and then again at a somewhat later date in the Gemara, the laws of Sabbath observance were formally set down by the great rabbis eighteen hundred years ago to remind Jews of the wondrousness of the creations of God. Acts of human creativity were not allowed; the laws prohibiting Jews from preparing food on the Sabbath or, for that matter, engaging in any other creative act as, for example, the separating of wheat from the chaff (winnowing), were based on this distinction.

Many of the Sabbath laws were tied to ancient agricultural practices. The one just mentioned—the law prohibiting the particular activity of separating grain on the Sabbath—was, therefore, extended to apply to all human creativity and work where separating was involved. This included cooking and baking and, interestingly enough, the eating of a fish where the bones were still intact. Since separating was considered human work, both pulling the bones from a piece of fish and then eating the portion remaining were prohibited. According to Orthodox ritual, however, Jews were (and still are) allowed to take the food from the bones.

If a Jew followed the growing custom of eating fish on the Sabbath *and* observed the prohibition of separation, eating a piece of fish was sure to become just what it was not supposed to be: a completely joyless event. Too much care and concentration would need to be taken to avoid separating the bones from the flesh. The joy of the Sabbath meal would then be sacrificed to watching for one's transgressions while merely eating a tasty mouthful of food.

The answer to all this was the creation of a boneless piece of fish, one that could be prepared before the Sabbath and eaten with relish without fear of violating the Sabbath laws.

"A pie of fish hash and flour," mentioned in the Talmud by the scholar Rabbi Papa of Naresh, in Babylonia, may have been the first solution to the boneless fish dilemma. Although he would never pray in a house where it was being cooked since its pungent odor disturbed his devotions, nor would he recommend it be eaten by nursing mothers, Rabbi Papa savored the taste of fish-hash pie on a Sabbath eve. There was no better trifle, he proclaimed, for it made the Sabbath a delight.

Just what besides boneless fish and flour went into the pie is unclear. But one good guess would be garlic, since it too was a beloved Sabbath food.

The recipe collection of the Roman glutton Apicius includes a dish called *Patina de Abua Sive Apua,* which is usually translated as "Smelt Pie" or "Sprat Custard." It calls for steaming a mixture of boned chopped fish, pepper, the strong and bitter herb called rue, fish broth, and raw eggs, a recipe not so very different from what Rabbi Papa's fish-hash pie probably contained, or what we know today as gefilte fish: the Yiddish name given to two boneless fish dishes eaten on the Sabbath since medieval times.

The first and most commonly prepared gefilte fish recipe is probably of German origin (with vague hints of Rabbi Papa's Babylonian delight). It consists of golf ball-sized pieces of ground and heavily spiced freshwater fish which are boiled in a fish broth and usually served chilled. The second, thought to originate in Roumania, is much more elaborate. A large fish is gutted and all the flesh is removed, leaving the skin and head intact. The bones are removed, and the boneless flesh mixed with spices and flour and stuffed back inside. The fish is then sewn closed, baked, and served "whole," but, of course, it has actually been stuffed with its own boneless flesh, hence the name "gefilte" or stuffed fish.

Just what an extraordinary culinary creation this is cannot be overemphasized. To be sure, recipes calling for boned fish have been prepared since the time of Rabbi Papa and probably before his time as well. And there is nothing nowadays as unremarkable as a fish stick or a quenelle. What is so remarkable is the way in which gefilte fish is more than what it seems to be. Fish bones are nowhere to be found in its melange of ingredients; but its historical essence is everywhere, as pungent and enticing as its taste.

GEFILTE FISH

6 pounds fish (2 pounds each of whitefish, bass, and pike—or a combination of at least two firm-fleshed fish)
6 onions, peeled
8 carrots, scraped clean
1 parsnip, cut into small pieces
Water to cover
Dash of salt
3 raw eggs
1 tablespoon sugar
Bread crumbs or matzah meal
1 tablespoon salt
1 teaspoon pepper

1. Skin and bone the fish, and place with the heads and tails in a large cooking pot. Add 4 sliced onions, 4 sliced carrots, and the parsnip. Add enough water to cover and a dash of salt. Cook until vegetables are soft, about 1 hour.
2. While the stock is cooking, chop or finely grind the boned fish. Grate or grind the remaining carrots and onions and add to the ground fish. Add the raw eggs, sugar, and bread crumbs or matzah meal to bind the mixture together, about ¼ cup. Add seasonings.
3. Knead the mixture together for 20 minutes.
4. Form into 3 or 4 large balls or 12 to 15 small balls and place in the boiling liquid. Reduce heat to simmer, cover, and cook for 1 hour.

5. Remove the fish balls and strain the liquid. Return the fish to the liquid and refrigerate. Serve with cooked carrots from the broth and *chrain*.

Makes 12 to 15 servings.

Gildene Yoich

See Chicken Soup.

Gipa

To hear an Iranian Jew talk of *gipa* (pronounced with a hard *g* like the *g* in geese, *geepa*) is much like hearing love poetry recited by one's intended; the phrases describing its taste are spoken with great tenderness and their sound mellifluous. Everything about the dish is better than the best food one has tasted: the texture, the intermingling of spices, the color (an amazing greenish-yellow), the gravy. And the way it is traditionally cooked is spoken of with particular reverence, in a stone pot cooked over a low open fire, and made only on the Sabbath.

The respect paid to *gipa* is greatest in those who, having left Iran, must remain content with less than the real thing. The major ingredient, tripe, is difficult if not impossible to come by nowadays; and beef casings are only second best.

Not willing to leave even one part of a slaughtered animal unused or uneaten, the Iranian-Jewish housewife remembers the time when she would spend hours cleaning the inside of a once-capacious cow stomach before mixing the ingredients to stuff it: onions, a leek, an entire bunch of parsley and just as much (or more) dill weed, depending on what the family liked, yellow split peas, oil, rice, a heaping tablespoon of cumin, and ample sprinklings of turmeric, salt, and black pepper. Using about a half cup of vegetable oil poured over all, she mixed and pressed the ingredients together, usually with her hands. Then she would stuff the mixture into 3 or 4 large pieces of tripe. Using a needle and thread, she sewed the sacks closed, placed the stuffed sacks in the stone pot, added enough water to keep the ingredients moist, and placed the *gipa* to cook on the Sabbath cook stove. Hours later, at lunch the next day, the stuffed sacks would be cut open and the *gipa* served.

GIPA

Although kosher tripe once was widely available commercially in the United States, it no longer is, making the preparation of an authentic *gipa* in this country an impossibility. However, the same stuffing ingredients can be used to fill beef casings, which are available. The result will be an oriental version of kishke.

1 leek
2 large onions
1 bunch parsley
1½ bunches dill weed
1 cup yellow split peas
2 cups uncooked rice
1 tablespoon cumin
1 teaspoon turmeric
1¼ teaspoons salt
½ teaspoon black pepper
½ cup vegetable oil, olive oil, or melted chicken fat
Kosher beef casings

1. Wash, trim, and finely chop the leek (top and bottom), dill, and parsley. Peel the onions and finely chop them. Add remaining ingredients except casings, and mix well.
2. Cut the casings into 12-inch-long pieces. Using a needle and thread, sew up one end of each casing.
3. Stuff the mixture into the casings. Sew to seal closed.
4. Place stuffed casings in a large Dutch oven or other thick-sided pot. Add about two inches of water and place in a 375-degree oven for 30 minutes, uncovered. Reduce heat to 250 to 275 degrees, cover, and slowly simmer for 3½ hours, adding water as needed until ready to serve.

Goat

One little goat, one little goat,
My father bought for two zuzim.
One little goat, one little goat.

—Chad Gadyo, an ancient Aramaic nursery rhyme, sung traditionally at the end of the Passover Seder

"So you want one of my goats, do you? [said Tema-Gittel of Kozodoievka, the teacher's wife]. Well, let me tell you this, my dear man. I'm not interested in selling the goat. For let's not fool ourselves: Why should I sell it? For the money you offer? Money is round. It rolls away. But a goat is always a goat. Especially a goat like mine. Did I call it a goat? A sweetheart, that's what it is! How easy it is to milk her! And the amount of milk she gives! And how cheap it is to feed her! What does she eat? A measure of bran once a day; and, for the rest, she nibbles the straw from the roof of the synagogue. Still, if you're ready to pay what it's worth, I might think it over. Money is—how do you say it?—a temptation. If I get enough money, I can buy another goat. Although a goat like mine would be hard to find. Did I call it a goat? A sweetheart, I tell you! But wait, why waste words? I'll bring the goat in and you'll see for yourself."*

And what did Shimmen-Eli of Zolodievka, member of the Tailors' Guild and president of his synagogue do when he saw the milk from the "sweetheart" that he had been pushed to buy by his wife, Tsippa Baila-Reiza? He licked his lips in anticipation of tasting its delicious sweetness. And when, after much haggling, the deal was consumated and Tema-Gittel had taken the money, spit on it to ward off the Evil Eye, and had led the tailor out on the road, the excited Shimmen-Eli had gone to take the goat back to Zolodievka and found the little beast reluctant to go.

Stubborn, the goat just would not budge. She bleated. She kicked her hind legs. "Koza," the children screamed at her in

*From "The Enchanted Tailor," by Sholom Aleichem, in *The Old Country; Collected Stories of Sholom Aleichem,* translated by Julius and Frances Butwin. New York, Crown Publishers, Inc., 1953.

Russian until she finally moved. "Don't give me a headache," Shimmen-Eli told the goat in so many words. "Once I, too, was free." Then, hurrying, he and the goat took off down the road connecting the two villages.

For him, Shimmen-Eli of Zolodievka, this goat would mean "crocks and crocks of butter, . . . delicious jugs of . . . buttermilk, . . . cream, . . . and clabber, rolls and biscuits baked with butter, sprinkled with sugar and cinnamon," delicacies to those both rich and poor but almost undreamed of luxuries to such a poor man as Shimmen-Eli. Oh, how anxious he was to taste these longed-for delights, even if they were to come from such a stubborn beast as the one he led!

Exalted by Eastern European Jews like the fictional Shimmen-Eli, for whom its acquisition meant a giant step up from the depths of poverty in which he and the millions of Jews he represented spent their days, a goat, ornery and cussed as it was, was also the stuff of which dreams were made. One's good fortune could be measured by a she-goat's presence in a *shtetl* household even if it ate everything in sight, smelled horrible, kept one awake all night with its bleating, and every now and then disappeared into some gully and had to be prodded and kicked for hours until it could be driven back to where it had come from.

The dramatic tension produced by its mixed bag of attractions and offenses became the subject for dozens of stories and legends, some told in Hebrew, others in Yiddish. Again and again, the goat would be assailed by some character or other, cursed, derided for all the indignities it rendered to all who had anything whatsoever to do with it. Yet, the very same goat that would just as soon kick over the pail of its own sweet milk would feed one's family, too. So it became an object of love as well as hate, a metaphorical creature, a literary stand-in for the diasporic Jew whose life was itself such a mixed blessing of sanctity and tribulation.

Sometimes it was a messenger as well as giver of life and health, as in the late-medieval fable of the she-goats of Shebreshin, the story used later by the famous Hebrew novelist, S. Y. Agnon, in his "Fable of the Goat." Shebreshin, a corruption of the Hebrew words *shev rishon* (meaning sit first!), was one of the nine Polish villages settled by Jews who had been expelled from Spain. It was thousands of miles from the city of

Jerusalem and yet, miraculously, became directly connected to the Promised Land by a tunnel traversed by two she-goats belonging to a poor Hasid and his wife. These poor Jews depended on the goats for their livelihood, for it was the goat milk, butter, and cheese which they sold to earn money.

One day the Hasid's wife forgot to tether the animals. Frantic, fearing that they would run away and the family would starve, she began crying and shouting. Her husband, as if anticipating future events, stopped her, saying, "Everything is from Heaven." And soon what he had said proved to be true.

The goats returned at sunset and gave more milk than ever before. The sick villagers who drank the milk which the Hasid's wife had run and sold to them became well after drinking it. Taking this as a sign that the goats had been blessed, the Hasid and his wife allowed the goats to go untethered again and again, until six days had passed. On the seventh day, the Hasid followed the goats, hoping to learn the secret of his sudden good fortune.

The goats led him into a cave. Once inside, he saw a distant beam of light; the goats scrambled toward it and he quickly followed them. At the other end of the cave was the holy soil of Israel. Full of awe, the Hasid threw himself to the ground, kissed the rocky soil and even the stones themselves, and thanked God. Then he wrote a letter to the Jews of Shebreshin and to all the Jews in the Diaspora. He tied the letter to the neck of one of the goats. Onto a fig leaf into which he had tucked the letter, he asked that the letter be handed to the rabbi of the village.

But when the goats returned without the Hasid accompanying them, the woman grew so worried that she never noticed the letter. Sure that robbers had killed her husband, she moved to the village and took the goats to be slaughtered. Only when the goats had been killed was the letter found and taken to the rabbi.

Weeping, the rabbi proclaimed a period of mourning, for only the goats had known the way to the Holy Land; now the path would never be found. The people would have to go on waiting for redemption in exile. Their bad deeds had made them overlook the letter which would have shown them the way out of their travail.

The goats had carried a message but the Jews had been too sinful to recognize it. No wonder they had found themselves the persecuted residents of such an alien environment. And look at what wondrous food the goats had brought; their milk had been lifegiving, healing. In haste, the Hasid's wife had allowed her passions to get the best of her. Rather than observe the goats carefully, she had killed the very creatures who would have saved her and led her "home." It's as though the goats had been sacrificed to atone for the sins of Shebreshin and metaphorically all Jews.

How intricate is the pattern of legend, scripture, history, and day-to-day reality of the Jews woven into this story about as seemingly ordinary an animal as a goat. But it should be clear by now that the goat has never been just an ordinary animal to the Jews; and, as is so often the case in Judaism, the reasons for its specialness are many.

From the scriptural roots of Judaism, the Bible, comes a multiplicity of images of the goat, first in Genesis as domesticated animal, usually raised in small herds for meat as well as milk, as in the story of Jacob and Esau. Jacob fetches two kids from the family flock to make a meal for an almost-blind Isaac while Esau is out hunting for the wild deer Isaac has asked to be brought to him (Genesis 27:9).

Even in this ancient Biblical passage, the goat is used for more than food. It is a substitute for another food, an unknowing participant to a subterfuge. Isaac eats and enjoys the savory meal, thinking all the while that it is the venison brought by Esau. Yet, it is the goat meat which Rebekah has prepared and that Jacob, dressed in goatskin to appear to Isaac as the hairy Esau, has put before him.

Then in Leviticus, the goat takes on a very special role as the carrier of the sins of the people: the scapegoat. One goat is presented by Aaron as a sin-offering to the Lord and another, the Azazel, is sent into the wilderness to carry off the sins of Israel (Lev. 16:8–10). At the time of the Second Temple, the Azazel which had been sent off, always on the Day of Atonement, was killed to ensure its never returning with its heavy burden of sin to the places where people lived.

In a later Biblical development, the cooking of chunks of young goat in a sauce of goat milk, oil, and onions similar to the present-day Italian dish *caldariello,* in the manner probably used by Rebekah to prepare the savory dish for Isaac, was prohibited once and for all. The custom of boiling a kid in its mother's milk probably dated from a much earlier time when ancient peoples served the dish at idolatrous fertility festivals. "Thou shalt not seethe [boil] a kid in its mother's milk" was first stated in Exodus, then repeated in Leviticus, and mentioned again in Deuteronomy. It became the basis for that particular Law of Kashrut which deals with the separation of meat and milk.

Also from the Bible comes the use of the goat (or a lamb) as the Paschal sacrifice. This sacrifice was the central event of the Passover celebrations at the Temple in Jerusalem, offered in commemoration of the lamb eaten at the first Passover meal in Egypt. The practice of offering sacrifices at the Temple is written about in copious detail in the Bible. This particular sacrifice was unique since groups rather than individuals brought the animals to the Temple and remained together to prepare the meal and to consume it before dawn of the next day. Thousands of animals would be brought to the Temple and sacrificed by their owners. Then the slaughtered animals would be carried off to be placed on spits of pomegranate wood and hung over clay stoves or "Pesach-ovens" which were located in the courtyards of every home in Jerusalem.

But, when the Second Temple was destroyed in the first century and the Jews were forced out of Israel (or even before that time if a Jew lived in the Diaspora and could not journey to Jerusalem to observe Passover), the sacrifice became represented by a roasted bone placed on the Seder or Passover plate. And so the goat became a symbol of not just one exodus—the first the Jews had made from Egypt—but of all succeeding ones as well.

Elevated, exalted, symbol of sacrifice, sin, and even destiny, a long list of attributes made the scrawny, bearded, black-colored *capra hercus mambrica* larger than life. It took the Talmud to bring it down a peg.

Armed robber. Thief. Crop-destroyer. The Talmudists wrote of the goat as if it had been one of the ten plagues. Symbol in one sense, yes, but to a person living one's life in third- or fourth-century Babylonia, a goat was nothing but trouble. Through the cornfields belonging to Rabbi Joseph or down the streets of Pumbadita and Mehuza, it went, eating everything in sight.

There was more. A he-goat of the town of Mehuza had busied himself at upsetting a cask, jumping on it, breaking it, and eating some turnips which had been lying on top of it. A woman had brought some dough to the bakehouse to be baked into bread. Before it could be placed in the oven, the baker's goat had eaten the dough and died. More still. The townsfolk of Pumbadita and elsewhere had brought their goats to the butchers to be slaughtered. Waiting until market day to slaughter them, the butchers had allowed the goats to roam the village streets, overturning all in their path.

The Aramaic equivalent of "Do something!" must have been heard by the rabbis throughout the land. Finally, they responded by proclaiming: "To the scholars that go up to Palestine and to those that come down to Babylonia, the following is the prevailing law regarding the goats that belong to the butchers which roam the streets and cause damage; the owners should be warned twice or thrice and, should they take no heed, the animals may be slaughtered and the meat given to the butcher to sell."

Was this to be an end to all the commotion? Impossible. A goat was still a goat. It would be counted on to spend the next fifteen centuries making just as much trouble as ever.

Over the centuries when times grew much worse, the law which permitted the slaughter of upstart goats was rarely enforced. As time passed and life for the Jews grew more difficult, the goats they could afford became fewer in number and the stories of their past glories and foibles multiplied. No longer herders but most often landless peasants, the Jews of the European Diaspora became as grateful as Shimmen-Eli for the shaggy presence of a goat and as savvy as Tema-Gittel at evaluating their preciousness.

The time when one's wealth could be measured in buckets of goat milk is gone forever. But its passing occurred not so many years ago, for, until thirty-five or forty years ago in Europe, there were places just like Kozodoievka and Zolodievka. In hundreds of Russian and Polish rural villages, there would have been a she-goat nibbling from the straw roof of the synagogue; and her owners, hating and loving her at the same time, would have called her sweetheart.

Gogl-Mogl

First comes the cracking voice, next the hoarseness, and then the bleary eyes, followed by the running nose, shallow cough, and fever. The diagnosis hardly matters (although to make one is easy enough) for the cure in many Jewish homes has been the one that's been used for years: *gogl-mogl* (say *gawggle—mawggle*), the potable comforter that is whipped up in the kitchen without a prescription from an egg, sugar, vanilla extract, and a splash or two from a bottle of the family brandy.

In a matter of minutes, the time it takes to beat its few ingredients into a yellow-white foam that has been heated to a temperature guaranteed to warm the innards of even the chilliest mortal, a *gogl-mogl* is ready for sipping. Then the women, who are as skillful at practicing medicine without a license as they are at cooking perfect meals without benefit of Cordon Bleu, scurry and fuss with the blankets, plump the pillows, and serve the brew that is in reality liquid custard, but in the Jewish imagination has become synonymous with motherly care and concern.

Jewish mothers (or fathers) from Eastern Europe have not always had such exclusive rights to the use of *gogl-mogl*. The Russians and Poles knew as much about its healing properties as the Jews did and of its inebriating qualities even more. Also, it is likely that the drink came into the Polish and Russian culinary sphere long before it beguiled the Jews, brought to Slavic lands by English traders and sailors during Elizabethan times who called its more potent rendition, huggle-my-buff.

Other terms are used more frequently nowadays to describe the Jews' much beloved *gogl-mogl*—flip, egg flip, creme Anglaise, milk punch. Even the names syllabub and posset are better known. But in thousands of Jewish homes throughout the world, none is so colorful and comforting as the one which in nonsense rhyme turns ordinary custard into potent, curing restorative.

GOGL-MOGL

To use as a remedy for sore throat or hoarseness, add only a tablespoon of liquor or if the patient is a child, add liquor only at your discretion. To make a *gogl-mogl* punch, add up to one cup of rum, brandy, or cognac.

4 egg yolks
½ cup sugar
1 teaspoon vanilla extract
4 cups (1 quart) hot milk
Rum, cognac, or brandy, to taste
Nutmeg, to taste

1. Beat egg yolks with sugar until frothy and pale yellow.
2. Stir in vanilla and slowly pour in very hot milk, beating constantly. Add liquor and mix well.
3. Pour into mugs, sprinkle with nutmeg, and serve.

Makes 8 drinks.

Goose

A goose that hears the Megillah (Book of Esther) you should drive out of the community.

—Old Yiddish saying

To read a paragraph which begins with the sentence "Geese is my business . . . "* is to know instantly that you have entered the tumultuous world of the nineteenth-century Yiddish story writer Sholom Aleichem's fictional village of Kasrilevke, just in time to listen to the goosekeeper's Chanukah lament.

Her story, fiction borrowing heavily from fact, was first recounted by Sholom Aleichem in Yiddish to be read by Russian-Jews living lives not very different from that of the goosekeeper. She was an imaginary woman who had a contemporary as well as an historical counterpart in almost every Jewish village in Europe, from the Middle Ages to the third decade of this century, simply because goosekeeping had been a

*From "Geese," by Sholom Aleichem, in *Stories and Satires* (Yoseloff, 1959).

traditionally Jewish and traditionally female occupation since Talmudic times.

Despite the spirit and holiday glow which surrounded this particular lady of the geese, one of Sholom Aleichem's most masterfully done character studies, she was the embodiment of despair.

The cycle of her life, totally out of sync with the cycle of the Jewish year, went like this. At Sukkot-time she bought the geese. Forced to take out a loan from an ignominious loan shark with a pot belly who called himself Reb Alter, she had to endure first the geese and then Reb Alter's threats to foreclose on her enterprise for nonpayment of his usurious interest rates.

And heaven forbid if she mistakenly bought a gander. "A goose'll give fat, a gander—plagues!" she exclaimed.

Then came the care and feeding of the inventory. If the geese weren't put in the coop before the new moon, they were ruined. Ditto if they were left in the cage during the day. And if she forgot to say, as she caged them up for the night, "I hope you get as fat as me," while pinching herself three times, all was lost. . . .

In the meantime her husband did nothing but sit and study Torah while she did all the work. Oh, the pain of it. . . .

Every year, she raised thirty geese; shlepped them to be slaughtered; plucked their feathers; salted, rinsed, and scalded the meat; separated the skin, the fat, and the giblets, trying to turn everything into money. How hard she worked and for what? . . .

While the citizens of Kasrilevke were building booths for Sukkot, she was buying geese. When the children were spinning Chanukah dreidles, she was frying kosher-for-Passover goose fat. Her world was topsy-turvy, a mess. Yes, absolutely upside-down. The profit, if there was any, came from the goose meat and the fat. If the price of meat was high, well and good. But if the butchers were having a price war, she'd make nothing for her efforts. . . .

Because of this, she also dealt in feathers. Her daughters, sitting at home waiting to get married even if they were only six and eight, nine and ten, helped her pluck goose feathers. And ate. "A little goose gullet, a gizzard, a head, a foot, a drop of goose fat." Sometimes, the smell of rendered goose fat was enough for them. They didn't even have to eat. . . .

So, the interest accumulated on her loan like "wild mushrooms," the children filled up on smells, and her husband filled up on Torah. The rich townsfolk chewed lustily on roasted goose at Chanukah time and anticipated the taste of a Passover matzah ball made with little drops of goose fat, while she continued to lament that there wasn't a drop of profit to be had.

Goose-raising may have been an unprofitable occupation for Jews living in the small rural villages of Russia in the late nineteenth century (what occupation wasn't?), forcing some Jews to live on smells rather than substance, but elsewhere, notably in German lands and at an earlier time, raising the scrappy birds was one of the ways the Jews kept themselves alive and in the good graces of the Christian communities in which they lived.

In the Middle Ages, particularly in the fifteenth and sixteenth centuries, goose-raising was a Jewish occupation. So good were the Jews at the task that they apparently supplied entire communities with fattened birds, especially for the Roman Catholic feast of Martinsmas. The "Martinbirds," as the holiday geese were called, were given, rather than sold, to the Christian townsfolk as payment of a tax or as some chroniclers infer, as a form of protection extracted from the Jews each year as payment for the modicum of tranquility the Christians had provided the Jews living in their midst during the preceding year.

The traditionally Jewish times of year for preparing geese were and still are the holidays of Chanukah, which comes in early winter, and Purim, which comes in the spring. A very old food custom associated with Chanukah has been the preparation of foods made with oil (like potato pancakes and fritters) or natural fats (usually fat roasted meat or a well-fattened fowl). The practice of serving goose on Chanukah, its eating still very much a part of Chanukah feasting today, definitely existed in sixteenth-century Germany and probably originated at a much earlier date, well before Sholom Aleichem's "Kasrilevkites" adopted the savory habit that filled them with goosemeat to the brim of their *streimels*.

ROAST GOOSE

Capon, duck, or a roasting chicken can be substituted if goose is unavailable.

A 4- to 6-pound goose
4 or 5 apples, quartered
Salt and pepper to taste
Paprika
3 onions, sliced
Juice of ½ lemon
1½ cups orange juice

1. Remove all the fat from the goose and salt the cavity. Sprinkle the apples with lemon juice and mix with sliced onions. Stuff the goose with the quartered apples and onions, and tie the cavity closed using a needle and thread or poultry pins. Salt and pepper it, and sprinkle with the paprika.
2. Put on a rack and roast in a 425-degree oven for 30 minutes.
3. Remove fat in the roaster. Baste with the orange juice.
4. Lower the heat to 325 degrees and continue roasting 20 to 25 minutes for each pound, basting the goose with the orange juice every 30 minutes. Serve with the apples and onions.

Makes 8 servings.

Goulash

The first bowl of goulash was prepared at least as long ago as the ninth century, somewhere in that vast expanse of flat land in eastern Hungary which is known as the *puszta.* There, cattle and sheep herders cut meat into cubes, cooked the meat with onions in a heavy iron kettle called a *bogracs,* and stewed the mixture until every drop of liquid had evaporated. Then the meat was dried in the sun, placed into a bag made of sheep's stomach, and stored until lunch or dinnertime when a piece of it would be mixed with some water and reheated—an early and surprisingly sensible-sounding method of reconstituting food. Goulash was the ninth-century answer to a ninth-century technological problem, just as space-food sticks and Tang are an answer to a twentieth-century one.

If a lot of water was added, the dish became *gulyasleves*, or soup; otherwise, it was *gulyashus*, or goulash meat, a simple stew seasoned mostly with saffron and a touch of caraway. Paprika replaced saffron sometime in the late sixteenth century, introduced into Hungary by the conquering Turks.

The word *gulyas* originally meant cattle or sheep herder, referring to the person who took care of the *gulya* or herd. In modern Hungarian, *gulyas* is one of the four traditional and distinctively different Hungarian stews. *Porkolt*, *paprikas*, and *tokany* are the names of the other three.

Hungarian gourmets never, never, never confuse the four. Not surprisingly, neither do Jewish cooks, gourmet or not, nor kosher cookbooks, since *gulyas* (invariably printed in English with a different spelling, g-o-u-l-a-s-h) is the only stew of the four types which can be prepared in the traditional Hungarian way without violating the rules of kashrut.

Added to an authentically prepared *porkolt* of chicken, veal, or fish, for example, are bacon drippings or lard; to a chicken *paprikas*, sour or sweet cream; and to beef *tokany*, smoked bacon, pork sausage, lard or sour cream, or a combination of the four. There is little wonder that goulash, because it called for none of these non-kosher ingredients while still emitting the voluptuous aura of real Hungarian cuisine, became so popular in Hungarian-Jewish households. If you view twentieth-century American-Jewish cookbooks as a reliable barometer of Jewish culinary tastes, goulash appears to be among the most popular of the foods eaten by Jews. There is hardly a Jewish cookbook without at least one recipe for it. Then, too, it is a rather simple mixture of meat, vegetables, and spices, cooked only in its own natural juices; there is no fancy brown sauce or wine to be added, no complicated multistep process to follow. Thus, goulash fits well into the traditional, ages-old method so dear to the Jews, of slowly stewing beef accompanied by little more than a few vegetables and some spice.

GOULASH

The extra tablespoon of spicy Hungarian paprika does make a difference and will improve the taste of this recipe; and don't use the mild American paprika for this recipe if you want to make goulash the way the Hungarian Jews do.

4 tablespoons vegetable oil
1 clove garlic
1 large onion
2 pounds lean beef chuck, cut into ¾-inch cubes
3 fresh tomatoes
2 green peppers
1 tablespoon Hungarian paprika
½ teaspoon freshly ground black pepper
1 teaspoon caraway seeds
1 teaspoon salt
4 medium potatoes, cubed

1. Chop onion, tomatoes, and peppers coarsely. Mince the garlic. Do not use green pepper cores.
2. In a large Dutch oven, sauté onions and garlic in oil until translucent. Stir to prevent them from sticking to the bottom of the pot.
3. Brown the meat with the onions and garlic.
4. Add tomatoes, peppers, paprika, caraway seeds, pepper, and salt. Mix well. Reduce heat to simmer, add 4 cups warm water, cover, and cook for 1 hour.
5. Peel the potatoes and cube them. Add to the goulash after the first hour, along with 2 cups warm water and an additional ¼ teaspoon salt. Cover and simmer for 30 minutes.
6. Taste for seasoning. Serve accompanied by little boiled dumplings or egg noodles.

DUMPLINGS FOR GOULASH

Called *galuska* in Hungarian, you may also know them as *nockerl,* or soup dumplings.

2 eggs
⅓ cup cold water
¾ teaspoon salt
⅓ cup sifted flour
½ teaspoon baking powder

1. Beat the eggs, water, and salt together. Add the flour and baking powder, mixing until smooth.
2. Drop by the teaspoonful into boiling salted water. Cook for 5 minutes, or until the dumplings rise to the surface. Drain well and serve.

Gugelhupf

Baked just long enough to come from the oven crusted and brown outside, with its protected contents tinged a golden yellow by a half dozen egg yolks and full cup of butter, and dotted with a mere handful of sweet white raisins, the *gugelhupf* continues to be lightly embraced and joyously savored by those who know its simple wonders. The cake is meant to be eaten with strong coffee or, if one must, a cup of lemony tea. Good for a Sabbath afternoon, thought the Viennese Jews who made it on Friday and looked after it until the time came to eat it.

The Jewish history of *gugelhupf*? It was a seventeenth-century borrowing, a perfect Sabbath afternoon sweet. Credit for the creation, some say, should go to a Viennese baker who wanted to celebrate the defeat of the Turks in 1683 and created a turban-shaped cake to make his point.

The Jews also adopted a close relative of the *gugelhupf* called *babka,* the Polish sweet cake, and made *bundtkuchen* a Sabbath institution. The only real difference in the three cakes is in the shape of the pan in which each is baked. The ingredients are virtually identical, down to the last golden crumb.

Popular? Centuries ago, *gugelhupf* was the delight of German, Swiss, Hungarian, and Austrian households. Now, it is well-known in Israel; the Americans have, however, almost forsaken it.

RICH GUGELHUPF

2 packages dry yeast
½ cup lukewarm milk
1 cup butter, softened
6 egg yolks
3 cups flour, sifted
½ cup sugar
¼ teaspoon salt
¼ cup raisins
¼ teaspoon cinnamon
1 teaspoon grated orange rind
Confectioners' sugar

1. Dissolve the yeast in the milk.
2. Cream the butter, then add the egg yolks and flour alternately, beating well. Add the sugar and salt, yeast mixture, raisins, cinnamon, and orange rind. Mix well.

3. Grease a Gugelhupf or Bundt pan. Place the dough in the pan. Cover and allow to rise in a warm place until double in bulk (1 hour).
4. Bake in a 350-degree oven for about 1 hour, or until crusted and well browned. Cool. Sprinkle with confectioners' sugar.

Gundi

Ah—the little round and aromatic mounds which accompany the chicken must be *knaidlach,* matzah balls, you tell yourself as you sit at the Sabbath table in a Persian household. Judging from their shape and pale brown color, you feel assured that you have spotted old friends in this new culinary environment. You are pleased. But wait. The color is too dark, the look not quite the same. A second and closer look has brought with it confusion and even more curiosity.

Gefilte fish, that's what this dish must be. But how does gefilte fish come to be served on the same platter as the chicken? And, as your helping comes closer, you know that this generously spiced food that is being placed in front of you hasn't a piece of fish in it.

Then, what is it? You must ask before you try it. *Gundi,* you are told; to serve it on the Sabbath in a Persian household is traditional. But there is no fish in it, no matzah meal, and no garlic. Instead, there is finely ground chicken, chickpeas pulverized to a fine powder resembling flour, a hint of turmeric, more than a hint of *hel* (cardamom), and pepper.

GUNDI (PERSIAN CHICKEN BALLS)

4 boned chicken breasts
¼ cup chicken fat
1 small onion, peeled
2½ cups dried crushed chickpeas*
1½ teaspoons salt

*Available at Middle Eastern food markets or pulverize the chickpeas at home, either by grinding them several times or putting them in the blender or food processor.

***Hel* is cardamom and is also available at any Middle Eastern grocery.

½ teaspoon pepper
¼ teaspoon turmeric
½ teaspoon ground *hel***
1 chicken, quartered
2 medium onions, peeled and quartered
4 or 5 small potatoes, diced
Salt and pepper to taste

1. Grind chicken, fat, and onion until the consistency of ground beef.
2. Mix with dried crushed chickpeas, salt, pepper, turmeric, and *hel.* Add about ½ cup water or until consistency of raw meatballs.
3. Form some of mixture into a ball the size of a golf ball.
4. Place chicken, onions, potatoes, salt, and pepper in a large soup pot. Add water to cover. Reduce heat to simmer and cook for 30 minutes.
5. Place the ball in the soup for 15 minutes. Ball should stay together. Add more chickpea powder to the gundi mixture, if needed.
6. Form remaining mixture into balls and cook, covered, for 15–20 minutes.
7. Serve, drained, as an appetizer or as a side dish to the chicken. Serve soup with pieces of boiled chicken.

H

Hamantaschen

Mohn (rhymes with *fun*) is both the German and Yiddish word for poppy seeds; *tasch* (rhymes with *gosh*), the word for pocket or purse. Put them together and the result is a pocket-like pastry of Germanic origin, triangular in shape, and filled with poppy seeds. Popular among German Jews and non-Jews alike in the late Middle Ages, *mohntaschen* (en is a plural ending) have always given the rabbis and the scholars something to really sink their teeth into, because a dish eaten by Jews has always been more satisfying if there exists some connection between it and the history of the Jewish people.

So, see in the word mohn a similarity to the word Haman, the villain in the Book of Esther (read each year on the holiday of Purim), and in *tasch* the metaphorical pocket of Haman's coat, the place where he carried the lots (purim) cast to determine the day on which the Jews of Shushan, Persia, would die. Replace mohn with *Haman,* keep the *tasch,* and the result is the word hamantaschen, the name given to the traditional pastries of Purim.

"There is a certain people scattered abroad and dispersed among the peoples in all the provinces of thy Kingdom," said Haman, a prime minister, one day several thousand years ago to his boss, King Ahasuerus of Persia. "Their laws are diverse from those of every people; neither keep they the King's laws; therefore it is not for the King's profit to suffer them. If it please the King, let it be written that they may be destroyed . . . " (Esther 3:8–9). But before the King could carry out Haman's nefarious plot, Esther, who was both Jewish and the favorite of the King, appealed to the King on behalf of the Jews. Justice prevailed. Haman swung from the same gallows he had prepared for Mordecai.

Since that time, Haman has become a worthy focus of

Jewish anger. The noise in a synagogue, the boos, shouts, and thunderous foot-stompings made each time his name is read as the Book of Esther is chanted each year, is a head-splitting cacophony of pent-up hatred for the likes of Haman and each and every other villain who has lived before him or since. And the eating of a food bearing his name is as close as Jews ever come to symbolically devouring their oppressors.

As extra justification for adopting *mohntaschen* and making them the traditional Purim pastry, it has been suggested that poppy seeds, the usual filling for this pocket food, were both a symbol of manna, the food God gave to the Jews wandering in Egypt before the Law was given to them, and one of the few foods Esther would eat in the Court of Ahasuerus since she would have been observing the Jewish dietary laws.

Today, traditional hamantaschen are still made with poppy seeds. But they can be filled with anything and still be called by that name. In addition to poppy seeds, *lekvar* (prune jam) and *povidl* (plum jam) are popular among Jews of Ashkanazic background.

RICH PASTRY HAMANTASCHEN

2 cups all-purpose flour, sifted
½ cup sugar
2 teaspoons baking powder
1 cup margarine
2 eggs
Grated rind of 1 orange
½ cup finely ground walnuts
2 tablespoons brandy

1. Sift the flour, sugar, and baking powder into a large mixing bowl. Using a pastry blender or fork, cut in the margarine.
2. Add the eggs.
3. Add remaining ingredients and work with your hands until the mixture forms a ball. Add more flour if the dough seems too sticky to handle. Wrap and refrigerate overnight.
4. Roll out to ⅛-inch thickness on a well-floured pastry cloth and cut into circles using a 3- or 4-inch diameter round cookie cutter or the rim of a drinking glass.
5. Mix filling ingredients well. Drop a teaspoonful into the center of each circle, and fold dough to form triangular pockets. Pinch edges together firmly.

6. Bake in a preheated 350-degree oven for 20 to 30 minutes or until the pastries are golden brown.

   Makes 3 dozen.

TWO TRADITIONAL FILLINGS

Povidl (Plum Jam):

1 jar (12 ounces) plum preserves
Grated rind of 1 lemon
¼ cup finely chopped walnuts

Lekvar:

2 cups prune jam (or 2 cups commercially prepared prune filling, Solo brand)
Grated rind of 1 lemon
1 teaspoon orange juice
½ cup finely chopped walnuts
¼ teaspoon nutmeg
1 teaspoon cinnamon

Haroset

How varied yet simple is the preparation of one of the symbolic foods of the Passover Seder, *haroset*—and how delicious the result. *Haroset* is the food which reminds each Seder participant of the hardships the Israelites endured as slaves in Egypt during ancient times when they were forced to build monuments to other men's beliefs.

Chopped coarsely and tinged red, the mixture is always prepared to resemble the mortar used to anchor the heavy blocks of rock hauled in place by men and women whose every movement was controlled by the whip held in the hands of a slavemaster. And yet the mixture, no matter in what region of the world it is prepared, has more than a hint of sweetness to symbolize a hard-won freedom, a freedom which is commemorated not only in this simple food but throughout the entire Seder and during the long Passover week.

Throughout the centuries, the method of preparing *haroset* has never changed; but the ingredients have been as varied as the places in which Jews have lived. Apples, walnuts, cinnamon, and wine go into a European *haroset,* while a typical

Yemenite mixture includes dates, figs, sesame seeds, almonds, ginger, raisins, and hot peppers. Moroccan Jews are likely to use pine nuts, almonds, and apples for *haroset;* and the Jews of Balkan lands have traditionally favored a combination of raisins and dates, mixed with walnuts, and flavored with nutmeg and cinnamon.

In Israel today, a favorite preparation calls for bananas, dates, apples, almonds or pine nuts, blended with orange juice and red wine.

HAROSET, ISRAELI STYLE

2 apples, peeled and chopped
4 bananas, chopped
Rind and juice of 1 orange
1 cup pine nuts or blanched almonds, chopped coarsely
10 dates, chopped
½ cup red wine
1 to 2 teaspoons cinnamon
Matzah meal
Pinch of salt
Sugar to taste

1. Combine fruit, fruit juice, rind, nuts, and dates. Add wine and blend thoroughly.
2. Add enough matzah meal to bind the mixture together. Add the cinnamon, salt, and sugar to taste.

Hazzenbluzzen

A dish of pure puffery—with folk etymologies filled with as much hot air as the food itself.

Some Jews call these little fried pastries *hoizenbluzzen,* a term which means pants blowing. Others call them *hazzenbluzzen* (say *haz* to rhyme with pa's—*zen*—*bluz* to rhyme with fuzz—*zen*). But there is little doubt that they are actually the Jewish variation of petit beignets, which found their way into the Eastern European Jewish diet from French cuisine several centuries ago. When they did, the fact that they puffed up when fried in very hot oil apparently reminded one pundit of a pair of pants blowing in the wind and another of the air the *hazan* (Hebrew for cantor) blew into the shofar (ram's horn) when he sounded it on Rosh Hashonah. And so another dish very un-Jewish became a convert in the usual way: first by being prepared for a specific holiday, in this case Rosh Hashonah, and then by having its name changed from the French, beignet, a word which originally meant a blow on the head, to the Jewish word *hazzenbluzzen.* The "blow" was still there all right, not on something but into something—in this case the shofar, an instrument which takes a lot of effort to make any noise at all.

Hazzenbluzzen are usually eaten on Rosh Hashonah when they are made from choux paste mixed with bits of shaved almonds, shaped to look like little shofars, fried in hot oil, and dipped in honey. Other traditional recipes for *hazzenbluzzen* call for rolling and cutting the dough into shofar shapes before frying them, but the final taste and texture are totally different from those recipes which use choux and are regional variations on the same theme.

HAZZENBLUZZEN #1

This is the most traditional Eastern European recipe, definitely not *haute cuisine.*

2 eggs
1 tablespoon sugar
1½ cups flour
Dash of salt
1 cup sifted confectioners' sugar
½ cup ground cinnamon

1. Beat eggs, sugar, and salt together. Add flour and mix well. Compress the dough and refrigerate overnight.
2. Cut small sections from the chilled dough and roll to ½-inch thicknesses. Cut into 3-inch strips. Shape into ties, bagel shapes, balls, or shofar shapes.
3. Deep fry at 375 degrees until golden brown. Cool.
4. Mix together confectioners' sugar and cinnamon, and shake or sprinkle over pastries.

Makes about 3 dozen pastries.

HAZZENBLUZZEN #2

Petit beignet, really, with a Yiddish moniker. Bake the paste balls (choux) in a 350-degree oven for 20 to 25 minutes and they are cream puff shells.

1 cup water
½ cup margarine
¼ teaspoon salt
1 cup all-purpose flour
4 large eggs
Toasted almonds
Sifted confectioners' sugar

Syrup:
½ cup water
¾ cup granulated sugar
2 tablespoons light corn syrup
½ teaspoon fresh lemon juice

1. Combine water, margarine, and salt in a saucepan and heat to full boil.
2. Remove saucepan from heat and stir in flour all at once. Stir until mixture forms a ball and pulls away from the sides of saucepan.
3. Using a processor, mixer, or by hand, add eggs one at a time and mix well. Dough will form a ball. Cool completely.
4. To make syrup, dissolve sugar in water over low heat. Add remaining syrup ingredients and bring to a boil.
5. Reduce heat and cook over moderate heat without stirring until mixture is slightly thick and shiny.
6. Form dough by hand into golf ball-sized balls and fry in deep fat until golden brown. Beignets will puff up as they are fried.
7. Drain on absorbent paper. Coat with syrup. Then sprinkle confectioners' sugar or shaved almonds over the tops of each and serve immediately.

Makes about 2 dozen pastries.

Helzel

Stretching yesterday's dinner into today's tasty leftover is usually the work of necessity. Yet, from the crumbs and scraps, bits and pieces, from all the food that is left behind, have come Jewish cuisine's best dishes. Bones and bits of cabbage and meat become a soup to be taken seriously; tough giblets become, miraculously, a tantalizing spicy stew. Liver, chopped and molded, transmogrifies into cocktail party flash. Even the tough neck of a goose, duck, or chicken is magically transformed into a dish called helzel (say *hell-zel*).

Helzel may have been born of necessity, but it has matured into something much more than just another way to disguise the seemingly unappealing. It is made with the rather thin but elastic skin which covers the neck of a fowl. This skin becomes a casing into which various imaginative, yet common and inexpensive, ingredients are stuffed. The helzel is then cooked in a variety of ways, sliced and savored. Sholom Aleichem wrote of Russian-Jewish cooks preparing helzel to be cooked together with meat in a sour soup or with a sweet meat and vegetable tzimmes.

Helzel also turned out to be a *ganif*, a thief, because when it was placed in the middle of a tasty dish, in a kugel which oozed with schmaltz for example, it "stole" the flavor from its surroundings. Far from this being considered a crime, it enhanced the appeal of the helzel even more.

Today helzel is made mostly from chicken or turkey and is sometimes roasted right along with the fowl itself. Over the centuries, its reputation for being a *ganif* has been reinforced. It steals flavor and also the hearts of all who appreciate its taste and economy.

Another name for helzel is *menalech*.

HELZEL, STUFFED

1 skin from a turkey neck, whole
4 medium potatoes, peeled
½ raw, peeled sweet potato
2 stalks celery, finely chopped
2 tablespoons chopped parsley
2 tablespoons chopped pecans or black walnuts, or a combination of the two
1 tablespoon honey
1 teaspoon paprika
1 teaspoon salt
½ teaspoon freshly ground pepper

1. Grate potatoes and drain well. Blend with sweet potato, celery, and parsley.
2. Mix nuts with honey and seasonings, and blend into potato mixture.
3. Sew up one end of neck skin and fill with stuffing, leaving about 1 inch at the top. Sew up open end, and roast with partially roasted turkey, at 325 degrees, placing it in the gravy to brown, basting often. The helzel should be completely cooked in 1 hour. Don't let it become dry. Remove when skin becomes golden brown and is still moist.

Herring

If Jews had the misfortune of coming from a place situated on a "crusty" hill somewhere between Mazelborscht (which was ruled by an emperor) and Gorshov (which was not), they were the colorful inhabitants of the fictional village of Chelm in Poland, a town immortalized in dozens of droll and ironic folk tales which parodied life as it was lived in the real villages of Chelm, Pisz, Lowza, or a thousand others about a century ago. They lived their lives rubbing elbows with the likes of a barefoot poet named Zekel, a female chauvinist called Yente Peshia, and a crew of nitwits variously named Sender Donkey, Zeinvel Ninny, and Treikel Fool.

Chelm had come into existence when, at the time of The Creation, the command had been uttered: "Let there be Chelm." Everything had gone downhill from then on. When they ran out of hairpins, the townspeople fought their wars with the pestles usually used for grinding matzah flour. Men were called upon to take over the tasks of cooking and baking. And, above all else, the wise members of the community were absolutely certain that the ocean, lakes, and rivers nearby were becoming saltier because of all of the herring that lived in them. The problem was centuries old, as old as the village of Chelm itself.

So much salt would be bad for the ocean, the wise men reasoned. Thus, for the Chelmers there could be no choice but to eat as much herring as possible lest the seas become overpopulated with herring and stay wretchedly, horribly, miserably salty. Why else, they proclaimed, would Jews go on eating so much herring!

Ridiculous reasoning, of course, a fantastic leap from the real reason for the Polish Jews' eating of so much herring. Poverty. Better to make light of the meagerness of one's diet and the topsy-turvy condition of Jewish life in the villages and towns of Poland than to constantly lament the inglorious fate of one's palate.

Hardly a meal in any poor Polish (Russian, English, German) Jewish household went by without a piece of herring, one day pickled, the next day baked, or fried, or grilled, or chopped, or dunked in sour cream. Sometimes a herring was smothered in sliced onions and pickled beets. Once in a while in the hands of a really creative cook, a simple piece of the fish was chopped, mixed with potatoes, and transformed into a pudding or wrapped up as filling for blintzes.

Plus, on the Sabbath when it was traditional to eat fish, if fresh fish wasn't available to make gefilte fish, a piece of boned salt herring would be chopped with apples, bread, eggs, and onions and called, not without a touch of irony, a savory and mouth-watering delight.

CHOPPED HERRING

2 1-pint jars herring in wine sauce
4 hard-boiled eggs
1 thick slice white bread, soaked in vinegar and then squeezed dry
1 sour apple
1 medium onion, grated
2 tablespoons sugar or to taste
¼ teaspoon pepper

1. Remove skin and bones from herring pieces. Reserve liquid.
2. Reserving one of the eggs, chop all other ingredients or put through a grinder. Season with sugar, pepper, and reserved liquid.
3. Serve on a bowl of lettuce and shape in the form of a fish. Decorate the fish with the grated yolk and white of the remaining egg. Garnish with black olives, parsley, and sliced tomatoes.

Makes about 4 cups.

Holoptsches

Cabbage is for sustenance and beets are for healing.

—The Talmud

If the value of a Jewish recipe could be measured by the total count of its various names, then *holoptsches* (say *hol* to rhyme with doll—*up*—*chuz*) would be the one most prized. Called also *praakes, holipce, geluptzes, holubtsi,* and *gelubtsy* in Eastern Europe (all but *praake,* a variant of the Russian word for little pigeon), stuffed cabbage is its name here and now.

Unpretentious in the extreme, its major claim to fame rests on the fact that it makes much of nothing much. Cabbage and other leafy vegetables have usually been plentiful in most parts of the globe but their appeal is limited. Meat has not always been bountiful but its appeal has usually been greater. Yet when cabbage is used as an edible wrapping for a small amount of meat which is mixed with spices and grain, there is a compelling palatability in the synergism.

As the ready availablity and the nutritional value of this dish became appreciated, it was introduced from one culture to another. Each region has left its own unique stamp on the basic recipe. The preference of Jews of Russian background is reflected in the sour-tasting cabbage and beef *holoptsches.* In the kitchens of Jews of Polish background, the dish takes on the sweetness so characteristic of the cuisine of that region. In Hungary, a peppery version is preferred. In Greece, grape leaves replace the cabbage, lamb the beef, and the dish is called *dolmades.*

HOLOPTSCHES

1 large green cabbage
2 pounds lean ground beef
2 eggs
1 large onion, chopped fine
½ cup matzah meal
Salt and pepper to taste
¾ cup tomato sauce
1½ cups water
¾ cup brown sugar
Juice of 1 large lemon
½ cup raisins

1. Remove the core from the cabbage. Separate the leaves and place them in a large dish. Pour boiling water over the leaves and set aside to soften for 5 to 10 minutes.
2. Mix together the meat, eggs, chopped onion, and matzah meal. Season to taste with salt and pepper.
3. Drain the water off the cabbage leaves and place a portion of the meat mixture on each. Roll, folding the ends in first.
4. Preheat oven to 300 degrees.
5. In a large oven- and flame-proof casserole, place the unused cabbage leaves. Place the cabbage rolls on top, seam sides down.
6. Add enough water to come to the top of the rolls, about 1½ cups. Mix the tomato sauce, brown sugar, lemon juice, and raisins, and add to the casserole.
7. Bring them to a boil on top of the stove and then bake, covered, for 1½ hours. This is a good dish to prepare ahead; reheating in a slow oven improves the flavor. If you are going to make this recipe in advance, store the food *in* the sauce and not separately. Skim off fat before reheating. Reheat slowly and simmer. Don't allow the mixture to come to a full boil, for this is a sure way to alter the flavor and change the consistency of the sauce.

Serves 4 to 6.

Honey

Honey and very sweet food enlighten the eyes of man.

—The Talmud

Wrestling with recipes somehow became one of the tasks which concerned Talmudic scholars. One of them, Raba bar Joseph bar Hama, headed a school near the Tigris River early in the fourth century. He was known not only as a teacher but also as a sensible man and an excellent debater. His view of

Jewish life was often the accepted one; and so one day seventeen hundred years ago, he found himself called upon to compare the recipe for a type of honey cake called *rihata* (made of flour, oil, and honey) prepared in one Babylonian village, with a different recipe for *rihata* prepared in another. Because one recipe happened to contain more of a particular ingredient than the other did, Raba bar Joseph bar Hama determined which blessing went with which recipe.

Yes, the Talmudists discoursed unceasingly on all that concerned them, including the selection of the blessing to be said before and after eating honey cake. But the uses to which honey had been put in one age would be remembered. Then, filtered through the experiences of a new age, its sweetness would be decanted into a new vessel more up-to-date and larger than the last.

It is not surprising that the Talmudists should have concerned themselves with honey. Date honey had been a very common ingredient in Jewish recipes from as early as Biblical times. In the Bible ancient Israel was referred to again and again as the "land of milk and honey," a metaphor which the Jews of every age took quite literally. Honey was *the* major sweetener used to make foods, particularly cakes, taste better. And it had been used throughout the ages as a preservative. Not until the Middle Ages did sugar become widely available. But, because in Europe its cost was fifty times as much as local flower or date honey, and because honey (and milk) were, symbolically, the land of Israel, honey was the more important sweetener for Jews.

In the Middle Ages, Jewish customs clung to honey's metaphorical essence like flies caught on sticky paper. Honey could sweeten one's love life if it were used to write incantations on the inside of a cup, dissolved in water, and then swallowed. Dribbled on a slate for a child to lick, it would bring him wisdom as he learned Torah, a practice inspired by the words of Ezekiel who tasted God's words in his mouth "as honey for sweetness" (Ezekiel 3:3). It could lend character to an unborn baby if the mother-to-be consumed copious amounts, and it could ensure a blissful marriage if the bride were met at the door of the home of the groom with a bowl of honey for her to use to anoint the mezuzah, doorposts, and threshold.

In the celebration of Rosh Hashonah, the taste of honey is

a double treat. Honey cakes (lekach), which are probably the first sweet pastry in the history of baking, are traditional. The custom is attributed to the Biblical quotation: "So David and all the House of Israel brought up the ark of the Lord with shouting and with the sound of the horn . . . And he dealt among all the people . . . of Israel . . . to every one a cake of bread and a cake made in pan and a sweet cake" (II Samuel 6:15).

Another traditional feature of every meal of this two-day holiday is the serving of sliced apples with an accompanying dish of honey. This combination anticipates the hope in the hearts of Jews everywhere that the days ahead will be fruitful and sweet and is, in Jewish mystical tradition, a combination symbolic of the Garden of Eden.

HOLIDAY HONEY CAKE

Once, long ago, in the early Middle Ages, honey cakes were inscribed with the names of angels and amulets were fastened to them.

½ cup vegetable shortening
3 eggs
1 cup sugar
3 cups all-purpose flour
1 teaspoon baking powder
1 teaspoon baking soda
½ teaspoon salt
1 cup honey
1 teaspoon grated orange peel
1 teaspoon cinnamon
2 tablespoons brandy
1 cup double-strength cold coffee
1 cup chopped walnuts or pecans
1 cup dried currants
2 teaspoons flour
½ cup whole almonds
Confectioners' sugar

1. Preheat oven to 350 degrees.
2. In a large electric mixing bowl, cream shortening and sugar. Add eggs, one at a time, beating well at medium speed. Add honey and orange peel, and continue to mix for one minute.
3. Sift flour, baking powder, soda, and salt into a separate mixing bowl. Add to honey mixture, alternating with coffee. When dry ingredients are thoroughly mixed, add brandy and cinnamon.
4. Place currants and chopped nuts in a small bowl. Add 2 teaspoons flour and coat the fruit-nut mixture. This will

prevent the mixture from sinking to the bottom of the pan while baking. Add to batter and stir in well.

5. Grease a 9″ × 13″ rectangular baking pan. Line bottom and sides with waxed paper. Then grease the waxed paper.
6. Pour batter into pan and distribute whole almonds evenly over the top. Bake for 45 minutes or until cake springs back when touched.
7. Place cake upside down on a large cake rack. Remove pan. When cake is moderately cool, remove waxed paper. When completely cool, sprinkle powdered sugar over top and cut into slices or squares.

HONEY CAKE

6 cups flour, unsifted
6 eggs
1-pound package brown sugar
1¼ cups oil
1¼ cups good quality honey
1¼ cups strong coffee
1 teaspoon vanilla
½ teaspoon salt
1½ teaspoons baking soda
1 teaspoon cinnamon
1 teaspoon allspice
1 teaspoon cloves
½ cup finely chopped walnuts
1 tablespoon sugar
½ cup raisins (optional)

1. Beat eggs thoroughly; add brown sugar and beat well.
2. Combine oil, honey, coffee, and baking soda, and add to eggs and sugar. Add liquids alternately with dry ingredients, beginning and ending with dry ingredients.
3. Add vanilla. Beat vigorously for 5 minutes at high speed. Stir in raisins.
4. Grease and flour 3 small loaf pans, and divide batter into 3 parts. Bake at 250 degrees for 2 hours.
5. Turn onto wire rack until cool. Sprinkle finely chopped walnuts and sugar over top.

Makes 3 cakes.

Horseradish

See Chrain.

I

Ingberlach

Tangy, chewy, crunchy morsels of ingberlach (say *ing—ber—lachk*) are traditionally served during the week of Passover. They are a particular favorite of the Jews who came to North and South America from Russia at the turn of the century. This very old recipe is prepared by bathing small bits of matzah in boiling honey, adding a sprinkling of ginger (*ingber* means ginger in Yiddish) and coarsely chopped pieces of walnuts. Then the mixture is cooled and molded to make an attractive after-dinner sweet. The Sephardim call the same dish *ahashoo.*

INGBERLACH

1 pound honey
1 tablespoon sugar
2½ cups matzah farfel
½ teaspoon ginger
¼ teaspoon water
2 cups broken walnuts

1. Pour the honey into a large saucepan. Add 1 tablespoon sugar. Bring to a boil, stirring constantly. Reduce heat.
2. Add the matzah farfel. Stir until the mixture is brown. Add water, ginger, and broken walnuts. Stir for several minutes more, or until the mixture becomes a deep brown.
3. Wet a large wooden board with water. Pour mixture out onto the board and with cold, wet hands, pat out to cover the board (to about ⅛-inch thickness). If the mixture is too hot to the touch as it comes from the pan, allow it to cool slightly, but work it before it begins to harden in the pan.
4. Break off small pieces and put into small paper cups to serve.

Makes 40 to 50 small, 1-inch-square pieces.

J

Jhalla

Jhalla is an Arabic word, pronounced as if it were spelled *jalla*, using a bit of a roll of the tongue on the "ll." Although it has often been used to describe a particular kind of Yemenite Sabbath or festival food, namely a plateful of fruits and roasted beans, *jhalla* actually refers to the ambience of a Yemenite get-together. To say the word is to evoke a scene of jovial companionship and animated conversation, enjoyed not at the corner café, but at one's home. Much as we might say, "Come over on Saturday evening for cocktails," and know as hosts that more than cocktails will be served or as the intended guests that it is really our company that counts, *jhalla* is a signal to Yemenite Jews that there's a party going on so be prepared to drink *arak*, beer, wine, or hot, strong coffee, and to nibble from trays piled high with dried fruit, beans, and nuts.

Most of the Yemenite community has been transplanted to Israel, colorful oriental customs and all. Even the cooking methods harken back to the days when Yemenite Jews did much of their cooking outdoors over open fires. In Israel today, one can visit homes where a typical food served at one of these festive gatherings, *adashim* or salted chickpeas or beans, has been prepared over an open fire built into the outside wall of a Yemenite Jew's home.

Soaked first in water for several hours and then drained and left to dry in the sun, the beans are placed in a hot frying pan which not a drop of oil has touched, placed over but not on the fire, and then shaken and tossed in the pan to keep them from burning. When the cook decides that the texture is just right, which means that the beans or peas are what the Italians would term *al dente*, she slips them from pan to plate, salts them, and serves them to her guests. Just this side of being pebbly and hard, they go down easily with a gulp of arrack or beer.

Juvetch

A melange of as many fresh vegetables as would fit into the most capacious casserole in the kitchen, a sprinkling of spices most prized by the cook and, if times were good, a hunk or two of spring lamb cut from the bone bubbled often in the sparsely furnished kitchens of Balkan Jews.

Time and time again, in Bucharest and Sofia, Istanbul and Skopje, and all the towns and hamlets in between, the open market would be visited or the garden plot searched carefully by the cook who would only be satisfied when she had found the firmest turnips. She would look for potatoes still smelling of the soft earth which had surrounded them only minutes or hours before, the most pungent leeks and reddest tomatoes, the most tender beans and tiniest peas.

She was preparing to make a vegetable stew called *juvetch* (from the German and Yiddish *gewächs*). The piquant taste has delighted Jewish palates for a thousand years at least; and, though it is commonly eaten by Christians and Moslems too, the Jews have made it a festive food, usually eaten in Turkey during the two days of Rosh Hashonah.

Without the meat, it is like an elaborate ratatouille; with it, it is a subtly flavored and filling main dish.

JUVETCH

To prepare, use only fresh vegetables, omitting those which are not in season or unavailable. Trim the meat well for this is not a robust cold-weather stew. Don't substitute vegetable oil for the pure olive oil. Olive oil imparts a unique flavor and, for this dish, an historically authentic one as well. Drizzle two tablespoons of lemon juice into the simmering mixture before deciding whether more is desired.

½ cup olive oil
1½ pounds coarsely cubed lean lamb
1½ cups chopped eggplant
2 cups water
½ cup chopped leeks, white parts only
2 stalks celery, chopped coarsely

2 turnips, cleaned and chopped
1 cup fresh green beans
1 cup fresh green peas
2½ tablespoons finely chopped fennel
4 tomatoes, peeled, seeded, and chopped
2 potatoes, peeled and sliced
1 cup zucchini or yellow summer squash, washed, peeled, and sliced
1 or 2 fresh okra, chopped
2 to 6 tablespoons fresh lemon juice
Salt, pepper, and fresh or dried basil to taste

1. Heat the oil and brown the meat in a Dutch oven. Remove the meat and fry the eggplant, leeks, and celery for 5 minutes, adding oil as needed. Remove and reserve.
2. Return the meat to the pot and add the water. Cook until tender.
3. Arrange the vegetables in layers in a large casserole dish. Mix the lemon juice and seasonings with the meat and pour over the vegetables.
4. Cover and cook at 400 degrees for 15 minutes. Remove cover. Reduce heat to 300 degrees and cook until vegetables are tender, about 45 minutes. Serve immediately.

Makes 8 servings.

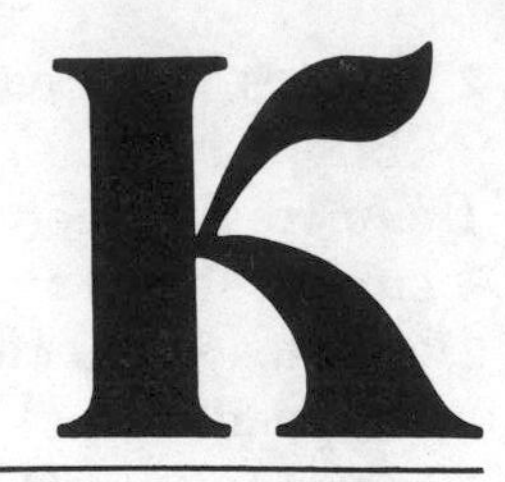

Kadaif

In Talmudic times, the word *katith* referred to a pastry or bread made of pounded wheat, a special delicacy made like no other. It is still true today that the dough is like no other, called shredded wheat for that is what it is. But referring to *kataif* or *kadaif* (say *ka—die—if*) dough as shredded wheat gives the misleading impression that the pastry when finished will taste like the food biscuits which once came dry and tasteless in a box of packaged cereal.

What could be further from the truth! *Kadaif* dough is made of flour and water which, after being mixed into a thin liquid, is thrown through a very fine mesh strainer to land on the other side of the strainer on a hot metal sheet. The dough doesn't get cooked in the process because it is removed from the metal sheet quickly and is cooled.

There are just a few steps to follow when making *kadaif:* preparing the syrup, preparing the filling, and putting the dough in the pan along with ample dribblings of melted butter or margarine. Then comes a slow bake in a warm oven and a quick bake in a hot one, followed by the drizzling of chilled syrup over the baked pastry and the most difficult task of all: waiting for the *kadaif* to cool.

There is another way to make *kadaif*, in small individual rolled pieces, a more time-consuming process.

The traditional fillings are a combination of pistachios and walnuts or just pistachios, or a heavy whipped cream filling seasoned with almond liqueur and cinnamon. *Kadaif* is often served to celebrate the Jewish New Year wherever Middle Eastern Jews reside.

KADAIF

1 pound kadaif pastry*

½ pound (2 sticks) unsalted melted margarine

Syrup:
1¼ cups sugar
½ cup water
1 tablespoon lemon juice
1 tablespoon orange blossom water

Cream Filling:
4 tablespoons ground rice*
2 tablespoons sugar
1 cup milk
2½ cups whipping cream

Walnut or Pistachio Filling:
2 cups pistachios or walnuts, or a combination of the two, coarsely chopped
2½ tablespoons sugar
½ teaspoon allspice
½ teaspoon nutmeg

1. Let the sugar, water, and lemon juice simmer until it thickens and coats a spoon. Stir in orange blossom water and cook for 2 minutes longer.
2. Cool and chill lightly in the refrigerator. Prepare one of the fillings.
3. *Cream filling:* Mix ground rice and sugar to a smooth paste with ½ cup milk. Boil the rest of the milk and add the ground rice paste slowly, stirring vigorously. Simmer, stirring until very thick. Then allow to cool, add cream, and mix well.
4. *Walnut or pistachio filling:* Mix the chopped nuts with the sugar and spices.
5. Put the kadaif pastry in a large bowl. Pull out and separate the strands as much as possible with your fingers so that they do not stick together too much.
6. Pour melted margarine over them and work it in with your fingers, pulling and mixing the strands so that each one is entirely coated with margarine.
7. Put half the pastry in a large 9″ × 13″ baking pan. Spread the filling over it evenly and cover with the rest of the pastry, evening it out and flattening it with the palm of your hand.
8. Using a sharp knife, cut the top layer into diamond shapes.

*Available at Middle Eastern food stores.

9. Bake in a preheated 350-degree oven for 45 minutes, then in a 450-degree oven for only 10 to 15 minutes longer, until it is a light golden color.
10. Remove from the oven and immediately pour the *cold* syrup over the *hot kadaif.* Serve hot or cold.

Makes 24 pieces.

Kasha

One can live without spices but not without grain.

—The Talmud

The man who earns water for his kasha *earns next to nothing.*

—Yiddish saying

In those good old days which preceded our own and stretched on and on before us for centuries, the Western Europeans made a staple diet of barley cereal and rye bread, the Scots had their oatmeal and oat porridge, the Greeks semolina, the American Indians maize, and the Poles and Russians had kasha, kasha, and more kasha (say *kash* to rhyme with *slosh—a* like *uh*). So did the Jews.

Technically speaking, the word kasha means cereal and can be made from wheat, oatmeal, barley, rice, millet, bulghur, and buckwheat. But when Jews talk about kasha, they almost always have the nutty tasting, brown, coarse buckwheat grain in mind. Yes, it's *retschene* kasha the Jews of Russian or Polish background are fond of—the kasha that was once eaten day after day for breakfast, lunch, and dinner, the kasha that once meant survival during a harsh Ukrainian winter.

Sometimes kasha is good eaten as a porridge cooked like hominy grits or cream of wheat (which may be good to eat but it doesn't taste as good as buckwheat kasha). Or kasha can be mixed with a beaten egg and fried onions and served along with meat or chicken as a side dish. But the absolutely best way to eat kasha is to mix it with fresh, homemade bowtie noodles and a little fat or *gribenes.* Call it by its Yiddish name, kasha *mit varnitchkes,* and then sit down to make an entire meal of it, without stopping to count calories consumed or to contemplate the sudden growth of one's belly.

KASHA

1 cup buckwheat groats
1 cup chopped onions
5 tablespoons chicken fat or vegetable oil
About 4 cups boiling water
1 teaspoon salt
¼ teaspoon pepper

1. Place the groats in a 350-degree oven to toast for about 20 minutes.
2. While the groats are baking, fry the onions in the fat or oil. Add the groats and stir.
3. Add the boiling water to the groats and return to the oven. Season with salt and pepper.
4. Cook homemade noodle dough in boiling salted water, drain and add to kasha. Serve hot.

Makes 6 servings.

KASHA VARNITCHKES

Noodle Dough:

2 cups semolina flour
2 eggs
¼ teaspoon salt
1 tablespoon water

1. Sift the flour and make a well in the center. Add the remaining ingredients and work into the flour. Knead.
2. Roll out the dough. Cut into rectangles and twist the dough to form a bow. Allow to dry while you prepare the kasha.

Kashrut

It is said that Rabbi Samuel of Babylonia who lived in the third century once sent to another rabbi, Johanan, thirty-nine camel loads of questions about the Jewish Dietary Laws. Extreme, perhaps, but also indicative of the great concern Jews have always shown for following the Laws of Kashrut.

First delineated in the Bible, particularly in the eleventh chapter of Leviticus and the fourteenth chapter of Deuteronomy, the Laws have been a major focus of rabbinic interpretation and practice (rabbinic and otherwise) ever since. It is these Laws which, governing as they do the preparation and eating of all foods, give the cuisine its raison d'être.

The Laws are somewhat complex but their purpose is not. They are, simply put, one very critical way for Jews to observe God's laws and commandments. They are intended to make Jews aware of God and their relationship to Him, and their relationship to all that God has created—in particular, all other living creatures and substances. Although they have also been interpreted as once providing the Jews with a more hygienic approach to eating than other ancient peoples, few modern rabbinical approaches to the interpretation of the Dietary Laws give much credence to this reason as being the primary justification for the Laws of Kashrut.

Rather, most look upon the Laws as hallowing God by the act of eating. Also, observing kashrut is a discipline offering those who observe the Laws the daily awareness of an act that otherwise might be taken for granted. Thought and planning must accompany the preparation and eating of each meal, and that is just the point. Yet as much as the observance of the Laws forces observant Jews to think about every bit of food eaten during a day, such thoughts are meant to be accompanied by an understanding of the commitment that is being made to carry out one of God's commandments.

The word kosher or *kasher* actually means "fit" for use. Its opposite is the term *t'refah,* which literally means "torn by a wild beast" but has come to refer to all foods, meat or otherwise, that are not kosher. The basic Laws are concerned with the following:

The detailing of permitted and unpermitted foods: Permitted are animals that chew the cud *and* have cloven feet—these include cattle, sheep, goats, and deer; all seafood that have fins and scales and the roe from them—these include anchovies, bass, halibut, herring, pike, salmon, flounder, tuna, sole, shad, and many others. Permitted are almost all domesticated fowl, including chicken, duck, goose, turkey, squab, pigeon, and capon. Also permitted are certain species of insects, including locusts; eggs from a kosher fowl; all fruits; and all vegetables. Not permitted are carnivorous animals or those that are wild, invertebrates, turtles, sharks, certain kinds of sturgeon, catfish, eel, reptiles, and amphibians.

The description of the way in which animals must be slaughtered and which portions of them may be eaten. The blood and certain cuts of kosher animals are not permitted.

The detailing of the way in which slaughtered meat must be soaked and salted ("koshered") before it is actually cooked.

The prohibition of mixing meat and dairy foods, based on the Biblical injunction: "You shall not seethe a kid in its mother's milk." Meat and dairy products may not be mixed together in a recipe. Nor may they be eaten together in a recipe. Nor may they be eaten together at the same meal, or cooked in a closed oven with one another. After eating meat, observant Jews do not eat milk or other dairy products for a prescribed period of time. *Parve* foods, those which are neither meat nor milk, are neutral and therefore may be prepared to eat with either meat or milk. Two complete sets of pots and pans, dishes, silverware, and other cooking utensils, dishtowels and drainboards must be kept—one set for meat, the other for milk.

On Pesach, the requirements for observance of the holiday are added to the requirements of kashrut.

Kishke

Kishke (say *kish* to rhyme with fish—*ka*) is the Yiddish word for a meatless sausage put together with a maximum amount of ingenuity and a minimum amount of food. Potatoes or bread crumbs, onions, and spices put inside a beef casing are all that are needed to make this traditional Jewish delight.

KISHKE

Spicy and aromatic, this recipe for kishke has been popular with Jews of Eastern European background for centuries.

½ cup schmaltz, nyafat* or vegetable oil
½ cup finely chopped onions
¾ teaspoon salt
½ teaspoon freshly ground black pepper
2 teaspoons paprika
1 cup all-purpose flour or fine bread crumbs
1 kosher beef casing or synthetic casing, cut into 6- to 8-inch lengths
2 large onions, sliced
¼ cup vegetable oil

1. Mix first six ingredients together in large bowl. Sew up one end of each piece of casing. Stuff mixture into beef or synthetic casings, leaving one inch at the end for expansion of the stuffing as it bakes. Sew up open end.
2. Plunge pieces of kishke into boiling water. Cook for 2 minutes. Remove kishke carefully using a slotted spoon. Drain on absorbent paper.
3. Place in baking pan with 2 large sliced onions and ¼ cup of oil. Bake at 325 degrees, basting often, until well browned, about 1½ hours.
4. Cut into slices about 1-inch thick and serve hot, as an accompaniment to roast fowl or beef.

Makes about 25 pieces.

Knishes

So fond are they of eating both sweet and savory filled pastries, that the Jews in their wanderings across the globe since ancient times have made these delights a major focus of their culinary efforts. Into pockets lined with everything from *filo* to *feuillitée, Muerbeteig* to paté a choux, have gone honey-glazed nuts or tart spinach, thick homemade jams or sweetened cheese, chili-laced ground meat or crunchy *kashe,* sometimes

*A hydrogenated vegetable oil available at kosher food stores.

prepared for a special holiday treat, but more often because the pastries are fun to make and even more pleasurable to eat.

Pin one name on these "pockets" and you're likely to think of another, and another, to make a list with almost as many entries on the page as pockets on a baking sheet. Leading it, in the minds of those whose background is Eastern European, are knishes (say *k'nishes* to rhyme with vicious) filled with everything from chicken mixed with *kashe* to pot cheese and pineapple, with the combination of mashed potatoes and fried onions being the most popular.

Second in line would come blintzes, and third, kreplach. Following on the list in no particular order would be *borekas* of spinach or feta cheese, wrapped in *filo* or a flaky dough and fried or baked; pirogen, more a meat roll than a pocket; *pompeshkes, punchekes, pelmeny, verenikes, shlonikes,* hamantaschen, *topfen,* and lastly, empanadas, all dough pockets filled with everything from poppy seeds (hamantaschen), curds (*topfen*), spiced beef and olives (empanadas), to whole apples (*punchekes*).

The origin of the so-called pocket foods is obscure, but food historians are fond of suggesting the Far East as source for these captivating treasures whose outards give little hint of what's within. It is quite possible that the Jewish Rhadanite traders whose routes took them overland from Europe, through Central Russia, India and the easternmost part of China, and back again during the ninth to eleventh centuries, brought the culinary idea for pocket foods to European cooks along with their more commercially profitable cargo of silks, spices, and pearls.

POTATO KNISHES

The gluten flour makes the dough crisp and light; the slow cooking of the onions gives the proper consistency to the filling. The recipe results in absolutely perfect, delicious knishes.

Dough:

6 tablespoons vegetable shortening
1¾ cups all-purpose flour
¼ cup gluten flour*
¼ teaspoon salt
4 tablespoons cold water
Yolk of one egg

*Available at all health food stores.

Potato Filling:

4 pounds (7 average-sized) white baking potatoes
1½ pounds (3 large) yellow onions
½ cup vegetable oil
½ teaspoon salt
⅛ teaspoon white pepper

1. In the food processor or by hand, combine flours, add shortening, and blend.
2. Dissolve salt in water and add to processor while running until dough forms a ball, or mix by hand until dough forms a ball. Let dough rest in the refrigerator while preparing the filling.
3. Peel and cube potatoes. Cook in salted boiling water until tender but not mushy.
4. Peel and slice onions thinly. Place oil and seasonings in a large pan and cook (do not fry) the onions over moderate heat until they are very soft, about 20 to 25 minutes.
5. Rice potatoes, add onions, and the oil in which the onions were cooked. Mix well and check for seasonings, adding more salt and pepper to taste, as necessary.
6. Preheat the oven to 500 degrees.
7. Roll out the dough on a lightly floured surface to ⅛-inch thickness. The sheet of dough should be approximately 2 feet square.
8. Using half of the potato mixture, form a long, straight mound of filling over the dough ½-inch in from the edges. Gently pat the mound to flatten it.
9. Bring up the edge of the dough to partially cover the filling and continue rolling the dough until the filling is completely covered. Using a sharp knife, cut the filled roll away from the remaining dough.
10. Cut the roll at 2¼-inch intervals. Place knishes on a well-greased cookie sheet, sides touching. Don't pinch the sides closed.
11. Brush with beaten egg yolk. Bake for 15 minutes and remove from oven as soon as they become golden brown. Repeat with remaining dough and filling.
12. The knishes may be frozen and then reheated at 350 degrees for about 25 minutes before serving.

CHICKEN KNISHES

Dough:

2¼ cups flour
½ teaspoon baking powder
1¼ teaspoons salt
1 cup vegetable shortening
5 tablespoons orange juice
2 eggs

Filling:

1 large onion, peeled and chopped
1 tablespoon oil or chicken fat
1½ cups cooked, boned, and finely cut or ground chicken
2½ cups cooked kasha (buckwheat groats)
1 egg, slightly beaten

1. Mix flour, baking powder, and salt together. Cut in the shortening as you would for pie crust, letting the dough form into pea-sized balls.
2. Add orange juice, one tablespoon at a time. Then add one egg.
3. Knead the dough with your hands until it is smooth and holds together in a ball. Wrap in waxed paper and refrigerate overnight.
4. Remove from refrigerator and cut into thirds. Return two-thirds of the dough to the refrigerator, letting one-third of it come to a good working temperature, about 10 minutes.
5. Roll out to a large square, ⅛-inch in thickness on a well-floured pastry cloth. Brush beaten egg yolk over the rolled dough. Cut into 2-inch squares.
6. Make the filling. Sauté the onion in the oil until translucent. Mix with the chicken, kashe, and egg.
7. Place a teaspoon of filling on each square. Seal all open edges to form a pocket.
8. Place on a well-greased baking sheet and glaze with slightly beaten egg white. Repeat the process with the other pieces of dough.
9. Bake at 350 degrees for about 45 minutes.

Makes 3 dozen.

BOREKAS

Dough:

3 cups flour
4 tablespoons white vinegar
4 tablespoons vegetable oil
1 teaspoon salt
Water
1½ cups chilled butter or margarine (3 sticks)
1 egg, beaten well

1. Mix flour, vinegar, oil, salt, and enough water together to work the dough easily. Knead dough until it is smooth and forms a ball. Divide the dough into thirds and refrigerate for 15 minutes.
2. Remove only one portion of the dough from the refrigerator. Cut butter or margarine into small bits, allowing ½ cup (1 stick) for each section of dough.
3. Roll out chilled dough on a well-floured pastry cloth or board. Add ½ cup of the butter bits onto the dough, fold dough into thirds, and roll again. Fold again into thirds. Wrap and place in refrigerator.
4. Repeat process with remaining sections of dough, making certain that the butter remains well chilled and the dough elastic. Refrigerate buttered dough sections for 30 minutes.
5. Repeat rolling and refrigeration process four more times. Refrigerate overnight.
6. Roll out and cut dough into 3-inch squares. Fill and fold to form triangles. Pinch edges together. Brush each triangle with a little of the beaten egg.
7. Bake at 450 degrees for 10 to 12 minutes.

Sweet Cheese Filling:

1 pound farmer's cheese or dry cottage cheese
3 eggs
1 cup sugar
1 teaspoon grated lemon peel
½ cup raisins

Mash the cheese with a fork. Add remaining ingredients and mix well.

Feta Cheese Filling:

1 pound crumbled feta cheese
½ teaspoon freshly ground pepper
3 tablespoons chopped parsley

Mix ingredients together and taste for seasoning before filling the dough.

Tart Cheese Filling:

1 pound Gruyere, Swiss, or mozzarella cheese
2 eggs, well beaten
3 tablespoons chopped parsley
1 teaspoon pepper

Grate the cheese. Add remaining ingredients and blend thoroughly.

Spinach and Cheese Filling:

2 pounds fresh spinach
1 pound Gruyere or Swiss cheese, grated
Salt, pepper, nutmeg

Cook spinach and drain well. Mix with cheese and add seasonings to taste.

Moroccan-Style Filling:

1 pound ground beef or lamb
1 medium onion, peeled and chopped
1 bay leaf
Juice of one lemon
1 teaspoon white pepper
Salt and pepper

Place ingredients in a heavy pot and barely simmer for 1½ hours. Drain liquid, discard bay leaf, and taste for seasonings.

EMPANADAS

Tinged red and ticklingly spicy from a hefty dose of chili powder, made sweet by yellow raisins and sour by bits of pickled pimento olives, all encased by a thin covering of dough, one empanada stands ready to be savored, sloshed around a bit by a sip of iced vermouth, and then followed by another and then another, until the serving plate is empty and the oven yields no more.

These little South American filled dough pockets, served particularly on Purim in Argentina but also all year-round, are tantalizing appetizers, the kind that suggest to a dinner guest that the cook is very much at home in the kitchen and interested in serving something slightly exotic and very special.

The dough is a modified puff paste, quick and easy to make. It freezes well.

Filling:

2 pounds ground beef
6 medium onions, finely chopped
3 dozen pitted green or pimento olives, finely chopped
1½ teaspoons salt
1 teaspoon black pepper
2 to 4 teaspoons chili pepper, depending on taste (3½ teaspoons makes the mixture tolerable and not overwhelmingly spicy)
3 hard-boiled eggs, finely chopped
1 cup yellow raisins

Puff Pastry Dough:

½ cup margarine
2 cups flour
½ teaspoon salt
4 egg yolks
7 tablespoons cold water
1 tablespoon lemon or lime juice

1. Brown the meat and onions. Drain off liquid. Mix well with other ingredients and set aside to cool.
2. To make the dough, using a pastry blender, cut the margarine into the flour, add salt, continue to mix, add yolks, water, and lemon or lime juice. Work until smooth.
3. Put on a lightly floured board. Roll out to a thickness of ¼ inch. Fold and let rest for 10 minutes. Repeat the rolling and folding process three times.
4. When you have completed the process, roll out the dough, cut 1½-inch circles, and fill with 1 teaspoon of the meat mixture.
5. Fold over into a semicircle and pinch edges together. Crimp edges with the tines of a fork.
6. Place on a greased baking sheet and bake at 350 degrees until golden brown, about 20 minutes. Or place unbaked pastries in freezer containers and freeze immediately. When ready to serve, place frozen pastries in a preheated 350-degree oven and bake for 30 to 35 minutes or until well browned. (If you like a shiny look, brush tops with water-diluted egg yolk before baking.)

TOPFEN

Dough:

4 cups all-purpose flour, sifted
1 cup cold butter
½ cup milk

3 tablespoons sugar
1 ounce yeast
2 eggs
1 teaspoon vanilla
Plum or grape preserves

Filling:
1½ cups creamed cottage cheese
3 tablespoons sour cream
4½ tablespoons all-purpose flour
1 egg, beaten
¾ cup superfine or granulated sugar
½ cup chopped almonds
2 tablespoons melted butter
1 teaspoon vanilla

1. Work 1½ cups of the flour and the butter into a paste.
2. Warm the milk slightly and dissolve the sugar and yeast in it. Beat the eggs and add them (reserve a teaspoonful for glazing the pastry later on). Add vanilla. Mix the remaining flour with the egg mixture.
3. Roll out the egg dough, thinning at the edges.
4. Cover top of butter dough with wax paper and roll into a small circle. Remove wax paper. Place butter dough on top of the egg dough. Overlap the butter dough with the thin edges of the egg dough. Fold in half and in half again. Put the dough in the freezer for 10 minutes. Then roll out, fold over, and roll out again.
5. Fold dough and refrigerate again for 20 minutes. Roll out again thinly, folding over as before.
6. Cut into 6-inch squares.
7. For the filling, mix all the ingredients to a smooth paste.
8. Place 2 tablespoons of filling on each pastry square. Fold corners into the center and pinch together tightly. Brush the pastry with the leftover beaten egg, top with a little plum or other dark jam.
9. Preheat oven and bake at 350 degrees for 35 minutes.

Koshnikes

It takes much less time to say *koshnikes* (rhymes with *josh—nick—kuz*) than it does to tongue-twist one's way haltingly through the double "k"s of kasha knishes which are what *koshnikes* are.

Kreplach

Kreplach (say *krep* to rhyme with pep—*lockh*) once were edible amulets with hopeful messages and mystical incantations carved into their doughy surfaces. "*Slikh, klin, liskh, lskh, khsil, skil*" were the words that at times would be clearly etched into them by the Jews of seventeenth-century Germany, in the belief that God's blessings would soon be forthcoming, and a world, often chaotic, could be briefly controlled by something as seemingly ordinary as a filled pastry.

Especially on Purim, Yom Kippur, and Hashonah Rabbah did the Jews of the late Middle Ages prepare the pocket food that might do more than satisfy the appetite. Sweet and filled with fruit, the dough for the small triangle-shaped pastries would be "kneaded with honey" and then baked or fried just as a crepe is made today. But today the food we call kreplach resembles wontons. The dough is more pasta- than pancakelike and devoid of incantations, the insides usually filled with meat or kasha, and their exposure to heat comes from being dunked into a pot of chicken soup, not a crepe pan or oven.

Hasidic tradition interprets the custom of eating kreplach immediately before or after Yom Kippur in a fascinating way: just as the filling is covered by a wrapping of dough, so will God's strict judgment regarding one's fate in the New Year be covered with mercy and kindness.

MEAT KREPLACH

Dough:

⅔ cup sifted flour
1 egg
½ teaspoon salt

Filling:

2 cups cooked beef, finely chopped or ground
1 medium-sized onion, chopped fine
1 teaspoon chicken fat
½ teaspoon salt
½ teaspoon pepper
1 egg

1. Beat egg slightly. Then add salt and flour.
2. Knead dough until it holds together in a ball. Roll out to ⅛-inch thickness on a lightly floured cloth. Cut dough into 2-inch squares.

3. Combine all of the filling ingredients and mix thoroughly. Place a teaspoon of meat filling in the center of each square. Fold one corner of dough over diagonally to form a triangle and press edges together with a fork. Work quickly so that the dough does not dry out.
4. Drop into boiling salted water and cook for 30 minutes.

Makes 20.

Krupnick

If krupnick *is food, then my village of Handrivke is a whole city.*

—Nineteenth-century Yiddish saying

Underfed, overworked, and tumbled down were the Jews of Anatevke, Swislocz, and a thousand Russian and Polish towns and hamlets in between. Anatevke, the fictional home of Tevye and Golde, Mottl and Chana, made it to Broadway; Swislocz, called Sislev in Yiddish, didn't survive World War II, except in the recollections of a few who left it many years ago and wrote about this Russian town, seventy versts from Bialystok, its appearance and people, its climate and, of course, its food.

In 1900, of Sislev's 4,000 residents, over 2,000 of them were Jewish, making do with what Sislevich had to offer—which more often than not wasn't very much.

Cobblestone streets in Sislevich numbered three; mud covered the others. Lining them was the typical assemblage of ramshackle buildings, all looking as if this day might be their last: the synagogue and the shops, the Talmud Torah, the secular elementary schools, the tanneries, the huge central market which covered two city-size blocks, the factories, and the homes. Sometimes if the residents were well-to-do, their *sislevecher* homes had two stories instead of one and a piece or two of wallpaper covered the plaster or wooden walls.

But money in Sislevich was not in abundance. What was abundant were potatoes; eaten three times a day (except on the

Sabbath) by the shoemaker and the tanner, the joiner and the rabbi, the leader of the labor union and the bagel maker. In fact, so given to eating potatoes were the residents of Sislevich that the town was known throughout the district as *sislevecher krupnick, krupnick* being the name of the hearty potato and barley soup eaten almost daily at the tables of Jewish *sislevechers.*

Imagine the dish for a moment. A combination of barley, groats, and potatoes; in summer perhaps a slice or two of mutton or beef added; in winter dried or fresh mushrooms, and some fat along with a bit of onion.

On Friday, breakfast was a bowl of *krupnick* prepared with kishke, accompanied by fresh rolls and potato pudding. At noon another potato would need to be faced, dunked in a sauce of a few bits of herring and lots of onions. (Only the rich could afford to eat a whole herring.) But on Friday evening, the Sabbath, both the potato pudding and heavy, filling, fattening, warming (and boring) *krupnick* were replaced by chicken soup. Who could have been disappointed?

KRUPNICK

This is a modern *krupnick* with more meat and fewer potatoes. Add four more potatoes and reduce the quantity of meat to a scrap clinging to a bone, and the recipe approaches authenticity.

1 large peeled onion
2 marrow bones
½ pound stewing beef, flanken, or lamb shoulder
⅓ cup pearl barley
3 cans sliced button mushrooms (or ½ pound fresh, washed mushrooms; or 1 cup dried mushrooms, soaked first for several hours)
5 carrots, scraped clean and cut crosswise
2 potatoes, peeled and quartered
1 large (28-ounce) can stewed tomatoes
1 tablespoon sugar
1 teaspoon salt
½ teaspoon pepper
Water to cover

1. Combine all ingredients in a large soup kettle and bring to a boil. Reduce heat to simmer and cook covered for 2 hours.
2. About ½ hour before serving, taste soup for seasoning.

Makes 6 to 8 servings.

Kubana

Kubana is the traditional Yemenite Sabbath breakfast dish usually prepared in a large lidded stoneware pot in an outdoor Sabbath oven. Eggs in their shells are often baked along with the *kubana;* they spend their cooking time atop the lid covering the *kubana* pot.

Kubana is unique in that only fine wheat flour is used to make it. Customarily, the dozen kinds of bread the Yemenite Jews are fond of preparing contain a mixture of flour and legumes blended in varying proportions.

KUBANA

Kubana is very similar to the spoon breads that are so popular in the southern part of the United States. This recipe makes a bread that is moist and slightly sweet.

1 tablespoon active dry yeast
2½ cups water
3 tablespoons thick jam or preserves
1 tablespoon salt
¼ pound (1 stick) softened margarine
7 cups all-purpose or unbleached flour

1. Dissolve the yeast in ¼ cup warm water. Add jam and let stand for a few minutes.
2. Make a well with the flour and add 2 cups water. Pour yeast over water and begin mixing dough with a spoon. Gradually add half of the margarine and continue mixing until all the flour has been absorbed. The mixture will look more like a cake batter than a bread dough.
3. Smear remaining margarine on the bottom and sides of a large casserole or heavy pot. Pour dough into pot, cover, and let rise until doubled, about 1 hour.
4. Bake in a 250-degree oven until it is raised and light brown in color, about 2 hours. Turn heat to 150 degrees and bake for up to 15 hours.

Kugel

Even if the kugel doesn't quite work out, you still have the noodles.

—Sholom Aleichem

eggs
white flour
kasha
marrow bone
meat
goose fat
pears
apples
beans
noodle leaves

A nineteenth-century Russian-Jewish shopping list in translation.

From the flour and eggs were made the traditional challah loaves; from the kasha, a cereal for the children. The marrow bone would be used for *p'tscha;* the goose fat and beef for a *tscholent.* The pears, pureed, made a fruit soup to eat following the *tscholent;* the apples were for the fermented drink, kvaas; and the beans, roasted and salted, would be nibbled as a snack called *bebelech.*

The noodle leaves, wide and flat, would go into a sweet pudding—a kugel, dotted with raisins, sprinkled with cinnamon, and bubbling over with fat.

So beloved was a lokshen (noodle) kugel that a really outstanding one was considered to be the work of an angel, beyond the culinary ability of mere mortals. Perhaps, to toast their good fortune at being able to eat such a delicious pudding which seemed to be made in heaven, the Jews of Central and Eastern Europe once had the custom of drinking liquor while they ate the kugel. "Whoever eats a lot of kugel must drink a lot of liquor" went one Yiddish saying. "Eat no kugel, drink no liquor" went another.

On another day, the kugel might be made from farfel or buckwheat kasha, potatoes, or rice. Or, like its ancient predecessor, *kutach,* mentioned in the Talmud, it would be made from bread crusts, sour milk, and oil.

Today, the eat-kugel—drink-liquor custom has few, if any, adherents. But the great affection that Jews have had for kugel—especially for sweet lokshen kugels mixed with eggs, butter, and cheese—continues, unabated.

KUGEL

½ pound fine noodles
½ pound creamed cottage cheese
½ pound cream cheese
5 eggs
½ teaspoon cinnamon
½ teaspoon nutmeg
¾ cup sugar
2 cups milk
1 teaspoon vanilla
⅓ pound butter
½ box white raisins

1. Soak raisins in hot water until soft. Cook noodles *al dente.* Drain. Add butter.
2. Cream cheeses and add remaining ingredients. Drain raisins. Stir cheese mixture and raisins into noodles.
3. Place in greased 11″ × 9″ pan and sprinkle top with cinnamon. Bake at 350 degrees 1 to 1¼ hours.
4. To freeze, bake for 45 minutes. Then freeze. When ready to use, remove from freezer and bake at 350 degrees for another 45 minutes. Or bake for 1½ hours and serve.

Makes 12 servings.

Kvass

Aging, stale crusts of pumpernickel once, long ago and far away, found their way into a curiously enticing brownish-colored liquid called kvass. Rather than being thrown to the birds, the dried-up pieces of tacky Russian black bread were pitched into a huge pot, covered with hot water, and soaked. Only after the last bit of moisture had steeped through them and was later squeezed out, were the bread bits discarded. But while the bread was now considered useless, the murky brown water was never more ready for kvass-making. To the soggy mush which remained after so much soaking, yeast, sugar, and mint would be added; and, so that it would foam and bubble as it was poured and sipped, a handful of raisins would be dumped into each bottle.

Every Russian-Jewish family had its kvass-maker, but there was nothing uniquely Jewish about the drink or its preparation. It was simply a great way to make spirited use of stale bread.

KVASS

1 pound stale dark rye bread or pumpernickel
8 cups water
1 package dry yeast
¼ cup lukewarm water
2 teaspoons sugar
2 teaspoons fresh mint leaves or 1 teaspoon dried mint leaves
2 tablespoons raisins
2 tablespoons honey or to taste

1. Break the bread into small hunks and place it in a large bowl or crock. Boil the water and pour it over the bread.
2. Mix the yeast with ¼ cup water and sugar, and let it double in bulk. Add it to the bread along with the mint leaves and stir well.
3. Cover the bowl and place it in a cool place for 24 hours.
4. Line a sieve with cheesecloth, and strain the last drop of liquid from the soggy bread. Discard the bread.
5. Stir in the raisins and honey.
6. Pour into two quart-sized bottles, cover with a towel, and place again in a cool place. Let stand for three days to allow sediment to sink to the bottom and the raisins to rise to the top.

Makes 2 quarts.

Lag Ba'Omer

And from the day on which you bring the sheaf of wave offering—the day after the Sabbath—you shall count off seven weeks. They must be complete.

—Leviticus 23:15

The thirty-third day of the counting of the omer is called Lag Ba'Omer. The omer or measure of grain is counted each day beginning with the second day of Passover and ending with Shavuot, the Feast of Weeks, 50 days later. During ancient times it was the custom to measure out this extra amount of grain (usually barley or wheat) on each of the 49 days between the two holidays. By marking each day before Shavuot, the holiday which commemorates the giving of the Law at Mount Sinai, the ancient Israelites became mindful of the awesome time that was to come.

The lore of Lag Ba'Omer includes stories of plagues and mysticism, mourning and celebration. One story, a midrashic tale, links the thirty-third day with the Exodus of the Israelites from Egypt. On the thirty-second day, the story goes, the people rebelled against Moses, blaming him for bringing food for only 61 meals, enough for only 31 days. Therefore, on the thirty-second day, there would be nothing to eat. But a miracle occurred when God commanded that manna fall from heaven on the morning of the thirty-third day, thereby saving the people from starvation. The names of Akiba, Bar Kochba, and Simeon Bar Yochai also loom large in the recounting of both the holiday's myths and truths.

Latke

Greasy, oniony, and salty is this luscious potato pancake traditionally eaten during the eight-day-long holiday of Chanukah. Gritty and predisposed to sog if reheated after being fried, an unattractive little latke (rhymes with *vot—ka*), eaten straight from the pan in which it has sputtered to doneness, promises satisfaction and heartburn with each tantalizing bite. And its culinary homeliness masks enough nimble and elegant mystical prestidigitations to intimidate even the most expert flapjack flipper.

Centuries ago in Talmudic times, Jewish mystics, devoting the entire length of their lives to the task of interpreting Jewish lore and history according to religious precepts, ignored the latke (they lived before the time when it was eaten) and concentrated their mystical energies on the oil in which it was fried. Even for those later mystics who did live during the age of potato latkes, a period dating from the sixteenth century to the present, after the potato was brought back to Europe from the New World, the oil had much more importance than the potato pancake fried in it.

For this, the mystics had their reasons.

The first: During the battle for Jerusalem in 165 b.c.e., the Syrians, eager to defile Jewish ceremonial objects inside the great Temple, stormed the huge structure and desecrated its vast interior. After a fierce fight, the Hasmoneans (Macabees) were finally victorious. They rededicated the Temple. In the process of repairing the damage, according to a tradition which seems to date from Talmudic times, the Hasmoneans (*Hashmonaim* in Hebrew) discovered a single cruse of oil which had somehow escaped destruction. The cruse, containing enough oil for only one day, burned for eight days and nights. That this could have happened amid so much mayhem was interpreted as being no less than a miracle. The eight candles of Chanukah are lighted to this day on Chanukah to commemorate the eight days of light that were the result of the miraculous cruse of oil.

The second: The Hebrew word for oil is *shemen,* a word remarkably similar in sound and spelling to the Hebrew word *shimona,* the word for the number eight. Both are similar to the word *Hashmonaim.*

Centuries after the cruse of oil story had circulated so widely that it became legend, Jewish mystics made much of the similarities. A mystical belief rooted in the lore of Kabbalah holds that, since the world was created by God's naming its various aspects first, i.e., "God said let there be light and there was light," and so on, the essence of all things is in their name (in Hebrew). Also, there is a mystical belief that each Hebrew letter of a word has a numerical equivalent. A word, therefore, is not only what it describes but the sum of its letters. If, in adding up the numerical equivalents of a word (an activity known as Gematria), two or more words were found to add up to the same or nearly the same number, they were considered to be divinely related, their equivalence much more than mere coincidence.

Not only did *shemen* (oil) and *shimonah* (eight) sound similar, they had almost the same value numerically.

Oil =		Eight =	
ש	= 300	ש	= 300
מ	= 40	מ	= 40
ן	= 50	נ	= 50
	390	ה	= 5
			395

It would be stretching the point to include the word *Hashmonaim* in this relationship of divine words. But then, the three words sounded remarkably alike, a similarity sufficiently strong, said the rabbis, to bond the three words into an everlasting mystical relationship.

On Chanukah, therefore, it is customary to tell the story of the *Hashmonaim,* to light the candles on eight successive days and, as if to add flavor to the miracle, to eat foods fried in oil.

The latke is an Eastern European contribution to the food lore of Chanukah. In Israel, the food fried in oil is soofganiyot, jelly doughnuts.

See also Chanukah.

POTATO LATKES

4 cups grated raw potatoes, drained
2 eggs
1 teaspoon salt
½ teaspoon baking powder
½ teaspoon baking soda
1 heaping tablespoon flour
1 small onion, grated
1 teaspoon minced fresh chives, parsley, or scallions

1. Combine all ingredients and mix well.
2. Drop by tablespoonfuls onto a hot, well-greased skillet. Fry on both sides until brown.

Makes 24 pancakes.

Legumes

If apples are the food of paradise, legumes are the food of paradox. Esau, acting precipitously and irresponsibly, sold his birthright to Jacob for a dish of them, yet the rabbis of the Midrash Rabbah tell us there is great joy in this Biblical story as well as sadness, for Jacob received what Esau had squandered. Ezekiel prepared his people for the siege of Jerusalem and the desperate famine and suffering that would follow. Yet survival would come in the form of legumes, made into a wheatless and heavy bread: "And take to thee wheat and barley and beans and lentils and millet and vetches and put them in one vessel," he said, "and make thee bread thereof" (Ezekiel 4:9). The inhabitants of the city would be gratified to have these legumes even in the midst of their suffering.

Like the egg, legumes, particularly lentils, according to extremely ancient tradition, were brought to a house of mourning. In fact, lentils were being eaten at the house of Isaac, Esau, and Jacob, according to ancient tradition, because the family was mourning the death of Abraham, Isaac's father. Their round shape represented life and the life cycle. Yet they also were thought to represent the silent mourners who, according to the Talmud, were so grief-stricken that they had no mouth to speak.

By the Middle Ages, the lentil gave way to the egg as the traditional food of private mourning after considerable rabbinic debate had been stirred up regarding the appropriateness of each. Yet legumes (as well as eggs) have continued to be the symbolic foods at times of communal grief and sorrow, at Tisha B'av for example, the day on which Jews mark the destruction of the Temple in Jerusalem, first by the Babylonians and again, centuries later, by the Romans. Before the fast begins on the eve of Tisha B'av, a meal including legumes is customarily served to those who will be fasting.

With intentional irony, reminiscent of the rabbinic interpretation of the story of Jacob and Esau, legumes were among the foods which were to be served at celebration feasts, a practice of medieval Jews which continues into our own times. Everpresent at traditional wedding feasts in the Middle Ages were beans or chickpeas placed on the table to remind people of life's contradictory, antithetical aspects, and the bittersweet feeling that tinges every joyous event. Also, since legumes were associated with mourning, they would appear at a Jewish medieval feast to fool the Evil Eye into believing that the people gathered at the happy occasion—particularly a wedding—were mourning and not to be envied. If the guests were perceived as grieving, the line of thinking went, the Evil Eye wouldn't bother them.

Today in some Orthodox communities, boiled peas are served at the joyous feast held on the Sabbath following the birth of a son, the Sholem Zocher. One group, the Lubavitcher Hasidim, believes that the legumes are served at the Sholem Zocher as sorrowful reminder that the newborn child has forgotten the Torah he once knew while still unborn. In such symbolism can be found the foisting into the modern age of the very old customs that link legumes, particularly the round varieties—peas, chickpeas, and lentils—to the paradoxical nature of life itself.

TO STEW GREEN PEASE THE JEWS WAY

To two full quarts of pease put in a full quarter of a pint of oil and water, not so much water as oil; a little different sort of spices, as mace, clove, pepper, and nutmeg, all beat fine; a little Cayan pepper, a little salt; let all this stew in a broad, flat pipkin; when they are half done, with a spoon make two or three holes; into each of these holes break an egg, yolk and white; take one egg and beat it, and throw over the whole when enough, which you will know by tasting them; and the egg being quite hard, send them to table.

If they are not done in a very broad, open thing, it will be a great difficulty to get them out to lay in a dish.

They would be better done in a silver or tin dish, on a stew-hole, and go to table in the same dish; it is much better than putting them out into another dish.

—Hannah Glasse, *The Art of Cookery Made Plain and Easy,* 1751

FELAFEL

Felafel is the ubiquitous street food of Israel and the Middle East. Tucked into a hollowed-out whole *pita* round, covered with salad fixings, and sauced with *tehina* (sesame paste), the little balls of spiced ground chickpeas are a snacker's delight.

3 large cloves garlic
2 teaspoons parsley, stalks removed
¼ teaspoon coriander seeds
1 20-ounce can chickpeas, well drained
3 tablespoons medium or fine ground bulghur wheat (burghul)
1½ teaspoons cumin
1 teaspoon salt
3 tablespoons flour
⅛ teaspoon ground chili pepper
4 cups vegetable oil for frying
Chopped tomatoes, scallions, cucumber, parsley

1. Using a blender or food processor, finely mince the garlic, parsley, and coriander seeds.
2. Add remaining ingredients and chop until peas are pulverized and mixture sticks together.
3. Form into balls about 1½ inches in diameter.
4. Using a large skillet, heat oil over medium heat. When oil is hot, add felafel balls and fry, turning occasionally, until balls are golden brown. Drain on absorbent paper. Skewer with toothpicks and serve as an hors d'oeuvre. Or stuff into *pita* bread accompanied by chopped fresh vegetables and *tehina*.

Makes 16 balls.

Liver, Chopped

So artless is this marvelous dish that it can be better explained by mentioning what it is not.

There it is on the dining table on a Friday night, a traditional Sabbath food served as an appetizer or on the sideboard at a cocktail party, molded into every conceivable shape known to humanity and the caterer. The recipe calls for no more than six or seven ingredients: broiled liver, hard-boiled eggs, fried onions, schmaltz or oil, sugar, salt, and pepper. Maleable and chilled, it stands practically bare in a copse of parsley, at the ready. When a knife bisects it, nary a truffle will be found imbedded in its interior, no slim slices of pork fat wrapped round its midsection, no crust caressing its naked state. It wasn't untinned from some trapezoidal can, nor would it ever be; and the only folks who rate it are its delighted eaters. They do so by heaping it on pieces of rye bread, pumpernickel, or challah, eating it hungrily and heaving great sighs of satisfaction.

So spare and simple is the recipe that it doesn't seem possible to admit that chopped liver (called by many *gehakte leber*, its Yiddish name) and paté de foie gras are culinary cousins, springing from the same ancient (probably Roman) source. But so it is. Once in the Middle Ages, chopped liver was made elegant by the Jews of France and Germany who added goose liver to a meat pie called pashtet, a dish much like a modern paté *en croute*. But this Sabbath dish was replaced long ago in the Jewish culinary repertoire by the more highly regarded Jewish "pocket" foods: knishes, pirogen, and kreplach.

CHOPPED CHICKEN LIVER

In order to prepare liver according to the dietary laws, it must first be coarsely salted and broiled to rid it of any excess blood. This does not mean it has to be incinerated to a point just this side of charcoal. It is sufficient to cook the livers until all pinkness has disappeared.

2 pounds chicken livers
4 hard-boiled eggs
3 medium onions
¾ cup schmaltz or vegetable oil
1 teaspoon sugar
Salt
Pepper

1. Using a small broiling pan, broil chicken livers until they are brown, 5 to 7 minutes. Remove from broiler and mash the livers with a fork.
2. Grate the onions. At medium heat, sauté onions in chicken fat until they are translucent and tinged brown. Add broiled livers.
3. Remove from the heat and grate the eggs into the liver and onion mixture. Add sugar; salt and pepper to taste.
4. Mix well. The mixture should be of spreading consistency. Add more schmaltz if necessary. Refrigerate until serving time. Serve on miniature rye slices or with salted crackers.

Lox

How very human it is to want to possess some outward sign that life has been generous, especially if it hasn't always been so. A status symbol, a sign that shows us, our family and friends, strangers even, that good fortune has come to visit and hopefully will stay around for a while. Lox (say *locks*) may not seem like the most dazzling choice. Nonetheless, these thinly sliced pieces of smoked salmon have become inextricably associated with success among the Jews of this century, particularly in the United States. The high cost of lox, even when it is of only indifferent quality, is greeted on Sunday mornings in the delicatessens of the world amid audible groans and inaudible feelings of self-satisfaction. As with so many other food preferences among Jews, there are reasons aplenty for plunking down so much cash for what seems to be just a mere piece of fish.

Even when fish wasn't expensive, Jews relished it. Few dietary laws were imposed regarding its eating. God said, "These you may eat, of all that are in the waters. Everything in the waters that has fins and scales . . . , But anything in the seas or rivers that hasn't fins and scales . . . is an abomination to you" (Leviticus 11:9–11). Free from the laws of slaughtering, fish could be enjoyed without elaborate ritual preparation. Over the centuries it also became the symbolic and mystical

Sabbath food of the faithful, tied to a belief in the coming of the Messiah.

Particularly in the Middle Ages, a time when mystical and superstitious beliefs abounded, fish became an important food for more than just its nutritional qualities. Fish (usually gefilte fish) seasoned with garlic was considered to be an aphrodisiac and became the everpresent Sabbath delicacy among European Jews of this time. In England it was a custom to eat fish on the second day after a wedding. In Salonika, the last day of the "seven days of fertility" following a wedding was called "fish-day."

When along the way one fish, salt herring, became the staple of the poor Jews in Eastern Europe, in Jewish minds it came to symbolize dearth—not fertility. Even as time passed and conditions improved somewhat for many Jews, they could not disassociate the unfortunate herring from its reputation. Then, early in this century and continuing to this day, many Jews began to enjoy prosperity, particularly in the United States. Anxious to forget their "herring" past and eager to find a fish which symbolized their abundant future but still tasted a bit like salt herring, Jews sought out lox which had a smoked (if salty) flavor and an elegant price tag. Lox on the table meant prosperity at the door.

Finally, to connect lox with the inevitable bagel, it should be mentioned that eating fish, including lox, was thought by Jews to be one protection against the forces of the malevolent Evil Eye. In a quite natural and superstitiously logical progression, then, lox became associated with bagels, another food with a long history of Evil Eye protection.

None of the above will be believed by those who, behaving like twentieth-century rationalists, are quick to point out that herring on a bagel or lox on a piece of sliced white tastes absolutely awful.

LOX

Very few people prepare lox at home since a trip to the local delicatessen to buy it is so much easier. But it is possible to prepare lox at home using a commercial or homemade smoke oven. The results will be far superior to what is commercially available; the flavor will be subtle and the product absolutely fresh.

3 pounds fresh salmon, bone in
¾ cup lemon juice
2 tablespoons garlic powder
2 tablespoons onion powder
4½ cups kosher salt
¼ cup brown sugar
2 tablespoons fresh dill (optional)
2 gallons water

1. Wash the fish and pat dry. Set aside and prepare brine.
2. Using a large pottery, heavy plastic, or glass crock (don't use wooden or metal containers), mix together all of the ingredients, stirring well to dissolve dry ingredients.
3. Place salmon in crock. Add brine. Cover and place a weight on top of the cover. Refrigerate for 24 hours.
4. Remove salmon from brine and gently rinse in salt water. Dry on wire rack that is covered with paper toweling. The fish should be completely dry before being smoked.
5. Start smoker and let it come to full temperature. Place salmon on an open rack and leave in smoker no longer than ½ hour. Too much smoking will actually cook rather than just flavor the salmon, changing the dish to smoked salmon (wonderful, but not lox).
6. Remove from smoker and serve with bagels and cream cheese, sliced tomatoes, and cucumbers.
   Note: Smoked fish may be kept frozen for up to 3 months and in the refrigerator for one week.

Maimouna

Maimouna (say *My—moo—na*). The sound of the word gives us a hint of its connection with the great Jewish scholar, Moses Maimonides, but nary a clue as to the importance given to it by the people who celebrate it. Observed mostly by Jews of Moroccan background, no matter where they currently reside, at the end of the last day of Passover, Maimouna is a glorious festival marking the end of one holiday season and the beginning of another. Plus, according to tradition, for hundreds of years it has become a way of commemorating the anniversary of the death of Maimonides' father, Maimon ben Joseph, who lived for a time in Fèz, one of Morocco's largest cities.

In Israel, Maimouna is a day for parading in the streets and dancing and picnicking in the large fields near the Knesset in downtown Jerusalem. Elsewhere, it is a day of feasting at a table set to dazzle both eye and palate.

Decorating the table are vases of flowers, fresh greens, and green wheat stalks gathered especially for the day. Set before the guests who go from house to house paying Maimouna visits to all their friends and family are dozens of trays laden with delicacies, mostly sweet and all having a special significance. There is even a special order to the table arrangement, for in the center there is always a pitcher of sweet buttermilk and a bowl of flour with beans, eggs, or coins set in it. The latter is the "lucky bowl"; during the celebration, the host will drop bits of flour taken from it onto the heads of each of the guests.

Surrounding the bowl and pitcher are the bowls of honey and fruit, salads and nuts, the delicate honey-butter pancakes called *muflita,* the nougat and orange candies, and the sweet breads and cakes.

Nearby is the couscous, a special meatless one for Maimouna, served with raisins, prunes, and cooked wedges of pumpkin. And as a symbol of fertility as well as abundance, there is also a whole fish, usually cooked, but occasionally brought out to the table very much alive and left to swim about happily in its bowl during the entire festivity.

Mamalige

While Christopher Columbus was busy discovering North America, Balkan peasants half a world away and totally unaware of his existence were even busier trying to stay alive. Columbus sailed across an ocean without falling off the world's edge and traipsed around the lush Bahamas and Cuba admiring the "simple souls" whom he found inhabiting the islands, all the while searching under every leaf and behind every hut for gold and spices to take back home to Queen Isabella.

The impoverished Balkan multitude, on the other hand, trudged despiritedly along the shores of the Black Sea, overland as far as the ridges of the snow-covered Carpathians, and up and down the banks of the Prut and the Dniester in search of anything that would keep a belly full.

Thinking not at all about the hunger of Russian and Roumanian peasants but solely about the economic fortunes of his queen and countrymen, Columbus, at the conclusion of his first expedition to the New World, had the good sense to take home with him a New World food which would ultimately benefit them all. With a load of corn seeds stowed deep in the hold of his ships, he sailed back to Spain and totally (and unwittingly) altered the diet and economic fortunes of most of Eastern Europe to this day.

From Spain the seeds went to Venice. The wily Venetians, who actually loathed the food, unloaded it as soon as possible to the Turks in Constantinople, and from there Jewish, Dutch, and Turkish traders sold it to points as far away from Constantinople as Cracow and Aleppo where it grew indifferently, and as close as Sofia and Kishinev where it thrived in the moderate Southeastern European climate.

Mamalige (say *mama—leega*), the peasants called the cornmeal that the Venetians had dubbed *meliga.* When cooked with water, it turned into filling, bland mush. But when the starving Jews who had been expelled from Hungary came to the region now called Moldavia S.S.R. at about the same time as the Venetians were selling off their maize, the Jews, grateful for any food at all, learned that this new food did for them what it did for all the other peasants who ate it. They became dependent on *mamalige* for survival, too, filling themselves up and out with mouthful after mouthful of its gritty, yellow tackiness. So much of it did they eat that the Jews of other areas, notably the potato-filled Litvacks up north, disparagingly referred to their brethren to the south as "mamaliges."

At first, plain porridge may have been sufficient for peasants, Jew or non-Jew, as a food which kept them from starvation. But when survival became more than a chance occurrence and good taste a concern, more than just water was mixed with the cornmeal and the results were absolutely stupifying! The Roumanians added buttermilk and hard-boiled eggs, chicken or goose and bits of bacon or pork fat. The Italians, who started growing corn shortly after they had made so much of a fuss about not growing it, called the mush *polenta* and added hard cheese to break up the dry monotony.

The Jews, taking advantage of *mamalige*'s being neither a milk nor a meat food, added to it or served following it rendered fat and roasted bits of *kodeh. Kodeh* was the meat from the tail of the fat-tailed sheep. The tail was so enormous that it had to be supported by a little cart attached to the sheep's body.

Cooking *mamalige* in a Roumanian-Jewish or Russian-Jewish household became a morning ritual. First, the *kukuruze,* the cornmeal, was tossed into a large pot, mixed with water, and then stirred constantly with a stick until it was thick and steamy-hot. Then out came the string to cut it—no knives allowed. And, finally, when it came time to say the final blessing after a meal of it, those who were able said grace with hardly more than the strength of a fly. *Mamalige,* Bessarabian Jews used to say, *men mischt mit a drik* (mixed with a stick), *men schneidt si mit a schtrik* (cut with a string), *un dernuch benscht men wi a flig* (and afterwards said grace with the strength of a fly). The word *mamaligos* is used to this day in Roumania to describe a person who is lazy or totally devoid of initiative. It's hardly surprising.

MAMALIGE

2 cups yellow cornmeal
¾ cup cold water
1½ teaspoons salt
Pepper, to taste
3 cups boiling water
¼ pound butter (1 stick)
2 cups grated sharp cheddar, *kashkaval*, pot, cottage, or *brinza* cheese

1. Mix the cornmeal and cold water until smooth. Add salt, pepper, and boiling water.
2. Let the mixture cook for 15 to 20 minutes over very low heat, or until mixture comes away completely from the sides of the pot. Stir to remove lumps.
3. Add butter and 1 cup of the cheese. Mix and pour into a small greased casserole dish.
4. Cover the top with remaining cheese and place in a preheated 375-degree oven for about 15 minutes or until cheese has crusted and the cornmeal mixture has become almost solidified.

Makes 8 servings.

Mandlen

So rare are old Jewish cookbooks that the recipe collections which do survive are to be devoured as if they were sweet and delicious crumbs, leftovers of precious ambrosia. Those published in the Yiddish language are the rarest of them all, for few were ever written and fewer still published. But here and there are manuscripts tucked away in dusty archival collections. And, occasionally, one can find a book, its pages discolored and brittle.

From one such book comes a recipe for mandlen, soup almonds, made with a single egg, pulverized almonds, a dusting of salt, and a bit of grated lemon rind. This is a recipe of great simplicity, as are the other hundred or so recipes with which it is included, all of them contained in *Instructions for Cooking and Baking*, published in New York City at the turn of the century. Written by Hinde Amchanitzky, a woman whose serious and authoritative-looking countenance appears in a photograph on the title page, the volume is a slice of social history even if it can be swallowed in a single captivating bite.

Hinde Amchanitzky may have written her book in Yiddish but her recipes are an amalgamation of Jewish Americana, circa 1901. Old Jewish recipes like the one for mandlen and others for stuffed spleen (*gefilte miltz*), butter rolls (*putterzemmeln*), and compote (*kislitse*) are described in a simple, straightforward style on several of its 50 pages, but so are recipes for macaroni soup, steak, peaches [*sic*] pie, and a dessert printed in transliterated Yiddish as "snawbawls," i.e., snowballs. Clearly, the author wrote her book not only for cooks who could read Yiddish better than they could English, but also for those who wanted to sample the foods of the American melting pot—French cutlets, English pot rolls, and "peaches pie"—along with their *miltz*, *putterzemmeln*, and mandlen.

MANDLEN FOR CHICKEN SOUP

Combine one yolk of a large egg, 1 cup finely ground almonds, a little salt, and some grated lemon rind. Beat the egg white until stiff and fold it into the almond mixture. Drop by teaspoonfuls into deep, hot fat and fry until golden. Drain on towel papers. Makes 1 dozen.

—Hinde Amchanitzky, *Instructions for Cooking and Baking*, 1901

Manna

About fifty years ago a world-famous zoologist led an expedition to the Sinai Peninsula in search of confirming botanical and zoological evidence of the ancient wanderings described in the Biblical Book of Exodus. In particular, he went in search of manna and found that it had indeed existed in Biblical times in the Sinai just as it does today: the honeylike sticky secretion of the tamarisk shrub produced by scale insects which infest the shrub, particularly during a two- to three-month period during the spring of each year.

As interesting as this discovery is, it is thoroughly beside the point to observant Jews whose interest in manna is anything but scientific. To them, manna is the food of deliverance, the food of foods, the food of legendary properties.

For the same reason, it is also beside the point that even today manna is gathered from tamarisks dotting the hills of Kurdistan and is made into a candy called *man'as Sama,* Manna of Heaven, in 50-pound batches to be sold by vendors in the streets of Baghdad. A piece of *man'as Sama* is not at all what Jews have in mind when they think of the manna of ancient Israel. Again, it is not important to know that manna has shape and substance and that one can touch, taste, and even eat it today. Manna is a symbolic food, one of the earliest ways in which the Lord demonstrated his love of Israel by causing manna to rain down upon the starving desert wanderers.

Who can imagine how it must feel to experience real hunger if one has just finished eating a rich, carefully prepared, five-course meal? But a starving person cannot refrain from fantasizing a thousand banquets, or dreaming of foods once eaten no matter how simply prepared.

To experience starvation is to realize that all other human activity ceases in the face of it, all activity but the mind's constant yearning for the foods which once satisfied even if they were signaled to be eaten with a whip and consumed with hundreds of others in a ditch of rubble, the yoke of slavery about one's neck.

Onions, leeks, cucumbers, and melons. Bread. Fish even. The wanderers in the wilderness of Sinai remembered what they had eaten in Egypt and rebuked Moses for leading them to such an arid and forsaken place. As recounted in Exodus, the memory of the taste of food grew stronger than the memory of sorrow and enslavement, the wish for food more captivating than the wish for freedom. The exiles from Egypt soon forgot who they were and what they had come out of Egypt to do.

Then, suddenly one morning they woke to find the ground around their encampment covered with a "fine flakelike thing, fine as the hoar-frost on the ground, and just as white." Stunned by its sudden appearance, they questioned one another seeking a name for the strange substance which now surrounded them.

"It is the bread which the Lord hath given you to eat," Moses told them. Manna. Some ran to gather it, eager to satisfy their hunger, claiming that it tasted like wafers made with honey. Others, doubting Moses, left their portion and it became wormy.

For forty years, according to the account in Exodus, until they reached Canaan, the wanderers would wake each morning to find that manna had indeed rained down around them, enough to feed them for the day. On the sixth day there would be enough for two days so that they could rest on the Sabbath. Quickly they would gather it up, grind and shape it into cakes to be baked and eaten. They would be kept from starvation by a food that had the quality of being many foods.

Soon the mysterious substance did more than satisfy hunger. It became nourishment for the soul as well, evidence of the Lord's special interest and commitment to the children of Israel, a commitment which to this day Jews remember in rather fascinating ways—by sprinkling sesame seeds on the Sabbath challah, by covering that challot with a white cloth, and even by sprinkling bread crumbs to feed the birds on the day of each year when the section containing the Song of Moses is read in the Synagogue.

Marzipan

When Jewish cooks turn to sculpture, they often use marzipan as their raw material, for this mixture of finely ground almonds, sugar, and subtle flavorings is as maleable a medium as clay and much more pleasurable on the palate. Less inclined to make the elaborately decorated candies that their Christian neighbors enjoy at Christmastime, they nevertheless participate in this thousand-year-old craft, particularly during the Passover holidays when desserts made with flour are forbidden and the substitutes, matzah flour or meal, seem comparatively colorless and pallid.

Marzipan is mentioned in European Jewish writings of the sixteenth century but there is every reason to believe that Jews knew about marzipan before it ever made its way to Europe via the Crusades. The delicacy was the most highly esteemed of all dessert foods of the Middle East (a major center of Jewish life) hundreds of years before it earned the same reputation in Europe. It originated in Persia and was brought to North Africa and the medieval Muslim empires of Damascus, Baghdad, and Konya (modern-day Israel and Jordan, Syria and Turkey, respectively) by the cooks who served the swashbuckling caliphs, their enormous courts and *hareems.* The taste and texture of marzipan enchanted everyone, including the daring Crusader knights who forced many a captured Arab cook to prepare the same tempting morsels within the stone confines of a Crusader castle as those culinary wizards had done so delectably in the tents of their marauding Muslim masters.

So, too, by the end of the first Crusade, there were to be found in the manor house and castle kitchens of Europe almonds by the sackful. By the end of the third Crusade almonds were almost as ubiquitous in recipes as salt. They were pounded, watered down for almond milk to be used as a popular substitute for cow's milk, added to thicken every sauce imaginable, and mixed into marzipan to mold into the famous subtleties and warners of the medieval European banquets, those spectacular, illusional between-course diversions, so dear to the hearts of medieval Europeans.

From hundred-pound batches of marzipan, one fifteenth-century historian recorded, were sculpted the likes of bobbing ships, elephants, *chateaux* with moats filled with orangeade, and even one huge pastry containing twenty-eight very lively and busily performing musicians!

Gradually this food of European princes, knights, and kings became available to the common folk, among them the Jews. Less spectacularly but just as elaborately, from marzipan (called *marchpane* in England, *marzepane* in German, and *martzepan* in Yiddish, from the Arab word *mataba*) now came confections shaped into miniature fruits, animals, crescents, and rounds.

Fruit tarts prepared in the Jewish and non-Jewish bakeries of Germany, England, France, and Italy were layered with apples or pears, filled to the brim with almond paste, and then sprinkled with kirschwasser or brandy.

In Poland, marzipan in a Jewish household eventually lost its original identity and became known as *teyglach.* Flour was inevitably added to the ground-nut mixture, and over several centuries, the food became more cookie than ground-nut candy, the amount of flour greatly exceeding the amount of nuts.

The most popular time of year for serving marzipan today is during the week of Passover, and in North Africa, particularly in Morocco, at the celebration which follows Passover (called Maimouna). Sprinkled lightly with rose water, orange water, or bits of lemon peel, the nut mixture is dyed with food coloring, saffron water, or turnsole, molded into exquisitely refined and sweet renditions of reality—into pears and apples, flowers, fish, and baskets of fruit—or stuffed into the fresh pitted dates, prunes, or sandwiched between giant walnut halves, to be served with strong, sweet Moroccan mint tea.

MOROCCAN MARZIPAN PETIT FOURS

Moroccan Jews have given their favorite dessert the French name petit fours, but these petit fours are totally unlike the small iced and decorated cakes the Americans and French call by the same name. In this recipe, the amount of almonds used is twice the amount of sugar and, unlike most marzipan recipes, the sugar is the granulated and not the powdered kind. If the almonds are oily, the egg yolks may not be needed.

4 cups blanched almonds
2 cups granulated sugar
Peel of ½ lemon
2 tablespoons orange blossom water (optional)
1 to 3 egg yolks, as needed
½ pound firm, unblemished dates, pitted
½ pound large pitted prunes
½ pound large walnut halves
Red, green, and yellow food coloring

1. Grind the almonds and lemon peel together with the sugar. Add the orange blossom water, if desired, and knead for several minutes. The mixture should have the consistency of soft clay without being sticky. If it is too

dry, add one egg yolk at a time until the marzipan reaches the proper consistency. Knead for several minutes and set aside.

2. Slit one side of each of the dates and prunes and remove the pits. Carefully enlarge the opening until there is enough room for about one teaspoon of filling. Assemble pairs of walnut halves.
3. Separate the marzipan into three parts and to each part add 1 or 2 drops of food coloring or enough to achieve a muted, pastel tone. Red, green, and yellow are recommended. Knead one color into each section of marzipan evenly, washing hands between each color.
4. Pinch off small pieces of marzipan and form into balls approximately one inch in diameter.
5. Fill each date with pink and green filling. Using the same colors, press a pair of walnut halves into opposite sides of each ball. Fill the prunes using the yellow balls.
6. Press the filled fruit into smoothly shaped petit fours, striating the tops by pressing into the marzipan with the tines of a fork.
7. Lightly coat petit fours by gently rolling them one at a time into granulated sugar.
8. Place in paper pastry cups and store in a cool place in a covered cookie tin or box for up to a week. In hot weather, store in the refrigerator.

Makes 48 individual petit fours.

Matzah

Walk the streets of Jerusalem's old city and know that you are walking over ancient streets others have walked on for tens of centuries. Receive a package of *shmurah* matzot (say *matz* to rhyme with dots—*ot* as in oat) from a gray-bearded rabbi who has taken great care to see that the wheat used, from the time of its harvesting to the preparation of the flat cakes for Passover, has not been exposed to excess heat or moisture, hence the reason for this special name, *shmurah,* meaning watched. Even one extra drop of water could result in leavened bread rather than the brittle cracker which each cake of matzah must become. Countless are the numbers of these flat matzot that have been baked for Passover in this city where a building that is 500 years old is considered new!

Stand at Herod's famed Phasael Tower at sunset, talking to a friend. For a few moments every object of the landscape becomes daubed in a mellow gold. Hear the sound of the *meuzzin* chanting the Islamic call to prayer or the melodious cadence of pious Jews chanting the early evening prayer. Touch the walls built in Suleiman's time. Listen to the meowing of a scrawny black cat as it sniffs the dry rubble underfoot, looking for its dinner.

Soon you will ask yourself the inevitable questions, each a variation of merely one: What has changed here? What has changed since David conquered the city and made it his capital? What has changed since thousands came to Jerusalem to celebrate the Passover feasts of ancient times? What has changed since the great Temple stood gleaming in the golden light of sunset?

Everything, you will say. But then, too, nothing at all.

Far to the north in the Upper Galilee where settlement is as scanty as summer rain, is it any different? Stand at the top of Mount Tabor on a still summer morning. What has changed since Deborah won a great battle there? Stand at the foot of Mount Meiron or on the wide plateau nearby. What has changed since the wise Rabbi Simeon ben Yochai and his son Eleazer walked from the mountain to the village below it or the other great rabbis who lived there discoursed on Jewish law, rendering important decisions that would affect every future generation of Jews, even those living today?

Recently, the remnants of life lived seventeen centuries ago in that village were unearthed by archeologists excavating the ruins of a large house. Among the ruins was evidence that the people of Meiron made matzot just like those distributed today in the streets of Jerusalem's Jewish quarter.

Nineteen hundred years ago, after the Romans destroyed the Temple, most of Judea, the homeland of the majority of Jews living during that time, was placed off limits to them. Living in Jerusalem, the center of Jewish life, was not allowed. Forced to search for new homes, some Jews settled in the

Upper Galilee, establishing several settlements, including the one at Meiron. Here the Jews were left alone to lead their own lives and to follow their religion. Land was fertile and winter rainfall ample. Houses were built in a simple yet comfortable style, organized for living a Jewish life.

In the contents of an ancient storeroom in a home owned by a citizen of Meiron was evidence that a life rich in Jewish tradition went on unaffected by the force of Roman law and might. In this little room, underneath the main level of the house, were found remnants of pottery vessels, dinnerware, and even food—peas, walnuts, barley—and, most important of all, a shard with the Hebrew "*esh,*" meaning fire, written on it. Perhaps, say the archeologists, the whole vessel on which the word had been etched had once contained the grain used for making matzah, grain that would first be parched by fire according to a tradition dating from Biblical times. Then, just as it is today, it would be made into a bread to be eaten during the Passover week in commemoration of the Exodus, that time when the Jews were brought forth out of Egypt "and they baked out of the dough . . . unleavened cakes" because, the Bible says, "they were thrust out of Egypt and could not tarry, neither had they prepared for themselves any victual" (Exodus 12:39).

Today it is no different. Matzah has taken on a new shape, going from round to square, thanks to the invention of the matzah machine. But the food and the reason for its being eaten are the same as they were yesterday and the same as they will be tomorrow.

MATZAH BALLS

4 tablespoons chicken fat
¼ teaspoon ginger
1 teaspoon salt
¼ teaspoon pepper
1 tablespoon chopped parsley
4 eggs
8 tablespoons water
1¼ cups matzah meal

1. Blend fat, ginger, salt, pepper, and parsley. In separate bowl, beat eggs slightly.
2. Add fat mixture, water, and matzah meal to the beaten eggs and mix thoroughly. Chill for several hours or overnight.

4. Remove from refrigerator about ½ hour before the matzah balls are to be cooked. Form into small balls and cook covered in boiling, salted water for 50 to 60 minutes.

Makes 20.

Mehren Pletzlach

Mehren pletzlach (to rhyme with *therein—let's—lock*) is a traditional Passover confection from Eastern Europe. It is ages old. Carrots are spread out on a board to harden after having been cooked in a bath of sugar syrup laced with ginger and tweaked with lemon juice. The mixture is flattened (hence the name *pletzlach* which means flat or board in Yiddish) and scored into a diamond pattern, just as baklava is marked before it is baked, and is left to cool.

Mixing coconut into the recipe is an American variation as is rolling the mixture into small balls and covering them with coconut.

MEHREN PLETZLACH

2 pounds carrots, cleaned and scraped
2 cups sugar
1¾ teaspoons powdered ginger
2 tablespoons fresh lemon juice
1½ cups coarsely ground almonds
1 cup shredded coconut (optional)
Sugar
Coconut

1. Finely shred the carrots.
2. Place carrots in large saucepan and add sugar. Add water to cover. Bring to a boil, then cook over very low heat until sugar is completely dissolved.
3. Add ginger and lemon juice; gently simmer until all of the moisture has evaporated (about 1 to 1½ hours).
4. Remove from heat and add chopped nuts and shredded coconut. Taste for seasoning, and add more ginger if a spicier taste is desired.

5. Sprinkle sugar over large platter or cutting board. Spread carrot mixture evenly over board and press to a ¾-inch thickness. Mark into diamond shapes and cool. Cut when completely cooled.
6. As an alternative, roll cooled mixture into balls, one inch in diameter, and coat with shredded coconut.

Makes 25 to 30 pieces.

Oublie

Close your eyes and imagine that you are standing amid the noisy crowd at a market fair at Troyes, France, sometime in the twelfth century. The day is warm, the mood exuberant, and the crowd friendly.

Suddenly you realize that you are hungry. Eagerly, you begin walking to one of the many stands selling food. But before you get to the nearest one, you hear a boy singing a little nonsense rhyme about an *oublie.* What, you wonder, is an *oublie*? (Rhymes with you—flee.)

You walk toward him and reach for one of the pieces of food he has spread out on a tray that he holds braced against his chest. He tells you how much it will be and you pay him.

Now imagine that you are savoring the sweet morsel that also tastes faintly lemony and smells of orange blossoms. Each bite brings your teeth in touch with a confection that is crusty and somewhat tough; the texture is like that of stale bread. Your teeth also encounter peaks and valleys in a regular pattern. The *oublie,* so common to the people of Northern France in the Middle Ages that they couldn't have lived a week without it, was the original waffle.

The word itself is a corruption of the word *oblaye,* a term used to describe a consecated communion wafer.

In Jewish rabbinic writings of the Middle Ages, the dish is mentioned again and again, usually called *oublie,* but sometimes called *obleit* or *oblaten.* The Jews apparently loved the food which was made from "forgotten" pastry, the extra pieces of dough or extra batter left over after a town baker had finished the day's baking.

The recipe for *oublies* is matter-of-factly Levantine, the culinary result of crusader contacts with the cuisine of the Middle East in the eleventh century.

OUBLIES

1 cup flour, sifted
1 cup sugar
1 egg
3 tablespoons butter, melted
1 teaspoon orange flower water
1 cup milk
2 teaspoons grated lemon rind

1. Mix together the flour, sugar, egg, melted butter, and orange flower water. Work until smooth and shiny.
2. Gradually add milk, stirring until smooth. Stir in the lemon rind and let stand for 1 hour.
3. Heat 1 or more wafer irons (a Scandinavian wafer iron may be used) until a drop of water sizzles on outside. Grease the iron, pour in 1 tablespoon batter, and cook over high heat, turning to cook evenly, 3 to 4 minutes on each side or until light golden color.
4. Remove wafer and roll into a cylinder while still hot or leave unrolled.

Makes 32 wafers.

P

Pashtet

Read about the history of western cuisine and come to the seemingly incontrovertible conclusion that, metaphorically, the dining table of the west was cleared somewhere in the Roman Empire in the late fifth century and wasn't set again with food worth eating until the fourteenth when Guillaume Tirel dit Taillevent, Chef to Philip VI of Valois, Charles V, and Charles VI, placed on it his heavily spiced creations of hare in *cameline* and capon in cinnamon broth.

If the political Dark Ages began in the west with the conquest of the western Roman Empire by the barbaric hordes from the north, then judging from a close reading of the history of western cookery, the culinary Dark Ages began then, too. While plundering and ransacking, slaughter and mayhem took place outside the prototypical European kitchen door, what went on inside was presumably not much better. Indeed, it is a commonly held assumption that by the sixth century the fall from the sumptuous, if profligate, repasts of Rome to the peas porridge (hot and cold) and thick cereal-like frumenty eaten by the barbaric peasantry was total and irrevocable. And what once had been two divinely pleasurable acts, cooking and eating, were by that time reduced to necessities accomplished with rude equipment in crude surroundings by notably crude and uncivilized people.

Except for the likes of Charlemagne and a few other persons of his ilk several centuries after him, all of whom apparently dined regally in decent if messy surroundings, the rest of the western world, we are led to believe because of the apparent paucity of extant records to the contrary, for nearly seven centuries haphazardly selected and unceremoniously tossed their few vittles into a stockpot. Then they stoked up the fire and made do with the result, never once making a mental note to repeat a dish that turned out well or to improve one that hadn't.

If one goes along with this line of reasoning, easy enough to support since traditional western scholarship has unearthed very few facts to resist it, cooking was until the fourteenth century little more than a spontaneous act, based on whim and totally devoid of the order and tradition that had characterized it in Roman times. Even when fresh foods were available—eggs, cheese, butter, milk, cabbage, wild game, domesticated fowl and other livestock, legumes, fruit, and fish—using them in specific quantities and combinations to prepare particular dishes was apparently a rare occurrence during this age of culinary bleakness.

In point of fact, rare were the written recipes from before the fourteenth century that survived the next centuries to emerge from some nobleman's or monastery's library in manuscript or book form. "If only they had survived," the culinary historians lament. Even if they had been in shreds, the ink blotted, the paper rotting, they would have provided historians with some insight into the cookery of Europe in the early Middle Ages. The earliest and therefore most greatly prized recipe manuscripts and cookbooks date from the late Middle Ages: *The Book of Cury* from England, *The Viandier of Guillaume* and *Le Menagier de Paris* of the fourteenth century; the cookbooks of Platina in Italy in the fifteenth century; Rupert de Nola's in Spain and Meissispugo's *Libro Novo* in Italy in the sixteenth century.

Often considering themselves dependent on these later works plus scattered economic records, personal histories, and church documents to put together a picture of what and how Europeans ate in the Middle Ages, food historians have continued to pick over a plateful of meager historical scraps overseasoned with conjecture, dispatching in a paragraph or two any discussion of the early period. Then they have gone on to write about the verve and splendor of the late medieval coronation feasts, the low-keyed and elegant repasts of the Italian Renaissance table, the fascinating recipes and culinary skills of Chef Taillevent, and the early burgeonings of regional cuisines which inevitably followed the emergence of the nation-states of Western and Central Europe, finding in these subjects more nourishing and factually substantial historical fare. It is difficult, after all, to write history without at least a few well-documented facts to support one's contentions.

Completely overlooked as a matchless source of firsthand information about the preparation of food, food customs, and social practices in the Middle Ages have been the thousands of legal opinions written not only in the Middle Ages but in every century of our epoch by learned rabbis who were continually being called upon by members of their communities to interpret and discuss Jewish law. These opinions, known collectively as the *Responsa* (in Hebrew, *she'elot u-teshuvot*, "questions and replies"), were written in order to make the law understandable and meaningful to the people who observed it.

Because the very purpose of these rabbinic judgments was to provide a guide for daily observance, the *Responsa* constitute a cornucopia of the commonplace, which is of course precisely why they are such a treasure trove of social history. Village life, family relationships, the treatment of widows, the feeding of infants, business relationships and ethics, the price of goods in the marketplace, travel on holidays, the education of women—the thousands of *Responsa* written wherever organized Jewish communities have existed miss nary a subject, including food.

Since the Jewish dietary laws have always been so important a part of religious observance, and because the daily performance of dietary ritual has always been so susceptible to inadvertent transgression, it is not at all surprising to find that in every century since the Talmudic Age, rabbinic commentaries concerning the ritual fitness of specific foods and food combinations have been strikingly numerous. You will never find recipes in the *Responsa*, but because knowing the contents of particular dishes was a prerequisite to a rabbi's ruling on their ritual fitness, the information about specific dishes is sometimes overwhelming in its thoroughness.

Pashtet, sometimes called *pashtida* or *pastata*, is one such dish. Eleventh-century rabbinic responses contain numerous references to it, some of them written by the famed commentator, Rashi (who spent much of his life in Troyes, France), his teachers, and pupils. So do later commentaries written from Mayence to Marburg, Rome to Rothenburg, going well into the seventeenth century.

There is no way of knowing the precise origin of *pashtet*.

The word itself sounds much like the middle Latin word *pasta* (meaning dough), but references in the rabbinic sources to *pashtet* predate general references to the word *pasta*. At the same time in the region south of the Danube (now in Austria), *pashtet* was called *brietling*, a word that sounds much like the German word *brodt*, and the English word bread. Both *pashtet* and *brietling* are, of course, decidedly un-Hebraic, obvious loan words used by the rabbis (who discoursed in Hebrew) to describe a food for which there was no Hebrew word. Sketchy as these etymologies are, they do suggest an early European and non-Jewish origin for *pashtet*. Today, the word *pasteten* is used in modern German as a general name for baked pastries.

But if the origin of the dish wasn't Jewish, we know from the *Responsa* that the Jews made the dish their own, preparing, cooking, and serving it in ways emphatically Jewish, from koshering the clay vessel in which it was to be cooked to making the proper blessing for it before it could be eaten. One rabbi even commented that its appearance suggested the layers of manna that fell in Sinai and served as food for the Jews during their forty years' wandering in Biblical times.

Pashtet, the earliest sources reveal, was the name given to the dish prepared by the women of the Jewish households of Provence and the Rhenish provinces every Friday for the Sabbath, usually in pottery vessels which they often shared with their non-Jewish neighbors!

The filling for *pashtet* would be prepared by pounding and chopping various cuts of meat and combining them. Undoubtedly, goose liver was included and occasionally cow or sheep udder was used, too. Then the meat was mixed with legumes and other vegetables. Unhappily, the rabbis didn't discuss their names or quantities; but, onions, garlic, shallots, peas, and broad beans would have been the likely choices. Cinnamon, ginger, salt, and sage (even pepper in the homes of the well-to-do) might well have been used to spice the mixture; and from the vineyards of Rashi and other Jewish vintners may have come a drop or two of wine.

Then, we are told, the dough was made from flour, goose fat, and eggs. The bottom of the clay vessel was smeared with goose fat, a layer of dough spread over it, the raw filling added, and a cover of dough placed over all. The cook then pierced the dough to make a small opening which she promptly covered with a hollow egg shell in order to keep the aroma from escaping. And if she had filled the *pashtet* with chopped udder meat, she marked the dough in some specific way to signify that she had done so. With the placing of the pot lid (called a *sterzel*) over the unbaked delicacy to protect it from the elements, the cook's work was completed, for she rarely baked her own *pashtet,* preferring to take it to the *dreyfus,* the communal oven located in the center of town. There it would be baked along with the *pashteten* made by her Jewish friends and neighbors. Later, after it was partially cooked (as specified by Jewish law), it was transferred to the warming oven or hung on a chain over the embers at home until the family members were ready to enjoy it the next day at the main noontime Sabbath meal.

What is so remarkable about this dish as described in the medieval rabbinic literature is its complexity, sophistication and, above all, its obvious similarity to that most enchanting of classic French recipes, *paté en croute.* There is abundant evidence that Rashi's wife (whom he acknowledges as his source) took the same basic steps to prepare *pashtet* as did Careme six centuries later in order to bring his *pièces montées* filled with foie gras and pheasant to Talleyrand.

Also remarkable is what the commentaries tell us about the care and concern for food during a time regarded traditionally as culinarily crude and base. We can infer that there was a dough used to make bread and one used to make flaky pastry or *choux* paste for *pashtet,* and that they were notably different. It is also apparent that several varieties of meats were mixed together to enhance the flavor of a meat dish. Goose fat, tasty and pungent and from yet another kind of animal, was used to moisten the mixture as well as to add to its flavor.

Unmistakable, too, are signs of a small but functional *batterie de cuisine.* A French-Jewish household of the twelfth century was equipped with specific utensils for pounding, dicing, cutting, and scraping the udder meat to make it ritually fit and rid of its milk. There were several types of cooking vessels and lids—clay for *pashtet,* iron for pot-au-feu. Chains hung from the hearth and ovens varied in size and function.

So, in an age reputed to have been known for its culinary simplicity—let's face it, witlessness—and from a totally neglected source, comes enough evidence of creativity and resourcefulness to regard the later versions of *paté en croute*, even those from classical French cuisine, as no more (nor less) than skillful and more elegant elaborations on a very old theme.

As a postscript, it is worth mentioning that as highly valued and carefully prepared as *pashtet* was in the medieval Jewish household (and in neighboring non-Jewish ones, too), this bellwether of French cooking survives in Jewish cuisine in name only. In modern Israel, *pashtet*, sometimes called *pashtida*, is the common word for pudding, the kind of pudding that is usually made with a sweet dough formed into a dumpling and set upon cooked dried fruit to be baked overnight in a slow oven.

PASHTET

In the Middle Ages, the schmaltz for pashtet was rendered goose fat, the eggs goose eggs, and the flour whole wheat. Cow udder was the favored meat, and pepper an extravagance few medieval French Jews could afford. This recipe is a modern one, based on discussions of the dish from rabbinic sources dating from as early as the twelfth century.

Puff Paste Dough:

2 cups water
1 cup schmaltz or vegetable shortening
1 teaspoon salt
2 cups unbleached flour
8 eggs

Filling:

1 pound lean ground beef
3 cloves garlic, peeled and mashed
½ cup shallots, peeled and chopped
1 teaspoon salt
¼ teaspoon ginger
1 teaspoon black pepper
½ teaspoon powdered savory
1 teaspoon dried tarragon
3 pounds chicken livers
¼ cup dry white wine

1. In a large skillet, brown the beef, garlic, shallots, and salt. Drain off the fat.
2. Add remaining seasonings and cook over low heat for 10 minutes. Cool.
3. Broil the chicken livers, 10 minutes on each side, or until they are lightly browned.
4. Place cooked livers in a bowl and add wine. Cool.

5. Prepare the puff paste: In a small saucepan bring water, schmaltz or vegetable oil, and salt to a boil. Lower the heat and add flour. Beat with a spoon until the dough forms a ball and no longer sticks to the sides of the pan. Remove from heat. Add eggs one by one, beating until the mixture is smooth and glossy.
6. When the livers are completely cool, drain and reserve the wine. Use the steel blade of a food processor or a meat grinder to chop or grind the livers.
7. Add chopped livers and wine to the chopped meat mixture and mix well.
8. Lightly grease a 4-quart pottery, stoneware, or glass oven-proof casserole. Thickly coat the bottom and sides of the casserole with puff paste dough.
9. Add meat mixture, smoothing the top, and spread remaining puff paste over the meat, encasing the filling completely.
10. Place a hole that is one inch in diameter in the center of the dough covering. Cover with half of an empty egg shell and bake in a preheated 425-degree oven for 20 minutes. Reduce heat to 325 degrees and bake for an additional 20 minutes. Serve hot or cold.

Makes 8 servings.

Passover

This important festival, like all the other major Jewish festivals, has ancient agricultural roots which predate its connection to the Exodus, as well as deep historical and spiritual roots. Its multiplicity of names reflects its diverse and ancient origins.

The eight-day festival (in Israel, seven days) which comes in the spring of the year (beginning on the fifteenth day of Nissan) is called Hag ha-Pesach, or Festival of the Paschal Offering, because the day in ancient times was marked by offering as a sacrifice the first offspring of the season. In a land of sheep and goat herders this would have been a lamb or young goat. The name Passover is linked to this sacrificial practice since it was the blood from these sacrificed animals that Moses told the Israelites to smear upon their doorposts in order to serve as a signal to God to pass over their homes "when He smote the Egyptians . . . " (Exodus 12:27).

The festival is also called Hag ha-Matzot or Festival of the Unleavened Bread. The festival in ancient times came at the end of a growing season, and just as young animals became the sacrifice of those who made their living from husbandry, grain became the sacrifice of farmers. Later, when the holiday became linked to the historical events of the Biblical Exodus, the bread eaten was matzah, the same kind of unleavened bread that had been eaten in haste during the Israelites' Exodus from Egypt.

Central to the observance of Passover is the theme of redemption—the historical redemption of the ancient Israelites who escaped from slavery in Egypt, wandered in the desert for forty years, and finally came to the Promised Land, and the redemption of all Jews who have met with adversity. The story of this redemption is told on the first two evenings of the holiday at a service conducted not at the synagogue but around the dining table. The service, detailed in a narrative of the Exodus called the Haggadah, has a specific and unvarying order. The service and the meal which is eaten during it are called the Seder, the Hebrew word for order. The Seder has fifteen parts, each of them symbolizing an aspect of the story of the Exodus.

In ancient times during the period of the First and Second Temple, immense crowds of worshippers gathered in Jerusalem to perform the paschal sacrifice and then, in large groups, roast the lamb or goat over pomegranate wood in special Passover ovens. Then they ate pieces of the roasted animal along with small cakes of matzah. They also ate bitter herbs to symbolize the bitter times endured by the early Israelites during their enslavement.

After the destruction of the Second Temple, the paschal offering ceased and a roasted egg (*bay'tza* or *chagigah*) became presented as a symbolic offering to Seder participants along with a roasted bone, called the *ze'ro'a;* the *ze'ro'a* symbolized the lamb itself. Rarely were the two ever eaten at the Seder; and, in fact, in many Jewish communities of the world following a custom of post-Second Temple origin, a lamb is never prepared to be eaten at the festive Seder meal. Yet in others it is considered a delicacy.

Today, invariably, each Seder table is set with specific foods and enough wine to provide each participant the four cups required by the Haggadah. On a large plate, or, as the Jews of Yemenite background do, on a mat of lettuce leaves and other leafy greens, are the symbolic Passover foods: *maror,* the bitter herbs, usually horseradish, endive, or radishes; *haroset,* a sweet mixture of fruit, nuts, spices, and wine, that symbolizes the clay and mortar with which the enslaved Israelites built the huge edifices of Egypt; the *ze'ro'a* and *bay'tza;* the *karpas,* usually parsley or celery, to symbolize the springtime season; and salt water to symbolize the bitter tears of those who were enslaved.

Another plate holds three matzot which, according to custom, represent the three divisions within the House of Israel: Cohan, Levite, and Israelite. A large piece of the middle matzah, the afikomen, another symbol of the paschal sacrifice, is customarily set aside early in the Seder to be "stolen" from the leader of the Seder by all the young children present and held in ransom until the very end of the Seder. Then it is redeemed with presents or money by the leader who passes pieces of it to everyone, making it the last morsel eaten at the Seder. The afikomen (a word of Greek origin thought to refer to the after-dinner entertainment at a banquet) has been invested with magical powers throughout its long history.

All of the other dishes, and there are many, are the outcome of the wedding of Passover law and local custom. Forbidden during the Passover week are leavening of any kind, grain except in the form of matzah or matzah meal, and the legumes from which bread can be made. In addition, the Jews of European background do not eat rice.

The foods of the Seder plate do not vary from community to community; haroseth ingredients, however, will vary somewhat.

Traditional Jews would find a Passover without a long list of special delicacies no Passover at all. On that list in the homes of Jews of European (Ashkanazic) background would be matzah balls, gefilte fish with *chrain* (horseradish), chicken soup, *rosl* borscht with or without meat, eggs in salt water, fried matzah, matzah puddings, and a huge number of baked or fried pastries that are made by substituting matzah, matzah meal, potato flour, nuts, and even carrots for the usual wheat flour. These include *chremslach,* matzah pancakes called *pompeshkes, ingberlach,* and carrot *pletzlach.* Years ago, the major drink of the Passover week in Eastern Europe was *vishniak,* a cherry liqueur made especially for Passover. Now it is less popular.

The Passover cookery of the Sephardim also makes good use of nuts, usually almonds in various torten and marzipan confections. Other specialties include pickled turnips, lamb stew, vegetable omelets, and raisin wine.

Pastrami

Chewy, tangy, and peppery, tingly on the tongue, glorious between two slices of Jewish rye already slathered with mustard, pastrami (say *pas—tra—me*), like corned beef and chicken soup with matzah balls, is Jewish soul food with a vengeance. Even a Jew who has almost forsaken Judaism will hang on to a lingering religious identification by sinking his or her teeth into a thick slab of pastrami, followed by enthusiastic munchings of a good kosher dill.

That "i" at the end makes pastrami look and sound like an Italian convert. But its origin is Jewish-Roumanian and its older relative is a heavily spiced marinated meat dish native to Turkey and the Caucasus called *basturma.*

PASTRAMI

For this recipe, you will need to use a smoker. The small electric smokers sold at specialty kitchen equipment stores do an excellent job of smoking pastrami.

3-pound piece of beef brisket
10 small cloves garlic
4 tablespoons whole coriander seeds
4 tablespoons whole peppercorns
2 teaspoons salt
½ cup vegetable oil
2 tablespoons brown sugar
¼ cup tarragon vinegar
1 teaspoon allspice

1. Trim most of the fat off the meat. Place 6-inch deep gashes in the meat at even intervals.
2. Mash the garlic and crush peppercorns and coriander seeds. (Do not use ground pepper or coriander.) Mix the garlic, crushed pepper, coriander, and salt together, and spread the mixture over both top and bottom surfaces of the meat and into the gashes.
3. Place in a roasting pan or glass container (don't use plastic unless you want your container to retain a lingering aroma of garlic) and refrigerate overnight.
4. Mix remaining ingredients together and pour over meat. Marinate for an additional 24 hours.
5. After marinating period is over, remove meat from marinade and pat dry. Place in smoker on the middle rack, and smoke for 1 hour or until meat has been cooked by the smoking process. Do not let the meat dry out.
6. Slice and serve.

Pletzel

Pletzel rhymes with pretzel and in some culinary circles is known by its older name, *bretzel.*

There is nothing pretzel-shaped or tasting about a *pletzel.* A *pletzel* is a flat piece of dough (called in the United States an onion flat) which when overbaked or stale tastes and behaves on the tongue and teeth as though it were made from the inedible wooden plank from which it derives its name. In the same vein, in some areas of Poland, little flat breads, *pletzlech,* used to be called *shilgelech,* a variation of *shildelech,* the diminutive of the word for shields or plates.

Plucked fresh from a hot oven and attacked while still warm by a good set of teeth set in a jaw that has chomped through endless numbers of water bagels and survived without dislocation, the warm *pletzel* while far from tender (it's obstinate, in fact) is unqualified pleasure, a true Jewish delicacy, a bread with guts.

The recipe for *pletzel* has not varied in seven hundred

years. Pieces of yeast dough are rolled thin, sprinkled with a mixture of chopped onions, poppy seeds, and coarse salt, and are baked until the dough becomes crusty and the topping has browned enough to look as if it might burn if left to bake one minute longer.

Such is the lore of the *pletzel* that eating the onion-covered bread requires a ceremonious smear of schmaltz (chicken fat) or cream cheese over its horizontal entirety to be really enjoyed, anything less constituting culinary boorishness. Eaten nowadays whenever the mood strikes, in medieval times a large *pletzel* or two was distributed to guests who attended the feast following a ritual circumcision.

PLETZEL

1 cup warm (not hot) water
1½ teaspoons salt
1 tablespoon sugar
1 tablespoon vegetable oil
2 packages dry yeast (2 tablespoons)
2 eggs
4 to 5 cups all-purpose flour, sifted
4 cups chopped white or yellow onions
1 tablespoon dry poppy seeds
2 tablespoons vegetable oil
1 teaspoon salt
¼ teaspoon ground black pepper.

1. In a large bowl, mix water, salt, sugar, and 1 tablespoon oil. Sprinkle yeast into mixture. Add 1 egg. Add 3 cups flour gradually, stirring to mix.
2. Add additional cup of flour and knead dough until it is smooth and elastic. Cover and set in warm place until doubled in size, about 1 hour.
3. Meanwhile, chop onions. Strain liquid and discard.
4. In a large frying pan, heat 2 tablespoons vegetable oil. Add onions and sauté for 10 minutes. Remove from heat and add poppy seeds, salt, and pepper.
5. To make small rolls, break off golf-ball size pieces of dough. Roll out on floured board to ⅛-inch thickness. Brush with beaten egg. Spread onion in the center of each flat piece of dough. To make large flats, divide dough into four pieces before rolling each piece to a flat circle or rectangle.

6. Preheat oven to 350 degrees. Place rolls on well-greased baking pans. Pierce all but edges with a fork. Bake for 35 to 40 minutes or until onions become brown and the crusts crisp and golden brown.

Pomegranate

In any American supermarket, D'anjou pears are piled halfway to the ceiling, the fat Concords and Ribier clusters bulge up and out of their plastic wrappings, and the Stayman, McIntosh, and Red Delicious vie for appetizing attention. And over in the darkest corner of the produce section, stuck between the boxed garlic buds and the collard greens, are the rouge-red globes that in ancient times would have been given the center spot.

Tough, leathery to the touch, the skin of each clutches too tightly to its cache of tiny red pips, making the surface strained looking and bumpy, mottled red like an old vagrant's face, ugly, unsymmetrical, and unloved. No matter that the fruit's innards glisten with blood-red seeds locked together, ripe for sucking. Mostly neglected and ignored nowadays, the outer skins will soon shrink and the seeds dry out. The withering globes will soon attract no one save the clerk who throws them away.

Yet life in ancient Israel must have been suffused with the scarlet juice pressed from those tiny seeds. From the hills of Judea to the coasts of all of its surrounding seas, great and small, the silent winds must have wafted the fragrance of bell-shaped blossoms into every dwelling, every field, every forest, making of ancient Israel as much an orchard of pomegranates as it was a land of milk and honey.

Representations of the pomegranate were skillfully woven into the robe of Aaron in colors of blue, purple, and scarlet, the Bible says in Exodus 28:33, interspersed and surrounded with bells of gold. Pomegranates of brass were fashioned onto the pillars of Solomon's great Temple in Jerusalem (Kings 7:18, 42), visual reminders of the land where the Lord had brought the ancient Israelites, the place of "wheat and barley," where fig trees and pomegranates grew, "a land of olive trees and honey; a land wherein thou shalt not lack any thing in it; . . . " (Deuteronomy 8:8).

Circling, encircling each priestly robe were pomegranates of colored thread. Circling, encircling each column of the Temple were pomegranates of brass in endless chains, two hundred of them on each massive treelike column. They would have gleamed in the white light of the Jerusalem sun, bedazzling and then reminding the viewer of the red essence that was as satisfying to the thirst as water, as piquant to the appetite as wine.

The taste lingered on the palate, the look enticed. Like no other fruit the essence of it enveloped the soul, making into sweet, sensual poetry all description of it, the words flowing in rivulets, sung, spoken, and then finally written down, blessedly, to delight and console:

> Thy lips are like a thread of scarlet,
> And thy mouth is comely,
> Thy temples are like a pomegranate split open
> Behind thy veil. (Song of Songs 4:3)

And,

> Let him bring a silver cup from the melter, fill it with the kernels of a red pomegranate, surround it with a crown of red roses, and put it between the sun and shade. He will then sense in its brilliance the beauty of Johanan.

Love poetry from the Song of Songs and a description of a person of great beauty from the Talmud so elegantly befitted a food whose very appearance in ancient days reminded one of the richness and abundance that life offered. The theme is constant in nearly every book of the Bible in which the pomegranate is mentioned, leaving a legacy in later generations which invariably links the pomegranate to romantic love and good health.

In Jewish folklore, drinking its juice has traditionally ensured fertility and a life brimming over with health and well being. In fact, with seeds that according to Kabbalistic tradition numbered 613 per fruit, the number equal to the commandments (mitzvot) derived from the Torah, it is the perfect fruit.

No ancient recipe comes down to us, but from the twelfth

century comes a recipe for an elixir concocted by Maimonides for his most famous patient, Saladin. The great Jewish physician and man of letters instructed that it be sipped following the bath, before making love, or falling asleep. This recipe, which was based on a Middle Eastern concoction and also circulated rather widely in Europe after the Crusades, calls for "pomegranate seeds, sugar, and hot spices" like clove or mace, or a syrup of roses or sorrel, with water of ox tongue.

MAIMONIDES' POMEGRANATE ELIXIR

The sugar, water, and spices combine to make a syrup similar to Maimonides' preferred rose syrup.

1½ cups water
1 cup sugar
½ teaspoon cinnamon
¼ teaspoon nutmeg
¼ teaspoon mace
4 whole cloves
1 tablespoon fresh lemon juice
1 quart fresh pomegranate juice made from 10 to 12 pomegranates

1. In a large pot combine water, sugar, and all spices. Bring to boil and gently simmer for 10 minutes. Remove the cloves.
2. Cut the pomegranates in half and squeeze the juice from them. Extract the juice from the lemon.
3. Add lemon and pomegranate juice to the spiced hot syrup. Bring to slow boil, then simmer 2 minutes.
4. Serve warm with a lemon wedge for each glass.

P'tscha

P'tscha is hot broth, gone cold.

A dish that in the Middle Ages was commonly called *gele* or *gelatina* and is now called aspic has been called for hundreds of years in the Yiddish-speaking world of Eastern Europe *p'tscha* (say *peh—chá*), *fisnogen*, or *cholodnyetz*. *P'tscha*, piquant and tart and made even more so by the traditional sprinkle of lemon juice over each slice, was once a typical first course of a Friday evening meal. But as years of this century pass, *p'tscha* falls deeper and deeper into culinary obscurity.

Particularly in the United States among the younger generations of Jews born in this country, *p'tscha* wins no popularity contest. But there is every reason to believe that at one time it was well-loved, especially in those climes cold enough to solidify it into the slightly quivering, gelatinous mass that distinguishes it from the rich broth it would be if placed over a fire and heated.

Five hundred years ago, the Italian gourmet, Platina, made *gelatina* from the meat of forty sheep feet, "the sharpest vinegar," white wine, water, and salt. Today, wherever there are Jews still interested in making it, the best *p'tscha* is made in virtually the same way (minus 39 feet), seasoned with cloves and pepper and molded into a dish along with slices of hard-boiled egg.

A clue to *p'tscha*'s medieval origins is the addition of an unusual ingredient—calves tongues—once as popular in the cuisine of Northern Europe in the Middle Ages as chicken livers are in our own.

Fish is also used to make a *p'tscha* but never in one that already has meat in it. The fish, traditionally carp, substitutes for the meat while all the other ingredients remain the same.

P'TSCHA

Most kosher butchers sell the calves feet and tongues used traditionally in this extremely interesting dish.

2 small calves tongues
6 pieces calves feet—about 1½ pounds
1 medium onion, peeled
½ teaspoon whole cloves
1 teaspoon salt
1 teaspoon whole pepper
1 bay leaf
2 tablespoons lemon juice
½ cup white wine
2 tablespoons white vinegar
Water to cover
1 teaspoon granulated sugar
3 egg whites, beaten well but not dry
2 hard-boiled eggs

1. Combine all ingredients but sugar, egg whites, and hard-boiled eggs in a large pot and simmer until liquid is reduced by half. Strain through a very fine sieve.

2. Remove the meat from the bones and cut into small pieces. Discard bones. Peel the calves tongues, and discard the peel.
3. Add half of the meat to the broth, and refrigerate overnight. Refrigerate remaining half of meat in a separate bowl.
4. On the following day, skim off all the fat. Bring broth to a boil. Add a teaspoon of sugar and 3 beaten egg whites.
5. Boil rapidly for 15 minutes. Skim and stir constantly. Taste for tartness and add more vinegar if needed. Strain liquid through the sieve.
6. Wet a small mold with about an inch of clear jelly, and chill. When it is well chilled, add pieces of meat, 2 sliced hard-boiled eggs, remaining jelly with meat, and the less clear jelly, to give the mold a layered effect.
7. Chill overnight. Unmold and serve on lettuce leaves, garnished with tomatoes and cucumbers.

Makes 6 servings.

Pumpernickel

So strict were bread-making regulations centuries ago in England and France that barely anything went into a loaf. And the Jews, careful about food anyway, produced *pain ordinaire* for everyday consumption or challot for the Sabbath that were usually simple but tasty examples of the baker's stock-in-trade.

In Central and Eastern Europe, life was a lot less organized. There were no regulations for a baker to heed, no complicated judicial procedures to fear if a baker decided to produce a bread that was the outcome of his or her enthusiasm for the task.

Presumably, what mattered most in Western Europe was who controlled and profited from selling bread and, to a lesser extent, the quality of the finished product. What mattered most to the medieval bakers of Eastern Europe was the taste and staying quality of the bread itself. Unorganized and not limited to using specific quantities of a very limited number of ingredients, they threw all but the kitchen sink (in the Middle Ages there were none of these anyway) into the dough and hoped for a favorable outcome.

For us, living in this age of culinary internationalism, this means that we can choose recipes from several basic bread-baking traditions. One tradition has produced such pristine formulas as brioche and puff pastry—recipes that call for only a few ingredients which must be measured out very carefully. Another has given to the world traditional loaves following rules for their baking set down in Biblical times. Yet another tradition has given pumpernickel to the world, the most striking example of culinary anarchy around.

In fact, the more that goes into a recipe for the clutter called pumpernickel, and the less "pure" it becomes, the better it gets. Molasses, vinegar, coffee, even cocoa lose their identity and become undetectable in the finished product. The white flour gets swallowed up, the fennel seeds just tweak the taste buds, and the onion gives only a hint of its presence.

A medieval Englishman would have cried "Adulteration," after tasting a good piece of pumpernickel. "Who can tell what is in this bread." The bakers, if they had been English, might have lost their jobs, while Russian, Polish, German, or Jewish ones would have gone on merrily producing the staff of life, giving it all that they had.

PUMPERNICKEL BREAD

2 packages active dry yeast
½ cup lukewarm water
2 cups lukewarm coffee
1 tablespoon sugar
1 tablespoon salt
¼ cup oil
¼ cup molasses
2 tablespoons white vinegar
¼ cup cocoa (optional)
2 tablespoons caraway seeds
1 teaspoon onion powder or minced onions (optional)
1 teaspoon fennel seeds
4 cups rye flour
5½ cups all-purpose flour

1. In a large bowl soften yeast in water. Stir in coffee, sugar, salt, oil, molasses, vinegar, cocoa, caraway seeds, onion powder, and fennel seeds.
2. Gradually blend in rye flour and enough all-purpose flour to form a stiff dough.

3. Knead dough on a heavily floured surface until smooth and elastic, about 10 minutes. Place dough in a greased bowl and turn to grease top. Let rise, covered, in a warm place until doubled in bulk, about 1½ hours.
4. Punch down and knead on a floured board. Divide dough into two pieces. Shape each piece into a smooth ball.
5. Place dough into two greased 9-inch pie pans. Cut a crisscross in the top of each. Let rise, covered, in a warm place until doubled in bulk, about 45 minutes.
6. Bake in a preheated moderate oven (350 degrees) for 45 to 50 minutes, or until loaves sound hollow when tapped. Cool thoroughly on a rack before slicing.

Makes 2 round loaves.

Pupik

"In matters of taste and smell don't argue" says an old Hebrew proverb—inspiration for its utterance, perhaps, the munching of a *pupik* (say *pu,* as in put—*pick*), that small morsel of a fowl's innards called a gizzard in English.

Certain portions of edible animals are ritually unfit. But what is not, particularly if the eater is poor, is absolutely edible. So it is not at all surprising that several of the best Jewish dishes are made from giblets or organ meats, especially liver and less especially kishke, helzel, and *pupikes.*

An edible *pupik* is a tough little customer, designed to help digest, not to be digested. Yet when softened in a bath of oniony broth, powdered with a dusting of spice, and then mixed with a helping of fresh noodles, to only a die-hard vegetarian could the taste of a *pupik* be a debatable matter.

SPICED PUPIKES

3 pounds chicken giblets (gizzards and necks)
Water to cover
2 or 3 medium onions, diced
2 teaspoons paprika
¼ teaspoon black pepper
Salt to taste
Garlic salt to taste

1. Wash giblets and put in a pot with water to cover. Bring water to a boil and allow to cook for 10 to 15 minutes.
2. Pour off water and wash residue off the pot and giblets. Replace only the gizzards in the pot, cover with water, and add onions.
3. Bring water to a boil, then cover pot and simmer for 1 hour. At the end of 1 hour, add necks, recover pot and simmer for another hour.
4. After second hour, add paprika, black pepper, salt, and garlic salt. Allow giblets and seasonings to cook for at least 30 minutes more.

If using only giblets, 2 pounds serves 6 persons.

Purim

More than two thousand years ago Haman, a man remembered by Jewish people everywhere as the villainous chief minister to King Ahasuerus of Persia, cast lots (called purim in Hebrew) to determine the date on which all the Jews of the kingdom would be put to death. But Queen Esther, a Jew, was able to convince the king that he had to spare her people, and thus Haman's plot was thwarted.

The dramatic story of Purim appears in the Book of Esther in the Bible. The Megillah (as the Book of Esther is called in Hebrew) is chanted each year on the thirteenth day of the Hebrew month Adar amid great noisemaking, merriment, and revelry, the events related in it symbolic of all of the many struggles between the Jews and the various enemies who have sought to destroy them. The festival was observed first in Persia and from there spread to other Jewish centers.

The customs associated with the holiday are fascinating. Influenced by Christian carnivals, European Jews of the Middle Ages turned Purim into as boisterous a festival as Mardi Gras. Particularly in Italy was the Purim carnival tradition strong. Its legacy: the children's masquerade, usually a long processional through the synagogue of children dressed up as personages in the Biblical story; the obligation, although few accept it, to drink wine and liquor until one can no longer tell the difference between a description of cursed Haman and Esther's stalwart relative, Mordecai; and the incredible din as the Book of Esther is read. Everywhere, in every synagogue, as Haman's name is read, the congregants shake noisemakers called groggers, shout boos and jeers, all to blot out the villain's name. And finally, there is the food, pastries mostly, symbolic of some aspect of the story of Purim.

Messeket Purim, a thirteenth- or early fourteenth-century parody written by the chief exponent of the Purim parody tradition, Kalonymos b. Kalonymos, mentions almost thirty different dishes to be eaten on Purim. One, sounding suspiciously like chicken soup, is also to be dived into in search of the piece of meat cooked with it. The other foods, mentioned in this early work, included gingerbread, turtledoves, pancakes, small tarts, chestnuts, roast goose, stuffed pigeons, ducks, partridges, ragouts, venison, quails, macaroons, salads, chicken, swans, macaroni, young turkeys, and bucks.

With each passing century the list of Purim foods became longer and longer, the traditions becoming as plentiful as the foods themselves. In some countries and among certain communities, Purim remains the biggest gastronomical event of the year.

The seventeenth-century dish called *Megillah-Kroyt,* literally Book of Esther-*kraut,* was made of sauerkraut, raisins, and sugar and served on Purim eve. From the same period, in Europe the women braided challah loaves, shaped to symbolize the ropes on which Haman was hanged. And gradually many food traditions developed: kreplach; Haman's ears (Oznei Haman), fried to a golden brittle doneness; Hamantaschen, Haman's pockets full of mohn (poppy seeds); *mohnplatzen,* cut square cookies covered with poppy seeds to symbolize Haman's pockets full of bribes or purim (lots), Haman's hat, his coat, or nose. In the Middle East there are *gorayebeh,* sweet cookies shaped into bracelets representing Esther's jewelry; halvah; honey cakes; *challot* shaped like turbans; and pastries shaped into miniature Esthers, Mordecais, and Hamans.

R

Rosh Hashonah

This day is holy unto the Lord your God, mourn not, nor weep.

(Nehemiah 8:9)

"Eat the fat," Nehemiah said. "Drink the sweet." Send portions to those who have nothing to eat. Celebrate, for this day is a holy one. On the day called Rosh Hashonah, literally, the head of the year, eating is as holy an act as praying. Sitting down to a splendidly laid table to welcome the new year is as meaningful as hearing the piercing sound of the shofar (ram's horn) in the synagogue.

The Rosh Hashonah "board" may groan under the plentitude of it all, yet gluttony has no place at a Rosh Hashonah meal. Tradition does. Remarkably in keeping with the words of Nehemiah, the foods traditionally eaten on this day are either fat, sweet, or are linked to various folk beliefs which have as their source other passages from the Bible and ancient rabbinic literature.

Ashkanazic and Sephardic traditions and food customs for Rosh Hashonah are quite similar. The "fat" is usually a roasted fowl or roast of lamb, preceded by chicken soup. And, of course, the "fat" can be interpreted as referring to the abundance of the entire festival meal and not just one food.

The sweetness of all sweet Rosh Hashonah foods is honey, served with a plate of sliced apples or pieces of challah. Dipped into the honey, the apples thickly coated with the honey become a symbol of the Garden of Eden; the bread dipped into the honey is symbolic of the longed-for sweetness of the year to come, a culinary metaphor for all of one's aspirations.

The sweet new year is also ushered in with foods prepared with honey as a major ingredient. Honey cakes (*lekach* and *lebkuchen*) and *teyglach*, baked dough dipped in honey, are the most popular of these sweet foods with Jews of European background. Baklava and *kadaif* are the traditional sweet pastries of Rosh Hashonah in the Middle East. Sweet fish dishes, honey-glazed carrots, beets, and beans are also popular.

There is a very old and rare custom of serving the head of a fish at the festival evening meal, brought to the table in remembrance of the sacrifice of Isaac, an event which according to tradition took place on Rosh Hashonah, the head of the year. Less frequently, since Isaac's ransom was a ram, a ram's or sheep's head is served to symbolize the sacrifice.

Since Rosh Hashonah is also a harvest festival, it is customary to bless a new fruit of the season. In the communities of North Africa and the Middle East, the fruit may be a fig, pomegranate, or melon; in Europe and North America, the apple or pear is usually served. Sometimes the fruits are eaten raw. Just as often they are stirred into a compote or tzimmes mixed with cardamom, cinnamon, sugar, and raisins and stuffed into a strudel, or layered into a kuchen or *fluden* along with sweetened cheese.

The festival bread, challah, is made for blessing and eating at the evening meal, shaped according to traditions dating from the Middle Ages. In certain Orthodox communities, one food is customarily avoided: nuts. Jewish mystical belief places great emphasis on the numerical equivalences of Hebrew words. Each Hebrew letter has its own numerical equivalent. *Egoz*, the Hebrew word for nut, is numerically close in value to *het*, meaning sin. Therefore, the two are related in a divine way. Particularly on Rosh Hashonah, the mystics have always felt, the time of the year when God's judgment will determine one's fate for the coming year, the divine relationship of words should not be ignored.

Rosl

Sometimes asking a simple question elicits anything but a simple answer. Some years ago, as part of the extensive information gathering activities connected to the eventual publication of a geographical atlas of the Yiddish language, a researcher asked a group of speakers of fluent Yiddish the deceptively simple question, *"Voz iz a rosl?"* (say *r-r-r-awsol*)—What is a *rosl*?—and needed a computer to sort out the answers.

"Soup with meat."

"Soup with beets and meat."

"Gravy."

"Tart gravy."

"Brine for pickling beets."

"Brine for pickling cabbage."

"Not just brine, but really sour brine."

"A sour."

"Beets in water, naturally fermented."

If the people who responded to the researcher's query had sat in a room talking about the meaning of the word *rosl*, the discussion might have gone like this:

"What is a *rosl*? That's easy," said the first. "It's what we in Pinsk used to eat for lunch in summer: a soup made with beets."

"Ridiculous," said the second. "In my village near Brest, there wasn't a beet in *rosl*. Only meat. My mother is turning over in her grave right now listening to you!"

"Come, come," said the third, "a *rosl* isn't soup at all, only the plain gravy from a piece of roast meat. That's what we called *rosl* in Kiev where I grew up."

"Gravy. Yes. That's what *rosl* is. Nice tart, slightly salty meat gravy," said the fourth, a former resident of Minsk, "not just plain gravy."

"But in Poland we called pickled beets *rosl*," said the fifth, growing thoroughly confused.

"And in Zitomir a *rosl* hadn't a beet in it," said the sixth, exasperated. "Other vegetables, cabbage and turnips, yes. But no beets."

Between the computer and the researcher, both of Solomonic temperament, the matter was settled in a manner reminiscent of a story from the fictional Chelm. Everyone, of course, was correct; the answer was determined by which one of the three distinctively different streams of Yiddish the interviewee spoke—Eastern, Central, or Northeastern—the categories determined to a great extent by geography and to a lesser extent by historical developments of the past seven centuries.

In North America, a hamburger is a hamburger is a hamburger. But in Eastern Europe a dish of *rosl* in a Jewish home of 60 years ago or even 250 years ago could be anything from a bowl of steaming hot soup which had a few ripe, red beets mixed into it, to a gravy from a piece of roasted meat (the meat itself called *roslfleysch*), to a dish of brined or naturally fermented beets, eaten especially on Passover, a custom which arose to call attention to mainstream Judaism's opposition to the Karaite practice of prohibiting the eating of *all* fermented food and drink on Passover. The traditional rabbinic practice prohibits just the eating of leavened bread on that holiday and the grains and legumes from which bread can be made.

In Polish, the source of the Yiddish word *rosl, rosol* (pronounced *rosow*), generally has seven meanings, a fact which probably accounts in part for the multiplicity of its meanings in Yiddish. Noteworthy is the absence of brined but otherwise uncooked meat from any description of a *rosl* as it would be prepared in a Jewish home. The rules of kashrut do not specifically forbid the eating of uncooked meat. But, since Jews customarily cook meat before eating it, it is not surprising to find that a Polish *rosol* will contain pieces of brined lamb or veal or a Russian *rosolye* will be made with pieces of beef, veal, or lamb, mixed with pickled cucumbers and beets, while a traditional Jewish *rosl* omits uncooked meat of any kind.

ROSL FROM BREST

This is a *rosl* made from naturally fermented beets. After the beets have been left to ferment for a month, they can be added to soups, eaten cold, or be used as the vegetable stock base for a hot soup or borscht to which meat or other vegetables are added.

6 to 8 large beets | **Water, boiled and cooled**

1. Remove tops and scrub beets thoroughly, removing every speck of dirt. Then peel, quarter, and place in a very clean, large earthenware crock, jar, or sterilized canning jars.
2. Completely cover beets with boiled water that has been cooled to lukewarm.
3. Seal tightly and leave to ferment at room temperature for one month.

ROSL FROM MINSK

This recipe is a modified "sour." The sauerkraut and pickles have been brined but not the beets. The outcome is a dish of marinated vegetables.

5 beets
3 large potatoes
2 carrots
1 cup sauerkraut
3 dill pickles, sliced crosswise
1 tablespoon caraway seeds
5 scallions, diced
¼ cup vegetable or olive oil
Salt and pepper to taste

1. Peel and cook the beets, potatoes, and carrots separately; cut into small pieces.
2. Add sauerkraut, dill pickles, caraway seeds, and scallions.
3. Add vegetable or olive oil and mix. Season with salt and pepper to taste.

Roslfleysch

Where in a *roslfleysch* (say *rawsol—flaysh*) are a *tscholent*'s rib-sticking, tummy extending combination of beans, eggs, chicken, and beef; the insouciance of a braised leek and the pinch of cumin of an Italian ragout; the Madeira, parsley, shallots, and orange peel of a hearty beef a la mode?

No mushrooms of a *stroganoff* lace its gravy. Nor is there so much as a hint of dill, a slosh in the pot of a cup of Burgundy, or some brazenly added teaspoon of hot chili pepper. There are no pieces of spicy beef sausage (chorizos or salami), as in a pot of *matambre.* And the spices, the cloves and cinnamon, have been left out too for no Middle Eastern kibbe is this dish either.

One searches in vain for a tomato, a carrot, a cabbage leaf, a raisin, olive or green pepper, a caper, pine nut or coriander leaf. What, the incredulous now ask, could be in the dish to make it worth eating?

In short, a *roslfleysch* is Jewish cooking at its simplest. Elaborate it is not, complicated it is certainly not. Hearty and filling it definitely is. And, surprisingly, with apparently so little to recommend it, *roslfleysch* is good. Once the tangy dish was the most popular meat dish among millions of Jews, the ones who lived in Russia's vast Ukraine until thousands of them migrated to Western Europe and North and South America early in this century.

Sometimes *roslfleysch* is prepared so that it comes to the table looking as if the meat has been converted to charcoal in some earlier epoch. But its appearance shouldn't deceive, for the taste makes *roslfleysch* a worthy competitor for sauerbraten or beef *bourguignonne.*

ROSLFLEYSCH

2 large onions, sliced
2 cloves garlic, minced
3 tablespoons vegetable oil
3 to 4 pounds chuck steak or fillets
2 tablespoons wine vinegar (optional)
1 tablespoon brown sugar (optional)
½ teaspoon salt
2 bay leaves
½ cup water
4 potatoes, quartered

1. In a large Dutch oven, brown the meat, onions, and garlic in the oil.
2. Add all the remaining ingredients except the potatoes. Cover; reduce heat. Simmer for 1 hour.
3. Add the potatoes. Simmer covered 1 hour longer, or until meat is tender.

Serves 6 to 8.

S

Sabbo

Sometimes a food is not nearly as interesting as the people who make it. So it is with *sabbo* (say *sah* to rhyme with ma—*bow* to rhyme with low).

In little villages that dot Ethiopia's grassy highlands, many of them situated only a few miles from the spot where the surging waters of the Blue Nile spill into Lake Tana, live the Jews who make *sabbo,* preparing this flat and brittle whole wheat Sabbath bread over an open fire each Friday morning for the evening Sabbath meal. Calling themselves the Beta Yisroel (the house of Israel)—although the world stubbornly clings to the term Falasha to describe these handsome people—they work, study, pray, cook, and eat in much the same way their ancient forebears did thousands of years ago, practicing Judaism as if they lived in the first century and not the twentieth.

According to one tradition, the Beta Yisroel came to Ethiopia from the ancient land of Israel with Menelike, son of Solomon, in the tenth century b.c.e. According to another theory concerning their background, the Beta Yisroel crossed the Red Sea from the Arabian peninsula in the years that followed the destruction of the Second Temple (66 c.e.) and over the centuries were gradually pushed into living in the highland areas by the Coptic Christian population who greatly outnumbered them, even in ancient times.

There, for at least twenty centuries and perhaps many more, they have lived a pastoral life that superficially resembles the life of non-Jewish Ethiopian peasants but which is vastly different in religious custom and observance. They have been almost totally untouched by the profound developments of the Jewish religion that have taken place since the Second Temple's destruction—the compilation of the Talmud and the writing of the vast compendium of rabbinic legal responses and interpretations, an evolutionary process which goes on to this day—and remain relegated to a lowly peasant status which has isolated them from most of their own countrymen as well.

The Beta Yisroel, like their non-Jewish neighbors, may speak Amharic, work the land as tenant farmers, and read the Bible in Ge'ez (the sacred language of the Coptic Christian church) but they practice monogamy exclusively, celebrate the Sabbath by praying in the synagogue, and practice the Jewish dietary laws as outlined in the Bible.

They also celebrate the holidays of Yom Kippur, Passover, Rosh Hashonah, and Sukkot, fast on Tisha B'av and the Fast of Esther, but do not celebrate Chanukah or Purim. It is because they do not celebrate the latter two holidays that historians place the group's dispersion from ancient Israel as taking place before the second century when these two holidays were included in the regular celebration cycle of the Jewish year.

They also prepare *sabbo,* a bread eaten only at the Sabbath meal. *Sabbo* is a curious food, not at all like a loaf of challah, the Sabbath bread made by most of the Jews of the world. Rather than being cooked in an oven like challah or on a griddle like the staple Ethiopian bread, *injera,* the *sabbo* dough is cooked over an open fire inside a casing of dry leaves. The finished bread is crusty on the outside and undercooked on the inside, its taste no match for the importance given it by this exotic group of African Jews.

Salt

In every age but our own, salt has been valued as highly as life itself. It has symbolized nothing less than absolute strength, power and wisdom, lasting friendship, sexual prowess and wealth, spiritual dynamism and eternal life. And to think that we have come to fear eating too much of it in the same way our forebears came to fear not eating it, not carrying it in the pockets, and not shaking it over their shoulders.

Modern English is sprinkled with etymological and linguistic remnants of salt's former importance: the word salary meant originally to be worth one's salt, in other words, worthy of a day's pay. The word salacious harkens back to salt's being connected to sexuality. Then there is the word cellar which actually once meant salt, so that to say salt cellar really is to say "salt-salt." And, in our culture, a person without salt is insipid and colorless, a "salty" person is one given to pungent or racy speech.

Yet these terms are no more than skeletal remains of a once vital and thriving body of religious beliefs, customs, and superstitions concerning salt, preserved in writings as disparate as *The Odyssey* and the Bible, the leaves of ancient Egyptian papyri and scholarly Jewish books, legends and stories. Truly astonishing is the importance peoples of all ages save our own have given to the substance.

The earliest Jewish references come, of course, from the Bible. The most important of these concerns the covenant of salt (symbolic of salt's capacity as preservative), made between God and the people of Israel (Numbers 18:19); the most colorful, the transformation of Lot's wife into a pillar of salt (Genesis 19:26); and the most somber, Abimelech's sowing the city of Shechem with salt (Judges 9:45) to ensure its permanent destruction.

From Biblical time to the early decades of this century, and especially in the late Middle Ages, so extensive was the rabbinic lore on the subject and so strong the belief in its powers that a day in the life of a Jewish family was guided by its use and even its presence in the house. A move to a new house became accompanied by a ceremonious transfer of salt and bread from the old dwelling to the new. Laying a cloth on the dining table was customarily followed by strewing salt on the cloth. Eating food sprinkled with salt meant ensuring the family's wisdom and health.

In a seventeenth-century European description of the powers of salt, Rabbi Zachariah Plungian of Zamosc declared that if salt were on the table, it would drive away the demons. Why did it have such power? Because, stated Zachariah, its numerical value was 78, equivalent to the numerical value of the word existence (*havayah*) which is 26 × 3. Therefore, during the meal one should dip food three times in salt!

Another medieval Jewish custom was to carry salt in the pockets of one's garments just in case it was needed to throw over one's shoulders to ward off the demons or, it is told, to defend against highwaymen. One writer, in fact, suggested that a handful of salt taken from one's pocket and flung at an attacker would render the attacker powerless, just as long as a proper incantation was uttered.

To this day in several North African Jewish communities, it is still the custom to rub a newborn's body with salt, both to symbolize the ancient covenant God made with Israel and to protect it from the Evil Eye.

Interestingly, the importance Jews gave salt was shared equally by their neighbors, first by the Romans and then by the Christians who in medieval times followed the practice of placing salt on a table before setting anything else on it. The Panter in a medieval castle controlled not only the bread but the salt as well. The person of highest status sat above the salt cellar that had been placed on the table. The witches feast, the medieval courtly banquet turned topsy-turvy, was composed of carrion, the flesh of hanged men and unbaptized children, deliberately prepared without salt.

Salt has always been used to make meat ritually fit for eating (kosher). Coarse crystals are spread over beef, lamb, and veal to assist in removing all of the blood from slaughtered meat, a practice thousands of years old, originally done by many ancient peoples to preserve meat but by the Jews to also perpetuate the original covenant of salt made with God.

In Jewish households today various folk customs may also be practiced but rarely as more than habit. For most Jews salt has lost its ascribed powers as demon thwarter and preserver of life and health; in short, salt has lost its salt. Only a few souls, remembering once-prevalent customs and still believing in them, would think to throw salt over their shoulders or put salt in their grandchildren's pockets in order to ward off the Evil Eye.

Schav

If the first taste is pithy and tart and it's as sour on the tongue as a teaspoon of lemon juice drunk straight up, there's been an authentic palate-seizing confrontation with *schav* (rhymes with bob). Sour are the sorrel leaves that give it its Russian name and the drops of lemon juice that are generously sprinkled into the dark green puree to heighten the flavor. A dollop of sour cream gives the cold soup its final whack just in case the sorrel itself or the lemon juice doesn't quite succeed in waking up the palate.

Between the *forspeis* (the appetizer) and a light dinner, before the plate piled high with herring salad and pickles has been passed to each hungry guest, comes the *schav*, a simple spring soup. It can be made from a mere half pound of sorrel, collected from the wilds or cultivated with ease. Milk sweetened with sugar is added to the sorrel along with chopped fresh parsley and small pieces of white potato. Then the melange is beaten into a puree and, as a last touch, is enriched with egg yolks.

Typically, *schav* has been prepared by Ukranian Jews and their descendants for Shavuot, the holiday commemorating God's giving of the Law to Moses at Mount Sinai. Its green color symbolized Mount Sinai, which, according to tradition, was a verdant mountain. Two of its ingredients, milk and sour cream, are among the dairy foods customarily eaten on the holiday. Also, there is an abundance of sour grass in the Ukraine in the late spring when the Shavuot festival is celebrated.

If, after the holiday, enough sorrel grass remains, it is chopped, mixed with bits of meat, parsley, and chopped dill pickles and simmered for *rassolnik*, a relative of *rosl*, and *botvinia*, sorrel soup augmented with pieces of fresh fish, usually salmon.

SCHAV

Sip *schav* when it's icy cold. Taste before adding the sour cream; the soup may be sour enough without it. A traditional Ukrainian-Jewish Shavuot feast began with *schav* and continued with blintzes or cheese knishes and a salty herring salad.

½ pound sorrel leaves*
2 tablespoons parsley
2 tablespoons butter
1 quart water

*Fresh sorrel isn't sold commercially in the United States. The only way to assure a good supply is to find it growing wild or to cultivate it. Most seed companies sell sorrel seeds. It is a perennial and easy to grow.

3 white potatoes
Salt and pepper
½ teaspoon sugar
2 cups milk
2 egg yolks
Juice of 1 lemon
Sour cream (optional)

1. Wash and remove stems from sorrel and parsley. Peel the potatoes.
2. Chop the sorrel, parsley, and potatoes. (A food processor is the ideal way to do this.)
3. Melt the butter in a large pot. Add the vegetables and cook over moderate heat for 10 minutes. Add water, salt and pepper to taste; stir and simmer for 25 minutes.
4. Strain the vegetables and reserve the stock. Using a blender, sieve, or food processor, puree the vegetables with the milk and sugar. Add to the soup stock.
5. Add lemon juice a tablespoon at a time. Check for taste.
6. Beat the egg yolks and add to the soup.
7. Reheat soup but don't let it come to a boil. Stir well and check for seasoning. Serve hot or cold accompanied by sour cream.

Makes 6 servings.

Schmaltz

Then Nehemiah said unto them: "Go your way, eat the fat and drink the sweet, and send portions unto him for whom nothing is prepared; for this day is holy unto our Lord; neither be ye grieved; for the joy of the Lord is your strength."

—Nehemiah 8:10

From the beginning, Jewish cookery has been well-oiled. In Biblical times it tasted of juicy, ripe olives that had been shaken from the gnarled, aged trees which dotted the Judean landscape, to then be bruised, crushed, and pressed into service. Pale, yellow-green oily pools made pebbly wheat into dough for little round flat breads and unleavened cakes, fine enough to offer to the Lord and to savor for food (Exodus 29:2).

Only a foolish man, the Bible says, would do without oil, for such a substance, as any wise man knows, is a treasure.

Yet, once the Second Temple was destroyed by the Romans in the first century and the Jews dispersed across Central Asia, Europe, and North Africa, the olive oil that they had used so lavishly in the Middle East was difficult or impossible to come by. Especially in Europe did the Jews have to find an alternate substance to lubricate their lentil stews, honey cakes and puff pastes, their "spongy cakes," Sabbath breads and *pashteten*.

They found it and called it schmaltz, the Yiddish word for fat or drippings (from the German word *schmalz*). Schmaltz is actually rendered fat, prepared using the globules of fat from a corpulent roasting chicken or a well-fattened goose. Rarely is it made from the fat of a four-legged animal, in part because of custom and in part because of the stringent dietary rules regarding the eating of fat taken from mammals. "Ye shall eat no [abdominal] fat, of ox, or sheep, or goat," the Bible states in Leviticus 7:23. And the fat of other ritually-fit, four-legged animals can be eaten only if it is taken from specific sections of a properly slaughtered, ritually-fit (kosher) animal.

If the Biblical age of Jewish cookery had been well-oiled, from the early Middle Ages on, it was definitely well-schmaltzed, oozingly so. The pale yellow-green streams were exchanged for yellow solidified cakes pungently scented with the lingering aroma of onions that had been fried to a crisp along with fat and skin, and then devoured eagerly.

In the Middle Ages in Europe, except for the use of nut oils in France and Germany, and butter in recipes made with other dairy products, Jews relied on schmaltz in their cookery and used it in breads and kugels, cakes, meat stews, and potato pancakes. Because meats could never be cooked in butter, nor could dishes which would be eaten with meat, schmaltz, available and easily prepared, was a perfect solution. So ubiquitous was it that it, too, like the olive oil it had replaced, became synonymous with good fortune and wealth.

Today, true chopped liver aficionados wouldn't be caught dead eating it without schmaltz.

SCHMALTZ

3 cups raw chicken fat and skins, cut into small pieces
1 medium onion, coarsely chopped

1. Cook fat and skins over low heat until the fat is almost melted. Add onion and continue cooking, stirring occasionally, until onion is golden brown and skins brown and crisp. Do not burn them! Remove from heat.
2. When partially cooled, strain skins and reserve fat in a covered glass jar. Refrigerate. Add the skins (called in Yiddish *gribenes* or *grieven*) to chopped liver or eat them as a snack.

Makes about 1 cup of rendered fat.

Shavuot

High, heavy-textured cheesecakes, enveloped in the freshest, ripest fruits of the season; ladder-shaped cookies so buttery they dissolve with the slightest touch of the tongue; blintzes filled with sweetened pot or cottage cheese, dotted with butter and sauced with blueberries in syrup or dolloped with thick sour cream: All are the foods of Shavuot.

Cheese-filled knishes and kreplach; round, flaky kolaches; *spanikopita*, cream soups of sorrel, beets and cucumbers; sweet choux paste puffs filled with ice cream and drizzled with melted chocolate or custardy creme Anglaise—the list goes on and on, transforming into culinary reality the Bible's description of Israel as the land of milk and honey.

The Shavuot holiday since ancient times has marked two important events—one unique and deeply religious, the other celebrated year after year with food as its major focus. The first event commemorates the Revelation at Mount Sinai, God's giving of the Torah to Moses and the waiting Israelites. The second celebrates the spring harvest, in keeping with the description in the Book of Exodus which commanded the Israelites to gather the first fruits of their labors.

Since ancient times an extensive Shavuot food lore has developed which reflects a marvelously sweet-toothed ingenuity as much as it reflects a love for the Law of Moses. Surprisingly, even with so many different dishes associated with Shavuot, all fit one of the following themes:

Dairy Dishes. Most use dairy products, usually cheese, but sometimes milk, sour cream, or yoghurt. The oldest of them may be *fluden,* prepared by the Jewish women of Northern France as early as the tenth century. In this country, following an Eastern European tradition of long standing, blintzes and cheesecakes are the most popular recipes; but almost any dish which includes a dairy product is customary. These might include cheese rolls, cheese pancakes (*chrematoten*), kreplach stuffed with cheese, sour cream cakes, or knishes. Some traditionalists hold that it is the whiteness of dairy foods that is in keeping with the purity of the Ten Commandments. Another reason for eating dairy foods has to do with the ancient Israelites having to wait so long at the foot of Mount Sinai for the revelation of the Law. While waiting, tradition has it that the milk curdled, leaving only cheese for cooking.

Cakes and cookies shaped like the Tablets of the Law. Rare in the United States, this tradition is well established in Sephardic communities in Europe, particularly in countries where Spanish Jews settled after 1492: Greece, Salonika, Bulgaria, and Italy. The icing for these cakes and cookies is traditionally white to represent the purity of the Law or the cloud at Mount Sinai. Jews of European background occasionally serve blintzes and knishes laid out in pairs on serving plates and decorated with lines of powdered cinnamon-sugar or poppy seeds to represent the writing on the Tablets.

Roses. The tradition of eating foods using rosewater, rose petals, or rose hip jam grew up in several Sephardic communities. Shavuot is known as the Feast of Roses in some communities, and desserts are prepared using the rose as both a decoration and as an ingredient.

Rice. This food is a Shavuot ingredient because of its whiteness and, therefore, symbolic purity. In Western Europe, it is served with milk and sugar. In the Middle East, it is eaten with a dollop of yoghurt and a little lemon juice, but no sugar. It is also mixed with spinach and cheese and served in *borekas.*

Borscht and other cold soups. The Eastern European Jews of

Ashkanazic background often include borscht, *chlodnik* (cucumber soup), and *schav* (sorrel soup) on their Shavuot menus. The borscht and *chlodnik* are served cold accompanied by large bowls of sour cream.

Sukkot

And ye shall take you on the first day the fruit of goodly trees, branches of palm trees, and boughs of thick trees, and willows of the brook; and ye shall rejoice before the Lord your God seven days.

—Leviticus 23:40

Traditional food for Sukkot: At least an olive's bulk of bread or its equivalent to be eaten on the first night of this week-long festival which comes five days after Yom Kippur and is the third festival of the New Year. Yet few Jews have been satisfied to eat just a small tidbit for Sukkot, for this holiday, now steeped in religious ritual and observance, originally celebrated a bountiful autumn seasonal harvest and was marked with rejoicing, prayers of thanksgiving, and feasting.

Yes, that small nibble has always been viewed as the mere beginning of a feast which is centered on recipes that can be eaten in a little outdoor booth called a sukkah. The sukkah is a temporary dwelling, its roof only partially covered with boughs, open enough so that it is possible to view the stars while eating a meal in it.

Rich, thick, hot meat and cabbage borschts, peppery goulashes, spicy kibbes, and casseroles filled with steaming hot stuffed cabbage leaves soaked in a sweet-sour tomato-y liquid (*holoptsches*) are all part of an American Sukkot celebration today. All of them are the foods of the countries where Jews have lived in the Diaspora. None are of ancient significance.

Two hundred years ago in Colonial times, the table in the "cabana," as the sukkah was then called by the Sephardic Jews of Newport, was covered with plates of fruit and bread and bottles of rum.

Five hundred years ago in Germany and France, a rich *fluden* was eaten on Sukkot, just as it is today by European Jews. The American Jews eat a variant of this medieval dish but call it strudel; the Sephardic Jews prepare baklava.

Throughout the centuries since ancient times, the ethrog (citron), one of the four species of trees which are gathered together and brought to the synagogue to be blessed during Sukkot, has been used by cooks to prepare candy or jelly following the last day of the holiday. And until recently, the ethrog's petiole, thought to possess special powers, was bitten off and held in the mouth of women in labor because it was thought that doing so would reduce the pain of childbirth.

The seventh day of Sukkot is called Hashona Rabbah. At the synagogue it has been customary since ancient times to beat the willow twigs (*hashonah*), one of the four species, on the ground. At home, in the kitchen, in preparation for the evening meal of this day, the custom of preparing kreplach to eat in chicken soup is still followed by a number of Jews of Eastern and Central European background. The origin of this custom is obscure but is thought to be associated with a fear of God's judgment and the attempt to "cover" the stringency of that judgment with mercy, in the same way that the dough of the kreplach covers up its filling.

Hashona Rabbah is perhaps the one holiday in the Jewish cycle that is inextricably linked in the minds of the superstitious with strange spirits, demonology, and the irrefutable will of God. In Eastern Europe women prepare a challah shaped to resemble the hand of man reaching to God, who, it was thought, confirmed on this day one's fate in the coming year.

The eighth day of Sukkot is called Shemini Atzeret. The day following is Simhat Torah, the ninth and last day of Sukkot. On Simhat Torah, the day on which the year-long cycle of Torah readings is completed, Jews celebrate the occasion by reading the last sections of the Book of Deuteronomy, taking all of the Torahs from the Ark in the synagogue and walking in a procession (called *hakafa*) around the synagogue at least seven times. The mood is joyous, sometimes even zany, and it is not unusual to see adults dancing with the huge scrolls as the congregation sings both traditional and modern Israeli Hebrew songs.

T

Teyglach

When tough, virtually tasteless hunks of dough become deliberately engulfed by a wave of honey laced with a flotsam of nuts and candied fruit, the result is a dish of Jewish ambrosia which stops just short of treacle. The recipe is called *teyglach* (say *tayg—lockh*), and the key to its origins is lost in the culinary eddies of time.

Perhaps this dessert, served traditionally on Rosh Hashonah when its sweetness becomes culinary metaphor, promising a sweet new year with each delicious crunch, had its origins in ancient Greece, when dough was bathed in sauces of all kinds and was praised as the food of the gods.

Goodness knows how many pieces of dough got themselves dunked and sauced at the tables of the Western World: pretzels in beer, bread crusts in wine (called *märde* in seventeenth-century German lands), *penitslech* of fine dried bread dipped in sugar and then in beer by the Jews of the same area, thin *filo* leaves or shredded dough laced with honey or date syrup. Or perhaps the dough itself evolved in the culture of Eastern Europe (from whence *teyglach* came to the United States) as a poor person's version of marzipan, devoid of almonds.

The best guess incorporates all these notions, adding to them a picture of utmost simplicity that focuses as much on the way of life of most Eastern European Jews over at least ten centuries as it does on the food itself. Scraps of dough were always in a kitchen and so was honey, set on a shelf in a jar, precious and full of sweet promise. Wasting nothing, Jewish cooks could preserve every scrap of dough they had, dropping each into honey which they had boiled to a syrup. Then they would store them on a higher shelf away from their scampering, sweet-toothed children until the next much-longed-for holiday feast.

TEYGLACH

Dough:

7 large eggs
⅔ cup oil
1 tablespoon honey
1 tablespoon sugar
¼ teaspoon salt
½ teaspoon ginger
5 to 6 cups all-purpose flour

Coating Syrup:

2 cups honey
2 cups sugar
1 cup minced candied fruit
4 ounces walnuts, coarsely chopped
4 ounces filberts, coarsely chopped

1. Preheat oven to 400 degrees.
2. In a bowl beat eggs, oil, honey, sugar, salt, ginger, and 5 cups flour with an electric mixer until flour is absorbed and mixture is smooth. Add enough additional flour to form a pliable dough that can be rolled.
3. Pinch off small portions of the dough and roll into long ropes. Cut into 1-inch pieces.
4. Bake for about 10 minutes. Cool on a rack.
5. To prepare coating syrup, in a large pot place honey and sugar and stir over heat until temperature reaches 260 degrees F. on a candy thermometer. Add fruit and nuts and stir thoroughly.
6. While syrup is hot, add pieces of baked dough and simmer for 5 minutes. Remove small amounts at a time with a slotted spoon and place on a greased cookie sheet in a thin layer.
7. Cool to lukewarm. Shape *teyglach* into a large mound on a serving plate to resemble a pyramid.

Makes 2 quarts.

Tisha B'av

And it came to pass, when Jerusalem was taken—in the ninth year of Zedekiah King of Judah, in the tenth month, came Nebuchadnezzar King of Babylon and all his army against Jerusalem, and besieged it . . .

—Jeremiah 39:1

The ninth day of the Hebrew month of Av is the traditional day set aside for the public mourning of the destruction of the temples in Jerusalem. The First Temple was destroyed in 586 b.c.e. by Nebuchadnezzar of Babylon, the Second Temple by the Romans in 70 c.e.

Central to the observance of Tisha B'av is a 24-hour-long fast which begins at sunset. Just as eggs are eaten at the meal following the burial of a loved one, the meal which precedes the Tisha B'av fast has customarily included a hard-boiled egg sprinkled with ashes to remind Jews that they are preparing themselves to mourn the destruction of their most important, hallowed sanctuary. As another symbol of the gravity of the fast to come, and unlike the meal preceding the fast of Yom Kippur which is a festive meal, the pre-Tisha B'av meal is deliberately light. One of the dishes served usually includes legumes, often lentils, which is yet another traditional and ancient symbol of mourning.

Tscholent

A Sabbath without tscholent *is like a king without a throne.*

—Traditional saying

In the collection of the Jewish Museum of New York is a well-used, heat-darkened, cast bronze cooking pot, lidless and minus its handles. Four centuries ago, *tscholent*, the most special of Sabbath delicacies, filled this capacious vessel to the brim.

Week after week, year after year, with the predictable regularity and sameness that is so much the major ingredient of a tranquil Jewish Sabbath, the redolence of the pot's confines eagerly drew a family to lunch after a long morning of prayer. The taste of the mixture within became the wondrous taste of the Sabbath itself, lingering long after the last mouthful had been chewed and swallowed.

It was the Poperts of Frankfurt, a family of German Jews living in the sixteenth century, who owned the cast bronze *tscholent* pot. The raised letters carefully hammered into the top of the pot just below the place where the lid would have fit spelled out the information that it contained the weekly Sabbath morsels prepared by Hirtz Popert's wife, the daughter of Moses Zur Leiter. Dismayingly, in keeping with the custom of the time, her own first name wasn't inscribed.

The Poperts' Frankfurt was a busy commercial center. In 1582, a year during which Mrs. Popert most definitely prepared *tscholent* in the special cast bronze pot, the Jewish community was at the peak of its prosperity. Although the Jews of Frankfurt were confined to living in houses constructed along either side of the narrow Judengasse in the area walled off from the remaining sections of the town, their Christian neighbors were at peace with them. In the waning years of the sixteenth century, all of the 1,200 inhabitants of Frankfurt, Jew and non-Jew, lived in relative calm. That meant that Mrs. Popert and her family ate many a Saturday Sabbath lunch in peace.

Early Friday morning, Mrs. Popert and her daughters would first make the Sabbath loaves, the challot, kneading and shaping them carefully. Then they would assemble the ingredients for the dish that would be eaten for lunch on the Sabbath, the much-loved *tscholent*. Pieces of goose or beef would be readied, along with broad or white beans, salt, garlic, onions, eggs in their shells, barley, potatoes, a little honey, a dollop of rich goose fat, perhaps a few prunes or carrots, and a dash of spice.

Each ingredient would be layered: first the beans to absorb the fat, then the meat and vegetables. At the top would go a large, melon-sized dumpling, the kugel or knaidel, called in later centuries the "ganif," the Yiddish word for thief, because it stole the flavor of the *tscholent*, absorbing into its spongy innards the *tscholent*'s fat gravy and vapors.

This done, Mrs. Popert would take some leftover dough from the morning's batch for challah, wet it, shape it into a narrow strip, and use it to seal the pot closed.

On Friday afternoon someone in the Popert household, perhaps a child or servant, would thread the metal handle through the rings attached to both sides of the pot, balance the sealed pot over both shoulders, and descend a narrow inner staircase to the street. Onto the bumpy Judengasse the culinary messenger would trudge, weighed down by both the contents and the pot.

Not far away was the bake oven, busy now with pre-Sabbath business. While the baker's assistant would line the *tscholent* pots along the sides of the oven, the baker, using a huge pallet, would take challot from the racks and distribute them to the pot carriers. The load home would definitely be lighter and would smell wonderful.

With such a clearly identified *tscholent* pot, Mrs. Popert's preparation, sealed by the wad of moist dough around its brim to keep the liquid from boiling over, would never become confused with other pots similarly filled and then delivered to the communal bake oven. There all of them would be kept warm all night. Basking in the radiated heat of fires banked especially for the Sabbath, fires that according to the laws of Sabbath observance could not be rekindled until after sundown on Saturday, the pot's contents would simmer all night, each ingredient insinuating itself onto another.

Almost a whole day later, the process would be reversed. It was time to eat! Empty-handed and hungry, after spending a morning at the synagogue, the person sent to retrieve the *tscholent* would return home excited by the prospect of sampling what was inside that wonderful sealed pot, elated by the promise of what would transpire once the lid was lifted from the pot and the contents spooned from the aromatic confines.

The *tscholent* with its beans and potatoes, bits of goosemeat and spice would be eaten every Sabbath, invariably, for the Poperts surely believed the ancient saying that "he who prepares, cooks, and encloses food before the Sabbath in order to eat hot foods is considered to be among those who will be fortunate to attain Redemption."

How unsurprising then, considering the reward, to find the Popert family eating many of the same hot foods that were specifically mentioned in the ancient legal writings where the laws of Sabbath observance were detailed. These foods—flesh, onions and eggs, spices, chickpeas, lentils, and oil—references to them scattered over several pages of the Mishnah, were mentioned to elucidate a particular point of law. Eventually these foods came to be cooked by all observant Jews throughout the world, not just the Poperts. Sometimes they would be cooked individually, the way they apparently were prepared in Mishnaic times. By the late Middle Ages, more and more Jews began cooking these ingredients together, in one large pot. Since there could be no cooking on the Sabbath, and since hot food was important to eat on the Sabbath, it became traditional to prepare the food on Friday, cook it partially, and then let it simmer unattended until it was eaten at noon the next day.

The Hebrew *khamim,* from the word *kham* meaning hot, meant "hot foods" in the early legal writings. Soon *khamim* referred to not just any hot food, but the special Sabbath dish with its predictable ingredients, baked or roasted in a single pot very, very slowly.

Tscholent, sometimes spelled *chulent* and also called *shalet* or *solet,* is the Yiddish equivalent of *khamim* and is the word of medieval origin used by Jews of Western and Eastern European background. It is thought to come from the French word *chaleur,* warmth, or *chald,* the Old French word for hot. There are those who prefer another, more colorful etymology and insist that *tscholent* comes from a combination of two Yiddish words, shul, meaning synagogue, and *ende,* meaning end—a wonderfully precise description of when this dish is served.

In the Middle East today, *tscholent* is still called *khamim. Adafina* or *d'fina* is the name given to it by Jews of Spanish (Sephardic) background. In Iran, the same basic ingredients—meat, legumes, grain, vegetables, and spices—are stuffed into sacks of tripe to cook overnight in a special Sabbath oven. The Iranian dish is called *gipa.* In Iraq, the traditional Sabbath dish was tripe, stuffed, heavily seasoned with cardamom, cloves, turmeric, and cinnamon, scattered with rose petals, and called *pacha.* The *pacha* was usually cooked in a wide-bottomed heavy copper pot over slow-burning embers. A thick, heavy cloth called a *jell* covered the pot and held in the warmth.

Each dish, no matter what its name, is essentially the same recipe with minor variations, whether or not it was made last week, last year, four hundred years ago in Frankfurt, or a thousand years ago in Palestine or Spain. Its preparation links Jews in every place and age, the metaphorical chain without end and fashioned from *tscholent* pots of earthenware and stone, copper, iron, glass, stainless steel, and synthetic twentieth-century alloys.

TSCHOLENT

2 cups dried lima beans, chickpeas, lentils, or haricot beans
3 pounds beef brisket, or goose, cut into coarse chunks
3 onions, diced
3 cloves garlic, mashed
3 tablespoons vegetable oil or schmaltz (chicken fat)
2 teaspoons salt
½ teaspoon pepper
¼ teaspoon ginger
2 teaspoons paprika
3 or 4 potatoes, cut in quarters
⅛ cup barley
4 unbroken eggs in their shells
1 pound kosher garlic sausage, cut into coarse chunks

1. Soak the beans for a few hours. Drain.
2. Use a heavy saucepan or Dutch oven and brown the meat, onions, and garlic in the fat. Sprinkle with the salt, pepper, and ginger. Remove from pan.
3. Place the beans, potatoes, and barley in the bottom of the pot and sprinkle with the paprika. Add meat, onions, and the unshelled eggs. Add enough boiling water to cover just above the mixture. Cover tightly.
4. Bake at 350 degrees for 2 hours. Reduce heat to 225 degrees and bake until meat and vegetables are tender. Or for quicker cooking, bake in a 350-degree oven for 4 to 5 hours.
5. Slice meat and serve with the beans, potatoes, and eggs.

Serves 8 to 10.

MIDDLE EASTERN KHAMIM

½ cup vegetable oil
2 tablespoons sugar
3 cups water
1½ cups raw, washed chickpeas
6 medium-sized potatoes, peeled and cut into cubes
4 pounds fresh beef tongue or short ribs
2 marrow bones
6 unshelled eggs
1 cup long-grained rice
2 cups water
½ teaspoon salt
½ teaspoon ground pepper
½ teaspoon turmeric

1. Coat the bottom of a large heavy pot lightly with vegetable oil. Spread the sugar over the bottom of the pan and brown it well over high heat. When it has turned brown, add 3 cups water.
2. Place the chickpeas, potatoes, meat, and marrow bones around the side of the pot.
3. Have ready a 10-inch by 9-inch sheet of aluminum foil. Fold the foil in half along its long edge and fold the sides over ⅛-inch on each edge to form a small pouch for the rice. Place the rice in the pouch and place the pouch in the center of the pot. The pouch should be partially submerged in the caramelized liquid.
4. Add the 2 cups water to the rice, place the unshelled eggs over the meat, cover and let simmer until the rice is steamed, about 20 minutes.
5. Add the seasonings to the rice and additional water, if necessary, to cover the meat, chickpeas, and potatoes. Place the lid on the pot, cover the lid with a cloth and place the pot over very low heat, 225 degrees, to cook overnight.
6. When ready to serve, peel the eggs and place them in a bowl with the potatoes. Place the chickpeas and rice in another bowl along with the sauce. Serve the meat in another bowl with the remaining sauce.
7. Since the *khamim* itself has not been seasoned, have ready at the table small bowls of cayenne pepper, cumin, and salt.

TSCHOLENT WITH A "GANIF"

Take a shin bone and a piece of [brisket], about three pounds; get a pint of Spanish beans, others will serve the same, and a pint of Spanish peas; put them in a brown pan, one that will fit the oven and put the beef, peas, and beans in it, and cover it over with water; add pepper, ginger, salt and a little cayenne pepper.

Make the coogle in the following manner: a quarter of a pound of currants, a quarter of a pound raisins, a quarter of a pound sugar, the same quantity of bread crumbs and suet, chopped fine, four eggs, a quarter of a pound of flour, some spices and a small piece of citron. Mix well together; put the coogle (or pudding) in a basin, place it in the pan with the peas and beans and cover the pudding basin with a plate. Let it cook a day and night, and dish up the soup without the meat.

—from Esther Levy's *The Jewish Cookery Book,*
Philadelphia, 1871

Tu Bishvat

The earth is full of the fruit of thy works.

—Psalms, CIV

Bokser, plums, pomegranates, pears, citrons, oranges, apples, dates, grapes, nuts, melons, apricots: All are the traditional fruits eaten on this holiday which is the yearly festival of trees. Celebrated in ancient times as the day on which the tithes of fruit were collected, in modern times Tu Bishvat is a minor festival day during which children are encouraged to plant new trees and adults bidden to chant the Biblical psalms which celebrate the fruitfulness of the land.

The Sephardic communities of Italy, Greece, Turkey, and North Africa refer to the holiday as the Feast of Fruits.

Since the holiday is celebrated on the fifteenth day of the Hebrew month Shevat, particularly in European communities before World War II, fifteen fruits were often set out to be eaten during the day.

Tzimmes

Make a tzimmes out of life and you make a fuss about it, a big to-do over nothing.

But make a tzimmes (say *tzim* to rhyme with brim—*mess*) from edible ingredients and you make a sweet stew, a traditional holiday dish served primarily for Rosh Hashonah but also whenever someone feels like making it.

The Yiddish word tzimmes comes from two German words, *zum* and *essen,* meaning "to the eating." So often did Jews go "to the eating" and find a sweet vegetable or fruit stew on the table that the stew itself took on the name tzimmes and so did any mixed-up, troublesome, or messy situation.

Straight from the late Middle Ages, perhaps even earlier, comes a dish of cooked carrots dusted with flour and glazed with sugar and cinnamon, a popular German recipe which became even more popular among Central and Eastern European Jews because of its color and a linguistic coincidence. This dish was (and still is) called *mehren* tzimmes. *Mehren,* the Yiddish word for carrots, became associated with another word, *mehrn,* which means increase or multiply. The Jews, fond of attributing to words magical and special powers which went far beyond their literal meaning, took the coincidence to mean that eating carrots would assist in their spiritual and economic good fortune. *Mehren* tzimmes or any dish made with carrots was even thought to be a remedy (*refu'ah*) for particular ailments and was mentioned as possessing special magical qualities because of its golden color. The color in Jewish folk tradition is often associated with good fortune because it resembles the color of coins.

There are other ways of making an even bigger tzimmes

over tzimmes—by adding meat or chicken to the sweet mixed compote. Usually prunes, plums, or apricots are the fruits used in a tzimmes. The vegetables are carrots, peas, and potatoes. Spice, usually cinnamon, and sweeteners, either sugar or honey, are added to heighten the taste. The custom of mixing somewhat sour food, like meat, with sweet vegetables or fruits was common in the Middle Ages, so much so that it became a distinct method of cookery, called "pointing."

The current custom is to serve tzimmes as a side dish in much the same way as one would serve lamb with chutney, fish with a thick homemade tartar sauce, or turkey with a raisin-apple stuffing.

CARROT, PRUNE, AND POTATO TZIMMES

1½ pounds brisket of beef
1 package (1 pound) carrots
1 large onion
3 sweet potatoes, pared
4 white potatoes, pared
½ pound dried prunes
1 cup water
2½ tablespoons honey
1 tablespoon salt
1 cup fresh or canned tomato juice
½ cup brown sugar
3 tablespoons granulated sugar
2 tablespoons water
1½ cups cold water

1. Trim most of the fat from the meat. Slice carrots crosswise. Slice onions thinly. Cut potatoes into medium-sized chunks.
2. Place meat into the bottom of a large pot; arrange layers of white potatoes, prunes, sweet potatoes, onion, and carrots.
3. Add water, honey, salt, tomato juice, and brown sugar; simmer for 1 hour.
4. Preheat oven to 350 degrees.
5. Heat 3 tablespoons granulated sugar and 2 tablespoons water over high heat until the sugar caramelizes; then pour cold water over the caramelized sugar and add the liquid to the tzimmes.
6. Place tzimmes in the oven and bake for 1½ hours.

Serves 6 to 8.

Yom Ha'atzmaut (Israel Independence Day)

On this day a meal of chopped "chicken livers" made by mixing together onions, vegetable or olive oil, bread crumbs, and fresh yeast, washed down by a glass of buckthorn juice would serve as the most striking and sad reminder of what life was like during the 1948 siege of Jerusalem, during those long, desperate days that preceded the founding of the State of Israel on May 14, 1948.

This was the food that was eaten by the thousands of Jerusalemites who were cut off from any source of supply during that bleak and dangerous time in Israel's history. Real food—bread, fresh produce, cheese, milk—was not merely scarce, it was almost nonexistent. *Khubeisa,* an herb, was also gathered, usually under gunfire, and boiled or blanched for "salad," and orange peels were fried and seasoned so that they took on the faint taste of chicken.

No longer must Israelis resort to eating wild plants and orange peels in order to survive. And so the celebration of the anniversary of the founding of Israel is a day when food in great quantities is nibbled and enjoyed with a kind of poignant gusto, particularly the portable "street foods" like felafel, stuffed into *pita;* skewered meats; and sweet, flaky pastries.

Yom Kippur

For on this day shall atonement be made for you; from all your sins shall ye be clean before the Lord.

—Leviticus 16:30

The holiest day of the year, Yom Kippur, is revered as the Sabbath of all Sabbaths, a twenty-four-hour period that is traditionally devoted to prayer, fasting, and atonement. Occurring on the tenth day of the Hebrew month of Tishri, it is the final day of the ten-day High Holy Day period which begins with Rosh Hashonah.

Since the focus of the day is on one's spiritual needs, physical needs are temporarily set aside in order to concentrate more fully on asking God's forgiveness for all the ways in which one transgressed during the year just past.

Because Yom Kippur is thought of as a Sabbath, work is forbidden. Cooking, therefore, is not allowed. And because it is a day where physical needs are denied, all but the very young, the sick, and pregnant women are required to fast throughout the day.

Yet, because Yom Kippur is a festival, the meal which precedes it has always been considered to be a feast. Challot are prepared for the meal, often shaped like birds, or having the wings of birds or angels, or ladders made of dough atop them to symbolize the flight of man's prayers to heaven. Because Yom Kippur is a time for a last look back on the old year so that the new year can be met with a clear conscience, the symbolic foods of Rosh Hashonah are also carried over to this evening festival meal. These include honey and pastries or main dishes made with honey. A fowl is usually roasted, and kreplach float in the soup made from its giblets. Fruits of the season are often mixed together and sauced with sweet wine.

One dish sometimes served by ultra-Orthodox Jews of European background on Yom Kippur is not found on the Rosh Hashonah table. It is soup made from a fowl, usually a chicken, which has been sacrificed on the day before Yom Kippur in the belief that the sins of the person who sacrificed it will be transferred to the fowl and therefore disposed of. The custom, called *kapparah,* the Hebrew word for expiation, was first mentioned in the rabbinic writings of the ninth century and its practice has always been a matter of heated disputation.

The meal following the day-long fast is usually light, since a sumptuous one would be too much of a shock after a day without food. Most traditional and ubiquitous throughout the world is the custom of serving brined or pickled fish. The custom apparently originated in ancient times; records from

Roman times are replete with references to its eating at this particular meal in the belief that salted fish restored salt to the body after a full day of fasting.

Zimsterne cookies, sweet with honey and tweaked with spices, are the first morsels eaten by the Jews in several areas of Central Europe, a practice that is thought to date from the Middle Ages. The name, *zimsterne,* meaning "to the stars," is thought to come from the appearance of the first stars of evening and, therefore, the end of the fasting period.

Z

Zimsterne

How often do we wish that what we treasure in our lives could last forever: a loving glance, a passionate kiss, the melodic, high-pitched trill of our children's laughter, or a day when our joyful mood seems to be matched by all that surrounds us. Knowing that the next moment will come with a relentlessness we can't control, we clutch the present one to us, savoring its sweetness before it becomes one more treasured memory.

So it is with the Sabbath, an all-too-short twenty-four-hour day when all of these, life's most tender experiences, are possible. Contemplating Sabbath's end is a bittersweet burden. We beg for time, wishing that tomorrow could be held at arm's length, if only for a few more minutes, just as Jews did many centuries ago when they lovingly created the ceremony of Havdalah. With its blessings, wine, braided candles, and spice box forged into a short ceremony at Sabbath's end, Havdalah has the power to distract us with its beauty from the inevitable pain that comes with the loss of something much loved and cherished.

Inevitably, the end of Sabbath comes with the appearance of three bright stars in the heavens. An ordinary day will follow but first there will be a sip of wine, a look at the bright light from the braided candle of Havdalah, and a breath of aromatic spice that will come from a little cache of cloves, mace, or perhaps cinnamon, held in a delicately crafted holder, the *hadas.* Before the ceremony is over, every sense will have been satisfied in order to emphasize that, yes, Judaism is a religion of prayer but also of action, pleasure, and joy.

One small culinary treasure comes down to us as being part of the Havdalah ceremony of Middle European and Eastern European Jews several centuries ago. Its origin is impossible to date but its raison d'être is easily understood. Called simply *zimsterne* (say *zim—stern—eh*), "to the stars" in Yiddish, it is a sweet, spicy morsel, an attempt to momentarily confine Sabbath's spiritual sweetness and piquancy to a tidbit which will evanesce on the tongue just as surely as day becomes night. It was also the custom to eat *zimsterne* to break the Yom Kippur fast.

Shaped like a star and tasting of honey and cinnamon, ginger and cloves, the *zimsterne*'s pleasant taste and all that had gone before it, it was hoped, would provide the spiritual and physical sustenance needed to face the days ahead.

ZIMSTERNE

4 tablespoons butter or margarine (½ stick)
1 cup sugar
3 eggs
½ cup honey
5 cups flour, sifted
¾ teaspoon baking soda
1⅛ teaspoons ground cinnamon
½ teaspoon ground cloves
¼ teaspoon ground mace or ground nutmeg
1 egg yolk plus food coloring

1. Using an electric mixer, cream butter and sugar. Add eggs and beat at medium speed until mixture is well blended. Add honey.
2. At low speed, add 4 cups flour, a cup at a time, beating until mixture is thick and flour has been completely absorbed. Add the last cup of flour and spices by hand. Refrigerate dough for 2 hours.
3. Preheat oven to 300 degrees. Roll out dough on floured board or cloth. Cut into star shapes. Make glaze with beaten egg yolk to which a few drops of food coloring have been added.
4. Line a greased baking sheet with wax paper. Place cookies on baking sheet; brush or smear a little of the glaze over the tops. Bake for 15 minutes. Remove cookies from wax paper while they are still warm.

Notes

ADAFINA

See Mishna Sabbath 4.1 and 4.2 for a discussion of hot foods prepared for the Sabbath.

ALBONDIGAS

Commenting on the assimilationist tendencies of American Colonial Jews, J.R. Marcus said of Gershom Mendes Seixas, the prominent *hazzan* of Congregation Shearith Israel (1768) and noted Jewish educator: "It is worth noting . . . that the only Iberian characteristics left [in Seixas] were his name and his Sabbath dish *albondigas*, meatballs."

ALMOND

The Talmudic passage regarding almonds appears in the Jerusalem Talmud, Ta'an 4:8, 68c.

APHRODISIACS

The following story about birds' brains and their importance to at least one individual living in the fourth century appears in Midrash Rabbah, Lamentations. R. Abbahu went to Bozrah and was given hospitality by Jose Resha. There were served to him eighty kinds of birds' brains; and the host said to him, "Let not my master be angry, but the catch [of birds today] has been insufficient!" People called him Jose Resha because his food was nothing else than birds' brains. (Resha means head in Aramaic.)

BAGEL

The Cracow Regulations of 1610 stated that bagels were among the gifts which could be sent "only to a woman who has given birth (the *kimptorin*) and the women who attend her."

BARNACLE GOOSE

Isaac ben Moses of Vienna, Rabbenu Tam, Samuel ha-Hasid, Judah ha-Hasid of Regensburg, Isaac ben Joseph of Carbiel, and Abba (of the *Zohar*) were the most prominent of the early discussants of the barnacle goose question. Rabbi Bernard Issachar Dov Illowy wrote his opinion denouncing those who would permit its eating in 1862.

Gerald of Wales was not the only non-Jew to write about the barnacle goose. So does Gervase of Tilbury. Records of their writings are preserved in extant English pipe rolls.

BOKSER

The quotation from the Talmud regarding Hanina comes from Ta'anit 24b.

BULKES

In the nineteenth century, according to writer Mordecai Spector, in the part of Russia-Roumania called Bessarabia, pregnant Jewish women prepared for their confinement by baking butter *bulkes,* placing them in a linen sack, and hanging the roll-filled sack from the rafters of their homes for at least a month. The result: rolls which would powder in the mouth but not be dried out!

CHICKEN SOUP

The quote from Maimonides appears in *Two Treatises on the Regimen of Health,* in Transactions of the American Philosophical Society, Vol. 54, Part 4, pp. 32–40.

Recently in a study conducted at Mt. Sinai Hospital in Miami Beach, Florida, scientists demonstrated that just as Maimonides claimed, chicken soup had medicinal benefits, or as the scientists stated, it rendered "efficacious upper respiratory tract infection therapy."

CHREMSLACH

Rabbenu Jehiel ben Joseph of Paris, French Talmudic scholar and commentator of the thirteenth century, also wrote of a food called *vermisist.* His legal opinion on it was able to set to rest a dispute that amazingly enough had entangled all those proverbial fine strands of Talmudic and post-Talmudic split-hairs for years: The question of whether or not one broke off a piece of the food before cooking it in observance of the ancient practice of presenting a portion of the ceremonial bread loaves to the priests of the Temple. No, said Rabbenu Jehiel, since bread was eaten with it. With that pronouncement the matter was settled, at least temporarily and only in France!

EGG

It was Rabbi Eleazar b. Rabbi Jose who told the story of the one hundred dishes made from eggs. Rabbi Judah ha-Nasi heard the story and said: "Such luxury we have never seen. Rabbi Simeon b. Halafta heard this and exclaimed, 'Such luxury we have never heard of!'" The passage appears in Midrash Rabbah, Lamentations III, 17.

FLUDEN

The Fox Parable Book, from which the introductory quote is taken, was originally written in Hebrew and called *Mishlei Shu'alim.* A Yiddish translation of it was printed in Freeburg in 1585 and later in Frankfort auf Main in 1687. A photographic facsimile of the 1687 edition appeared in Berlin in 1925.

The earliest known reference to *fluden* occurs in the following passage authored by Gershom ben Judah Me'or Ha-Gulah of Mainz (960–1028): "And Rabbi Shimon refers to Rabbi Yehuda Ha-Cohen b. Rabbi Meier, who is Rabbi Leontin, who stated that aroma is the essence. And Rabbi Yehuda, his contemporary, disagrees and teaches that 'aroma is not the essence' and permits the eating of the bread with meat even if it was baked in an oven with a cheese dish called *fluden.*" (*Or Zaru'a Piskei Avoda Zara,* Sect. 256, p. 67)

GARLIC

According to the fifteenth-century chronicler, Andris Bernaldez, the Conversos never lost their tastes for "eating . . . stews . . . of onions and garlic fried in oil . . . to avoid lard . . . and they themselves had the same smell as the Jews." Bernaldez, not content to blame the smell of the Conversos' breath only to their liking for garlic, suggested that the odor was due also "to their not being baptized." The quote appears in Trachtenberg's *The Devil and The Jews.*

There are dozens of references to garlic in the Talmud; most are endorsements of garlic as love philter or substance. The phrase "to eat garlic" when used in the Talmud, was a euphemism for the sex act. Rabbi Ezra is quoted in TJ, Meg. 4:1175a. The passage concerning Judah-ha-Nasi the Prince can be found in Sandhedrin II. See also Yoma 18a and Shabbat 118a, and Baba Kama, 82.

For a discussion of garlic eating in the Middle Ages, see p. 166, of Abrahams, *Jewish Life in the Middle Ages.* A discussion of garlic as a remedy appears in Trachtenberg's *Jewish Magic and Superstition.*

GEFILTE FISH

A detailed discussion of the significance of the Leviathan from the rabbinic point of view is available in the Pesikta de Rab Kahana, pp. 467 ff.

A fascinating discussion of the Leviathan meal appears as part of Goodenough's extremely comprehensive treatment of the symbols of the post-Biblical period.

Rabbi Papa, brewer, wealthy landowner, and Talmudic disputant was obviously also fond of food for he is often quoted on the subject. See Baba Bathra, Shabbat 118b and Erubin 65a for what he had to say about fish and fish-hash pie.

Apicius, commenting on his recipe for smelt pie, added the following amusing note, so typical of a Roman cook's need to disguise foods by transforming their shape or dousing them with sauce or seasonings of questionable taste: "Sprinkle with ground pepper when done and carry into the dining room. Nobody will be able to tell what he is enjoying."

GOAT

A narrative account of the fable, "The Two She-Goats from Shebreshin," appears in Hebrew folklorist Dov Noy's *Folktales of Israel,* the Agnon story in the December, 1966, issue of *Commentary.* See also the goat fables in the classic work by Louis Ginzberg, *The Legends of the Jews,* and in Ausubel's, *A Treasury of Jewish Folklore.*

On the subject of that one line which first appears in Exodus 23:19, "Thou shalt not seethe a kid in his mother's milk," Frazer writes most authoritatively and compellingly, taking a rather wide-ranging look at the reasons for the prohibition. Food historian Waverly Root's view, that the "Hebrews" once in a "territory they could call their own . . . began to eat not wisely but too well so that the dietary law had to be imposed on them," has not one grain of truth in it; his conjecture that the recipe which inspired the prohibition, a dish similar to the southern Italian *caldariello,* in the absence of an on-the-spot observation, is as good a guess as any.

The care and treatment of goats is discussed again and again in the Talmud, attesting to their importance in the agricultural life of Babylonia from the second to the fifth centuries of this era. (See Baba Metzia 23b and Baba Kama 20a and 23b.) As mentioned in the text, when the Jews lost their lands in Babylonia after the rise of Islam in the sixth century and as their lives became more and more confined in Europe, North Africa, and the Middle East, they rarely had the wherewithall to keep goats in herds.

GOGL-MOGL

Other etymological possibilities include the one given in one Russian etymological dictionary which suggests that *gogl-mogl* comes from the English word combinations *hugger-mugger* or *cugger-mugger.* One meaning of this term of many meanings is "whispering in a low voice," hence the possible connection to *gogl-mogl,* a drink which has always been given as a remedy for sore throat, hoarseness, and laryngitis.

HAZZENBLUZZEN

Yiddish linguist Mordecai Kossover once posited another etymology for this intriguing word, saying that *hoisabluza* was the name of a particular freshwater fish of Central Europe. However, he wasn't sure of just how the name of a fish was also used to name a small, fried puffed-up pastry.

HONEY

The quote from the Talmud appears in Yoma, following 83b.

HOLOPTSCHES

The introductory quote appears in the Talmud in Berakoth 44b.

KADAIF

The reference to *kataif,* dating from Talmudic times, can be found in *Midrash Tehillim* (Midrash to Psalms) XV, 1, a commentary on the Psalms of the Bible which was compiled over a period of at least ten centuries (!) beginning in the third century c.e. (in Jastrow, p. 681).

LEGUMES

The two key rabbinic sources where the link between lentils, eggs, and mourning are made occur in the following two passages. The first appears in the Talmud, Baba Bathra, 16b: "'And Esau came into the field and was faint.' It has been taught [in connection with this] that that was the day on which Abraham our father died, and Jacob our father made a broth of lentils to comfort his father Isaac. Why was it of lentils? In the West they say in the name of Rabbah b. Mari: Just as the lentil has no mouth, so the mourner has no mouth [for speech]. Others say: Just as the lentil is round, so mourning comes round to all denizens of this world. What difference does it make in practice which of the two explanations we adopt? The difference arises on the question whether we should comfort with eggs."

The second appears in Midrash Rabbah (Genesis) LXIII, 14: "'And Jacob gave Esau bread and pottage of Lentils' (XXV, 34). As a lentil is wheel-shaped, so is the world like a wheel. As a lentil has no mouth [opening] so a mourner has no mouth, for a mourner does not speak (on ordinary topics). As a lentil symbolizes mourning, yet also joy, so here too there was mourning—because of Abraham's death, and joy—because Jacob received the birthright."

MANNA

See Friedrich Simon Bodenheimer, *Ergebnisse der Sinai Expedition* 1927 (1929).

PASHTET

In the Soviet Union, the name *pashtet* describes a dish prepared today exactly as it must have been prepared in the Jewish households of the Middle Ages: a variety of meats, chopped and blended with herbs, and then enclosed in a pastry case.

The Romans knew what it took to make sophisticated meat pies, an art which obviously was the basis for the later *pashteten*. Pantropeon described a pie invented by the Roman Emperor Verus. It consisted of sow's flank (sumen), pheasant, peacock, iced ham, and wild boar's flesh enclosed in a laboriously worked crust.

POMEGRANATE

An important Kabbalistic work written by Moses Cordovero of Safed in the sixteenth century has the title (in Hebrew) *Rimmonim,* Orchard of Pomegranates, an illusion to the totality of God's creations.

Sounding more like the language of the Bible than the Talmud, the description of Johanan comes from the Talmud, tractate Baba Metzia 84a.

P'TSCHA

Platina, famed for his comprehensive collection of recipes called *De Honesta Voluptate* (about 1475) includes the following recipe for *Gelu (Gelatina) in Pattina*, "Jelly in a Dish."

"If you want two plates of that dish which we commonly call *gelatina*, take forty sheep feet from which the skin and bones have been removed and soak them in cool water for three or four hours; then rinse them and put them in a cauldron where there is one part sharpest white vinegar and as much white wine and two parts water; and add enough salt."

Fisnoga, another name for *p'tscha*, has a humorous connotation, since it is a combination of the Yiddish word for feet (*fis*) and the Russian word for feet (*noga*).

SALT

Plungian, the kabbalist, teacher and writer of the *Sefer Zekirah* (1707), is quoted on page 105 in Herman Pollack's exhaustive work, *Jewish Folkways in Germanic Lands* (1648–1806). Pollack's notes contain several other *midrashic* references on the subject of salt from the same period.

For those who have a Freudian bent, Ernest Jones' paper on salt is must reading but take him with a grain of salt, for according to him there is little that salt does not symbolize.

TSCHOLENT

The laws governing Sabbath observance are first mentioned in the Bible. The seventh day was to be "a Sabbath of the Lord" which the Israelites would come to honor in many ways. The earliest reference to food preparation for the Sabbath is in Exodus, where the Israelites are told by God to gather a double portion of manna which would be enough to feed them for two days, one of them the Sabbath (Exodus 16:22). The laws codified in the Talmud detail ancient Sabbath practices and prohibitions. Many of the foods mentioned in the Mishnah, Sabbath 1–22, are the ones which have come to be included in a pot of *tscholent*.

Heinrich Heine's poem, Princess Sabbath (*"Prinzessin Sabbat"*), is perhaps the only poem ever written about *tscholent*. Heine calls the dish *schalet* and in flowery, effusive language sings its praises, calling it a "ray of light immortal," "ambrosia," and the "very food of heaven which on Sinai God himself instructed Moses in the secret of preparing."

ZIMSTERNE

"So much was the use of myrtle (leaves) identified with the Havdalah ceremony that up to this day the spice box used at the ceremony although it contains other spices and not myrtle is still designated by the name *hadas,* the Hebrew word for myrtle" (Lauterbach, p. 92).

Bibliography

Abrahams, Israel. *Jewish Life in the Middle Ages.* New York: Meridian Books, and the Jewish Publication Society, Philadelphia, 1958 (1911).

Abramowicz, Hirsh. *Fashvundene Geshtalten* [Food Among the Jews of Lithuania]. Buenos Aires: (no publisher given), 1958 (in Yiddish).

Acton, Eliza. *The Best of Eliza Acton.* Harlow: Longmans, 1968.

Adler, Marcus Nathan. *The Itinerary of Benjamin of Tudela.* London: Oxford University Press, 1907.

Agnon, S. Y. "Fable of the Goat." Translated by Barney Rubin. *Commentary* 42 (December 1966): 42–43.

Aguilar, Jeannette. *The Classic Cooking of Spain.* New York: Holt, Rinehart and Winston, 1966.

Ain, Abraham. "Swislocz: Portrait of a Jewish Community." In *YIVO Annual of Jewish Social Science,* Vol. IV, pp. 86–114. Edited by Koppel S. Pinson. New York: YIVO, 1950.

Aleichem, Sholom. "The Enchanted Tailor." In *The Old Country: Collected Stories of Sholom Aleichem.* Translated by Julius and Frances Butwin. New York: Crown Publishers, 1953.

Amchanitzky, Hinde. *Instruction Book of Cooking and Baking.* New York, 1901 (in Yiddish).

Anderson, Matthew Smith. *Britain's Discovery of Russia, 1553–1815.* London: Macmillan, 1958.

Apicius. *Cookery and Dining in Imperial Rome.* Translated by Joseph Dommers Vehling. Chicago: W. M. Hill, 1936.

Arberry, A. J. "A Bagdad Cookery Book." *Islamic Culture* 13 (1939): 21–47.

Arrington, L. R. "Foods of the Bible." *Journal of the American Dietetic Association* 35 (1959): 816–20.

Austin, Thomas, ed. *Two Fifteenth-Century Cookery Books,* Vol. 91. London: Early English Text Society, 1888.

Autumn, Violeta. *A Russian Jew Cooks in Peru.* San Francisco: 101 Productions, 1973.

Axford, Lavonne Brady. *English Language Cookbooks 1600–1973.* Detroit: Gale Research Co., 1976.

Baer, Yitzack. *A History of the Jews in Christian Spain,* 2 Volumes, translated by Louis Schoffman. Philadelphia: Jewish Publication Society, 1966.

Bar-David, Molly Lyons. *The Israeli Cook Book.* New York: Crown Publishers, 1964.

Barrows, Anna. *An Outline on the History of Cookery.* New York: Teachers College, Columbia University, 1925.

Beck, Leonard. "A Note on the Librarian—Author of the First Cookbook." *The Quarterly Journal of the Library of Congress* 32 (July 1975): 238–53.

Berger, Abraham. "The Literature of Jewish Folklore: A Survey with Special Reference to Recent Publications." Reprint of *Journal of Jewish Bibliography* 1 (October 1938–39): 12–20.

Berger, Graenum. American Association for Ethiopian Jews. Personal correspondence, 1977.

Bermant, Chaim. *Walled Garden; The Saga of Jewish Family Life and Tradition.* New York: Macmillan Publishing Co., 1974.

Bernstein, Ignaz. *Judische Sprichworter und Redensarten.* Warschau: Gedrukt bei Josef Fischer in Krakau, 1908.

Bernstein, Mordecai. Two Remedy Books in Yiddish from 1474 and 1508. In *Studies in Biblical and Jewish Folklore,* pp. 289–305. Edited by Raphael Patai, et al. Bloomington: Indiana University Press, 1960.

Blanksteen, Jane. *Nothing Beets Borscht: Jane's Russian Cookbook.* New York: Atheneum, 1974.

Bodenheimer, Friedrich Simon. *Animal and Man in Bible Lands.* Leiden: E. J. Brill, 1972.

Bodenschatz, J. C. G. *Aufrichtig Deutsch Redender Hebraer,* 1756. Frankfort and Bamberg: M. Gobhardt, 1756.

Bodenschatz, J. C. G. *Kirchliche Versassung der Heutigen Juden, Sonderlich derer in Deutschland.* Frankfort and Erlang: J. F. Beckers, 1748–49.

Bourne, Ursula. *Spanish Cookery.* London: Futura Publications Limited, 1974.

Braham, Randolph L., ed. *Hungarian-Jewish Studies.* New York: World Federation of Hungarian Jews, 1966.

Brande, William G., translator. *Pesikta Rabbati; Discourses for Feasts, Fasts and Special Sabbaths.* New Haven and London: Yale University Press, 1968.

Briggs, Richard. *The New Art of Cookery According to the Present Practice*

Being a Complete Guide to all Housekeepers on a Plan Entirely New; consisting of thirty-eight chapters. Philadelphia: printed for W. Spotswood, R. Campbell and E. Johnson, 1792.

Brothwell, Don and Patricia. *Food in Antiquity.* London: Thames and Hudson, 1969.

Buonassisi, Vincenzo. *Pasta.* Wilton, Connecticut: Lyceum Books, 1973.

Caro, Joseph. *The Kosher Code of the Orthodox Jew.* Translated by Solomon I. Levin and Edward A. Boyden. Minneapolis: University of Minnesota Press, 1940.

Chambers, William. *Chambers' Etymological Dictionary.* London: W & R Chambers, 1882.

Corominas, Juan. *Diccionario Critico Etimologico de la Lengua Castellana.* Madrid: Editorial Gredos, 1954.

Cosman, Madeleine Pelner. *Fabulous Feasts: Medieval Cookery and Ceremony.* New York: George Brazeller, 1976.

Croly, Mrs. Jane (Cunningham). Jennie June's *American Cookery Book.* New York: The American News Co., 1878.

Danby, Herbert, D.D. *The Mishnah.* London: Oxford University Press, 1938.

Davidson, Israel. *Parody in Jewish Literature.* New York: Columbia University Press, 1907.

Efron, Z. "Loaves of Bread in Jewish Tradition." *Ariel* 26 (April 1970): 18–19.

Encyclopedia Judaica, 1972, second printing, 1973. s.v.: Almond, Apple, Carob, Ferrara, Food, Goat, Italy, Lag Ba'Omer, Manna, Midrash Tehillim, Pomegranate, Spain, *Tscholent,* Venice.

Epstein, Louis M. *Sex Laws and Customs in Judaism.* New York: Bloch Publishing Co., 1948.

Escola, Theodor Herzl. *Cozinha Tradicional Judaica.* 2 Edicao, *Belo Horizonte,* 1967.

Faitlovitch, Dr. Jacques. "The Falashas." Reprinted from *American Jewish Yearbook 5681.* Philadelphia: Jewish Publication Society, 1920.

Fisher, M.F.K. and the Editors of Time-Life Books. *The Cooking of Provincial France.* New York: Time-Life Books, 1968.

Fishman, Joshua A. "Yiddish in America: Socio-Linguistic Descriptions and Analysis." *International Journal of American Linguistics* 31 (April 1965): 87–94. Bloomington: Indiana University Press, Publication of the I.U. Research Center in Anthropology, Folklore, and Linguistics.

Frazer, Sir James George. *Folk-lore in the Old Testament; Studies in Comparative Religion, Legend and Law.* New York: The Macmillan Company, 1923.

Frazer, Sir James George. *The Golden Bough; A Study in Magic and Religion,* Volume 1, Abridged Edition. New York: Macmillan, 1951.

Fredman, Ruth. "The Passover Seder: A Study of Identity, Maintenance and Modification, 1976." Paper given at the Annual Meeting of the American Folklore Society, Philadelphia, November 11–14, 1976.

Freedman, Rabbi Dr. H. and Simon, Maurice, editors and translators. *Midrash Rabbah.* London: Soncino Press, 1939.

Friedenwald, Harry. *The Jews and Medicine: Essays,* Vol. 1. Baltimore: The Johns Hopkins Press, 1944.

Friedlander, Joseph, compiler. *The Standard Book of Jewish Verse.* New York: Dodd, Mead and Company, 1917.

Gaster, Theodore H. *The Holy and the Profane.* New York: William Sloan Associates, 1955.

Gaster, Theodore H., ed. *Myth, Legend and Custom in the Old Testament.* New York: Harper & Row, 1969.

Gaster, Theodore H. "Pagan Ideas and the Jewish Mind." *Commentary* 17 (1954): 185 ff. on 1–III.

Gaster, Theodore H. *Passover: Its History and Traditions.* Boston: Beacon Press, 1949; rev. ed., 1964.

Gaubert, Henri. "What Abraham Ate." *Jewish Digest* 16 (October 1970): 72.

Geertz, C., ed. "Deciphering a Meal." *Daedalus* (Winter 1972): 61–82.

Gil, Moshe. "The Radhanite Merchants and the Land of Radhan." *Journal of the Economic and Social History of the Orient* 17, Part 3 (September 1974): 299–329.

Gilbert, Martin. *Jewish History Atlas.* New York: Macmillan, 1969.

Ginzberg, Louis. "Jewish Folklore: East and West." Lecture delivered at the Harvard Tercentennial Celebration in 1936, in L. Ginzberg, *On Jewish Law and Lore* (Cleveland and New York: Meridian Books, 1962): pp. 61–73.

Ginzberg. Louis. *The Legends of the Jews,* translated by Henrietta Szold. Philadelphia: Jewish Publication Society, 1909.

Glasse, Hannah. *The Art of Cookery Made Plain and Easy.* London: privately published, 1751.

Goitein, Solomon D. *Jews and Arabs, Their Contact Through the Ages.* New York: Schocken Books, 1964.

Goitein, Solomon D. *Letters of Medieval Jewish Traders.* Princeton: Princeton University Press, 1973.

Goitein, Solomon D. *A Mediterranean Society: The Jewish Communities of the Arab World as Portrayed in the Documents of the Cairo Geniza.* Berkeley and Los Angeles: University of California Press, Vol. I, 1967; Vol. II, 1971.

Goodenough, Erwin Ramsdell. *Jewish Symbols in the Greco-Roman Period.* New York: Pantheon Books, 1956.

Goodman, Hanna. *Jewish Cooking Around the World; Gourmet and Holiday Recipes.* Philadelphia: Jewish Publication Society, 1973.

Granado, Diego. *Libro del Arte de Cocina (1599).* Introduccion por Joaquin Del Val. Madrid: La Sociedad de Bibliofilos Españoles, 1971.

Greenbaum, Florence Kreisler. *The International Jewish Cookbook.* New York: Bloch, 1918.

Grinstein, Hyman. *The Rise of the Jewish Community of New York.* Philadelphia: Porcupine Press, 1976.

Grossfeld, Bernard. *The Targum to the Five Megillot.* New York: Hermon Press, 1973.

Grunfeld, (Dayyan) J. *The Philosophical and Moral Basis of the Jewish Dietary Laws.* London: Soncino Press, 1961.

Grunwald, Max. "Various Charms and Magical Recipes." *Edoth I* (1946): 241–48 (in Hebrew).

Gutstein, Morris Aaron. *The Story of the Jews of Newport.* New York: Bloch Publishing Company, 1936.

Haboucha, Farha-Joyce. *The Sephardic Cookbook.* Mount Vernon, New York: Ad-Infinitum Press, no date.

Hacohen, Devora and Menahem. *One People; The Story of Eastern Jews.* Bat Yam, Israel: Sabra Books; New York: Funk & Wagnalls, 1969.

Hazelton, Nika Standen. *The Cooking of Germany.* New York: Time-Life Books, 1969.

Hertz, Rebekka. *Israelitisches Kochbuch.* Berlin: L. Lamm, 1905.

Herzog, Marvin I. *The Yiddish Language in Northern Poland: Its Geography and History.* The Hague: Mouton & Co., 1965.

Herzog, Marvin I.; Ravid, Wita; and Weinreich, Uriel. *The Field of Yiddish* (Third Collection). The Hague: Mouton & Co., 1969.

Iny, Daisy. *The Best of Baghdad Cooking, with Treats from Teheran.* New York: Saturday Review Press, 1976.

Irfan, Orga. *Turkish Cooking.* London: Andre Deitsch, 1958.

Jacob, Heinrich Eduard. *Six Thousand Years of Bread.* Translated by

Richard and Clara Winston. Westport, Conn.: Greenwood Press, 1944.

Jacobs, Joseph. *The Jews of Angevin England; Documents and Records from Latin and Hebrew Sources.* London: David Nutt, 1893.

Jastrow, Marcus, compiler. *Dictionary of the Targumim, the Talmud Babli and Yerushalmi, and the Midrashic Literature.* Brooklyn, New York: Traditional Press, 1903; rev. ed., no date given.

Jewish Encyclopedia, 1902. S.V. Apple, Childbirth.

Jones, Ernest. "The Symbolic Significance of Salt." In *Essays in Applied Psycho-Analysis,* pp. 22–109. London: International Psychoanalytical Press, 1951 (1923).

Jones, George Frederick. "The Function of Food in German Literature." *Speculum: A Journal of Medieval Studies* 35 (January 1960): 78–86.

Kasdan, Sara. *Love and Knishes.* New York: Vanguard Press, 1956.

Kettner. *Book of the Table.* London: 1887; rev. ed., published as *Kettner's Book of the Table.* London: Centaur Press, 1968.

Kosover, Mordecai. *Yiddishe Makholim.* New York: Yiddish Scientific Institute (YIVO), 1958 (in Yiddish).

Krauss, Samuel. *Talmudische Archeologie.* Leipzig: G. Foch, 1910–12.

Kravitz, Nathaniel. *3000 Years of Hebrew Literature.* Chicago: Swallow Press, Inc., 1972.

Kuper, Jessica. *The Anthropologists' Cookbook.* New York: Universe Books, 1977.

Lang, George. *The Cuisine of Hungary.* New York: Bonanza Books, 1971.

Lauterbach, Jacob Zallel. "The Ritual of the Kapparot Ceremony." In *Jewish Studies in Memory of George A. Kohut,* pp. 413–22. New York: Alexander Kohut Memorial Foundation, 1935.

Lauterbach, Jacob Zallel. *Studies in Jewish Law, Custom and Folklore.* New York: Ktav Publishing Co., 1970.

Leibowitz, J.O.; and Marcus, S. *Moses Maimonides on the Causes of Symptoms.* Berkeley: University of California, 1975.

Leslau, Wolf. "Black Jews of Ethiopia: An Expedition to the Falashas," *Commentary* 7 (March 1954): 216–224.

Leslau, Wolf. *Falasha Anthology; the Black Jews of Ethiopia.* New York: Schocken Books, 1969.

Lestschinsky, Jacob. *Jewish Migration for the Past Hundred Years.* New York: Yiddish Scientific Institute (YIVO), 1944.

Levi-Strauss, Claude. *The Raw and the Cooked.* London and New York: Harper & Row, 1970.

Levy, Esther. *Jewish Cookery Book.* Philadelphia: W. S. Turner, 1871.

Lewicki, Tadeusz. *West African Food in the Middle Ages.* London: Cambridge University Press, 1974.

Lieberman, Saul. *Greeks in Jewish Palestine; Studies in the Life and Manners of Jewish Palestine in the II–IV Centuries, C.E.* New York: Jewish Theological Seminary of America, 1942.

Leibman, Malvina W. *Jewish Cookery From Boston to Baghdad.* Miami: E. A. Seemann, 1975.

Loewenthal, Rudolf. "Jewish Merchants Between East and West: A Review of Rabinowitz, L. I. '*Jewish Merchant Adventurers.*'" *Historia Judaica* 11 (October 1949): 163–65.

Lohman, Tina, ed. *Book of Jewish Recipes.* Toronto and Montreal: The Jewish Standard, 1942.

Lokotsch, Karl Dr. *Etymologisches Worterbuch der Europaischen Worter Orientalischen Ursprungs.* Heidelberg: Carl Winter's Unwersitatsbuchhandlung, 1927.

Löw, Immanuel. *Die Flora der Juden.* Vienna-Leipzig: R. Lowit, 1924.

Lubavitch Women's Organization: Junior Division. *The Spice and Spirit of Kosher Jewish Cooking.* Brooklyn, New York: Lubavitch Women's Organization, 1977.

Maimonides, Moses. "Treatise on Sexual Intercourse." In *Studies in Judaica: The Medical Aphorisms of Moses Maimonides,* Vol. II. Edited by Fred Rosner, M.D. New York: Yeshiva University Press, 1971.

Maimonides, Moses. "Two Treatises on the Regimen of Health." Translated from the Arabic and edited in accordance with the Hebrew and Latin versions by Ariel Bar-Sela, M.D., Hebbel E. Hoff, M.D., and Elias Faris. Philadelphia: *Transactions of the American Philosophical Society,* July, 1964.

Maimon, Moses Ben. "Maimonides on Sexual Intercourse." In *Medical, Historical Studies of Medieval Jewish Medical Works,* Vol. I. Translated by Morris Gorlin. Brooklyn, New York: The Rambash Publishing Co., 1961.

Mann, Jacob. *Texts and Studies in Jewish History and Literature.* Vol. I: Cincinnati, 1931; Vol. II: Philadelphia, 1935; reprint ed., with an introduction by Gerson D. Cohen. New York, 1972.

Marcus, Jacob Rader. *The Colonial American Jew, 1492–1776.* 3 vols. Detroit: Wayne State University Press, 1970.

Meissisbugo, Christoforo di. *Libro Novo Nel Qual Sinsegno a Far Ogni Sorti di Vivandi.* Venice, 1559.

Meyers, Eric M. and Meyers, Carol M. "Digging the Talmud in Ancient Meiron." *Biblical Archaeology Review* 4 (June 1978): 32–42.

Midrash Rabbah. See Freedman, Rabbi Dr. H. and Simon, Maurice.

Millgram, Abraham Ezra. *Sabbath, the Day of Delight.* Philadelphia: Jewish Publication Society, 1944.

Moldenke, A. L. *Plants of the Bible.* Waltham, Massachusetts: Chronica Botanica Co., 1952.

Montefiore, Claude G. and H. Loewe A., compilers. *Rabbinic Anthology.* New York: Schocken Books, 1974.

Morgenstern, J. "Lag Ba'Omer, its Origin and Import." *Cincinnati Hebrew Union College Annual* 39 (1968): 81–90.

Nahoum, Aldo. *The Art of Israeli Cooking.* London: Gifford, 1970.

Narkiss, Bezalel. *Hebrew Illuminated Manuscripts.* Jerusalem: Encyclopedia Judaica, Macmillan Company, 1969.

Newman, Louis. *The Hasidic Anthology.* New York: Schocken Books, 1963.

Newman, Rabbi Julius. *The Agricultural Life of the Jews in Babylonia Between the Years 200 c.e. and 500 c.e.* London: Oxford University Press. 1932.

Noble, Shlomo. "Yiddish Lexicography." *Jewish Book Annual* 19 (1961–62): 17–22.

de Nola, Ruberto. *Libro de Cozina.* Toledo: Aramon de Petras, 1525.

Norman, Barbara. *The Spanish Cookbook.* New York: Atheneum, 1966.

Norman, Barbara. *Tales of the Table.* Englewood Cliffs, New Jersey: Prentice-Hall, Inc., 1972.

Noy, Dov. *Folktales of Israel.* Edited by Dov Noy, with the assistance of Dan Ben-Amos. Translated by Gene Baharav. Chicago: University of Chicago Press, 1963.

Papashvily, Helen and George. *Russian Cooking.* New York: Time-Life Books, 1969.

Patai, Raphael. *Tents of Jacob.* Englewood Cliffs, New Jersey: Prentice-Hall, Inc., 1971.

Peretz, Isaac Leib. "Bontshe the Silent." In Howe, Irving and Greenberg, Eliezer, *Selected Stories of Isaac Leib Peretz.* New York: Schocken Books, 1974.

Peretz, Isaac Leib. "Bontshe Schwieg" ["Bontshe the Silent"]. In *The Complete Works of Isaac Leib Peretz* (Yiddish). New York: Ferlag Yiddish, 1920.

Pesikta de-Rab Kahana. *R. Kahana's Compilation of Discourses for Sabbaths and Festal Days.* Translated from Hebrew and Aramaic by William G. (Gershon Zev) Braude and Israel J. Kapstein, 1st ed. Philadelphia: Jewish Publication Society of America, 1975.

Petachia ben Jacob (fl. 1175–1190). "Travels." In Adler, Elkan, ed., *Jewish Travelers.* New York: Hermon Press, 1966.

Picart, Bernard, illustrator. *The Ceremonies and Religious Customs of the Various Nations of the Known World.* No publisher, 1733–37.

Platina. *De Honesta Voluptate* [On Honest Indulgence and Good Health] (The first dated cookery book). Venice: L. De Aguila, 1475; rev. ed., St. Louis: Mallinckrodt Chemical Works, 1967.

Pollack, Herman. *Jewish Folkways in Germanic Lands (1648–1806): Studies in Aspects of Daily Life.* Cambridge, Mass.: MIT Press, 1971.

Pozerski, Edouard. *Cuisine Juive; Ghetto Modernes.* Paris: A. Michel, 1929.

Pullar, Phillippa. *Consuming Passions.* London: Hamilton, 1970.

Rabinowitz, Louis Isaac. "Eldad Ha-Dani and China," *Jewish Quarterly Review* 36 (January 1946), 231–38.

Rabinowitz, Louis Isaac. *Jewish Merchant Adventures; A Study of the Radanites.* London: Edward Goldston, Ltd., 1948.

Rabinowitz, Louis Isaac. "Notes of the Jews of Central Asia (Khorasan)," *Historia Judaica* 8 (April 1946): 61–68.

Rabinowitz, Louis Isaac. "The Routes of the Radanites," *Jewish Quarterly Review* (January 1945): 251–80.

Rabinowitz, Louis Isaac. *Social Life of the Jews of Northern France.* London: Edward Goldston, Ltd., 1938.

Raphael, Chaim. *A Feast of History; Passover Through the Ages as a Key to Jewish Experience.* New York: Simon & Schuster, 1972.

Rappoport, Dr. Angelo Solomon. *The Folklore of the Jews.* London: The Soncino Press, 1937.

Regelson, Stanley. "The Bagel: Symbol and Ritual at the Breakfast Table." In *The American Dimension,* pp. 124–138. Edited by W. Arens and Susan Montague. Port Washington, New York: Alfred Publishing Co., 1976.

Richardson, Henry Brush. An etymological vocabulary to the *Libra de Buen Amor of Juan Ruiz, Arcipreste de Hita.* New Haven: Yale University Press, 1930; reprint ed. New York: AMS Press, 1973.

Roden, Claudia. *A Book of Middle Eastern Food.* New York: Alfred A. Knopf, 1972.

Rogers, Ann. *A Basque Story Cook Book.* New York: Charles Scribner's Sons, 1968.

Root, Waverly. *The Food of Italy.* London and New York: Atheneum, 1958.

Roskies, Diane K.; and Roskies, David G. *The Shtetl Book.* New York: Ktav Publishing House, 1975.

Roth, Cecil. *The History of the Jews of Italy.* Philadelphia: Jewish Publication Society, 1946.

Roth, Cecil. *Venice.* Philadelphia: Jewish Publication Society, 1930.

Saketkhoo, Kiumars; Januszkiewicz, Adolph; and Sackner, Marvin A. "Effects of Drinking Hot Water, Cold Water, and Chicken Soup on Nasal Mucus Velocity and Nasal Airflow Resistance." *Chest* 74 (October 1978): 408–10.

Samuel, Maurice. *In Praise of Yiddish.* New York: Cowles Book Company, 1971.

Schaecter, Mordecai. *Food: A Yiddish Terminology.* Hamden, Connecticut: Judah Zelitch Foundation for a Living Yiddish, 1976 (pamphlet).

Schauss, Hayyim. *Guide to Jewish Holy Days; History and Observance.* Translated by Samuel Jaffe. New York: Schocken Books, 1938; reprint ed., 1962.

Schauss, Hayyim. *Lifetime of a Jew; Throughout the Ages of Jewish History.* Cincinnati: Union of American Hebrew Congregations, 1950.

Scholem, Gershom. *Major Trends in Jewish Mysticism.* New York: Schocken Books, 1941; reprint ed., 1954.

Schwartz, Rosaline B. "The Geography of Two Food Terms: A Study in Yiddish Lexical Variation." In *The Field of Yiddish.* Third Collection, Edited by Marvin I. Herzog, Wita Ravid, and Uriel Weinreich. The Hague: Mouton & Co., 1969.

Schwarzbaum, Haim. *Studies in Jewish World Folklore.* Berlin: de Gruyter, 1968.

Schwarzbaum, Haim. "Some Recent Works on the Ethnology and Folklore of Various Jewish Communities." *Jewish Book Annual* 19 (1961–62): 23–32.

Shulman, Abraham. *The Old Country.* New York: Charles Scribner's Sons, 1974.

Shulvass, Moses. *The Jews in the World of the Renaissance.* Leiden: E.J. Brill, 1973.

Simon, Andre. *Dictionary of Gastronomy.* New York: McGraw-Hill, 1970.

Simon, Solomon. "Gimpel's Golden Broth." In *The Wise Men of Chelm and Their Merry Tales,* [by] Solomon Simon. New York: Behrman House, 1945; revised ed., 1967.

Simoons, Frederick J. *Eat Not This Flesh; Food Avoidances in the Old World.* Madison: University of Wisconsin Press, 1961.

Singleton, Mack. *The Book of the Archpriest of Hita (Libro de Buen Amor).* Madison, Wisconsin: Hispanic Seminary of Medieval Studies, 1975.

Skeat, Walter W., compiler. *A Glossary of Tudor and Stuart Words.* Edited by A. L. Mayhew. Oxford: Clarendon Press, 1914.

Smallzried, Kathleen Ann. *Everlasting Pleasure, Influences on America's Kitchens, Cooks, and Cookery from 1565 to 2000.* New York: Appleton-Century-Crofts, 1956.

Snowman, Jacob. *A Short History of Talmudic Medicine.* London: J. Bale Sons and Danielson, 1935.

Soyer, Alexis. *The Pantropheon.* London: Simpkin, Marshall & Co., 1853.

Spector, Johanna. "Bridal Songs and Ceremonies from San'a, Yemen." In *Studies in Biblical and Jewish Folklore,* pp. 255–84. Edited by Raphael Patai, *et al.* Bloomington: Indiana University Press, 1960.

Stobart, Tom. *Herbs, Spices and Flavorings.* London: Newton Abbot, David & Charles, 1970.

Strack, Hermann. *Introduction to the Talmud and Midrash.* Philadelphia: Jewish Publication Society, 1945.

Tannahill, Reay. *Food in History.* New York: Stein and Day, 1973.

Trachtenberg, Joshua. *The Devil and the Jews; the Medieval Conception of the Jew and its Relation to Modern Antisemitism.* New Haven: Yale University Press, 1943.

Trachtenberg, Joshua. *Jewish Magic and Superstition.* New York: Behrman House, 1939.

Unterman, Isaac. *The Talmud; an Analytical Guide to its History and Teachings.* New York: Bloch Publishing Co., 1971.

Wason, Elizabeth. *Cooks, Gluttons and Gourmets; A History of Cookery.* New York: Doubleday, 1962.

Waxman, Mordecai. *History of Jewish Literature.* New York: Thomas Yoseloff, 1960.

Wedeck, Harry E., *Dictionary of Aphrodisiacs.* New York: Philosophical Library, 1961.

Weinreich, Beatrice Silverman. "The Americanization of Passover." In *Studies in Biblical and Jewish Folklore,* p. 341. Edited by Raphael Patai, F. L. Utley, and Dov Noy. Bloomington: Indiana University Press, 1960.

Weinreich, Uriel. "Mapping a Culture." *Columbia University Forum* 6, no. 3 (1963): 17–21.

Die Wirthschaftliche Israelitische Kochin. 2nd rev. ed., 1873.

Wischnitzer, Mark. *To Dwell in Safety; The Story of Jewish Migration Since 1800.* Philadelphia: Jewish Publication Society, 1948.

Wiswe, H. *Kulturgeschichte der Kochkunst.* Munich: H. Moos, 1970.

Wolff, Flora. *Koch-und Wirtschaftsbuch fur Judische Hausfrauen.* Berlin: Siegfried Cronbach, 1888.

Wright, Thomas, compiler. *Dictionary of Obsolete and Provincial English: Pre-19th Century.* London: Henry G. Bohn, 1857; reprint ed., Detroit: Gale Research Company, 1967.

Zborowski, Mark; and Herzog, Elizabeth. *Life is With People.* New York: Schocken Books, 1962.

Zimmels, H. J. *Ashkenazim and Sephardim: Their Relations, Different Problems as Reflected in the Rabbinical Responsa.* London: Oxford University Press, 1958.

Zlotnick, Jehuda L. [Elzet]. *Yiddishe Macholim* [Jewish Delicacies]. Warsaw: Lewin-Epstein, 1920 (in Yiddish).

The Zohar. Translated by Harry Sperling and Maurice Simon. London: The Soncino Press, 1931–1934.

Index